Kiss the Hand
You Cannot Sever

– Footprints & Shadows –

Adrienne Brady

Published by

**MELROSE
BOOKS**

An Imprint of Melrose Press Limited
St Thomas Place, Ely
Cambridgeshire
CB7 4GG, UK
www.melrosebooks.com

FIRST EDITION

Cover designed by Richard Chambers
Cover photograph © Adrienne Brady

ISBN 978-1-906050-60-3

Printed and bound in Great Britain by:
Biddles 24 Rollesby Road, Hardwick Industrial Estate
King's Lynn. Norfolk PE30 4LS

To the memory of my parents, James and Beatrice Brady, who spent a good part of their lives overseas in Egypt, India and Burma, instilling in me a passion for travel to untamed lands.

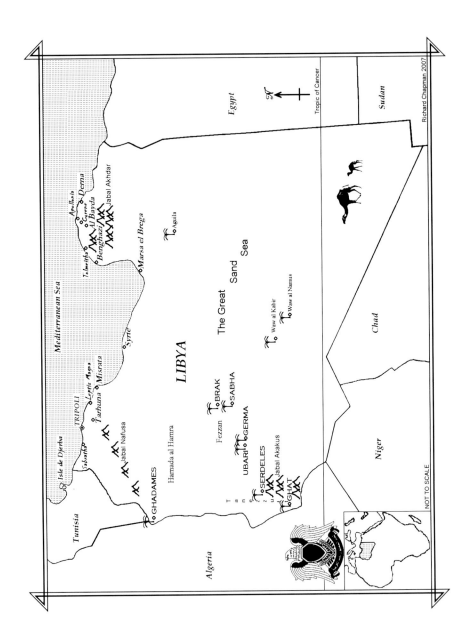

Richard Chapman 2007

Acknowledgements

I am indebted to my fellow expatriate residents and travel companions in Libya. Without them life in Libya would have been intolerable and exploring Libya impossible. In order to protect identities I have used fictitious names and, in some instances, have made other changes in the same interest. With the reader in mind, my story is a record of the highlights of the time I spent in Libya; therefore not every person I met, socialised or even travelled with has been included. Although I have long been out of contact I retain warm memories of the friendship of strangers.

I am grateful to my family for accepting with equanimity my decision to live and travel in such a politically unstable country. Thanks to the idle and ill-tempered security guards manning my prison-like compound in Libya, they were as impotent as I was in making telephone contact; the one means of communication that should have been available to us.

My heartfelt thanks to my partner and travel companion, Richard Chapman, with whom I have spent the intervening years in the Emirates. Richard's help and support (he wears many hats) have been instrumental in the Libyan memoirs reaching their final stage. The delay has been the result of work, our extensive travels through the wilds of beautiful Oman, Namibia and Botswana, as well as travel-writing assignments for various UAE newspaper supplements and magazines before returning to settle in the UK in 2005 and work on this book.

My thanks also go to Tatiana Wilde, the commissioning editor of Tauris Parke Paperbacks. Tatiana's enthusiasm for my manuscript and her insistence that there was a publisher 'out there' who would take it fuelled my determination to continue searching. I am also grateful to Rodger Witt – friend and the managing editor of *Sailing Today* – for his suggestions and encouragement in the early stages; Melanie Newman, for her thoughtful design work in the production of a publicity flyer; and expatriate friends Peter Foster and Jerome Harris for linguistic advice on the vagaries of Libyan/Arabic spellings and translations into English.

I would also like to thank Austin Kehoe, the commissioning editor of Melrose Books, for his warm and positive response to my manuscript as well as the editorial, production and promotion team of Melrose Books for their work in bringing *Kiss the Hand You Cannot Sever* to fruition.

Finally, I wish to acknowledge the following from which I have quoted:

Extracts from *The Histories* by Herodotus (copyright © John Marincola 1996) reprinted by permission of Penguin Group (UK).

Extracts from *The Antiquities of Tripolitania* by Denis Haynes (published in Libya – copyright laws do not apply).

Extracts from *Libya Handbook* by James Azema (copyright © Footprint Handbooks Ltd 2000) reprinted by permission of Footprint Handbooks.

I have drawn upon a wide variety of sources both during my time in Libya and since. Like Herodotus I merely repeat what others say! I am especially indebted to the writings of Denis Haynes and Richard Goodchild, the primary sources I have drawn from for background and descriptions of the Graeco-Roman sites and pre-Islamic Libya.

Every effort has been made to trace the copyright holders of additional quoted material. In the event that there are inadvertent omissions these can be rectified in any future editions.

Contents

Foreword

A copy of Jung Chang's *Wild Swans* was lying on my bedside table. I have a habit or intuitive sense that guides me to choose a book appropriate for my forthcoming travel plans. On my way to Brunei I'd selected Bruce Chatwin's *What am I Doing Here?* and spent the following two years asking myself the same question first coined by Rimbaud when isolated in the Arab city of Harar in neighbouring Ethiopia.

Now, immersed in *Wild Swans*, I was reminded of the thoughts of Colonel Gaddafi in his *Green Book*. In spite of Gaddafi's rejection of both capitalism and communism and his declaration that his was the Third Way, he had no qualms about swapping green for red and adopting a range of communist methodologies for his own brand of cultural revolution.

From the moment I first set foot on Libyan soil in September 1993 I was in a state of shock. Madhouse is the word that came to mind. It is hardly surprising therefore that my memoirs frequently read like bizarre fiction. At this time of extreme political tension I accepted a teaching post in Tripoli. The underlying reason was my keen interest in exploring a country that, at that time, was virtually impossible to get into. A residency was a passport to travel.

Just one of the problems I faced was the difficulty of getting hold of up-to-date travel information. Libya was not a tourist destination and few pre-revolution guidebooks survived the bonfires. Under the guise of eliminating the forces of evil, book-burning orgies were held as public demonstrations of ridding the country of imperialist influences. The military were responsible for weeks of bonfires fuelled by 'Imperialistic Texts' removed from the libraries of all institutions, heaped outside and set fire to by soldiers brandishing Kalashnikovs.

A number of guidebooks still in private circulation during my stay survived by being hidden away or taken out of the country and smuggled back in. In addition to a copy of Denis Haynes's *Antiquities of Tripolitania*, the second text I had the good fortune to get hold of was *An Historic Guide – Cyrene and Apollonia*. I later discovered that my copy, acknowledging neither the author nor the publisher, was the work of Professor Richard Goodchild. Without this invaluable pocket book I would have been lost in Cyrenaica, a region not covered by Haynes. As for the rest of Libya, apart from the writings of Herodotus, this was to remain terra incognita!

Getting into Libya was another story. At this time, without a residency, the country was virtually impossible to enter. In fact, the only foreigners in Libya were embassy staff and workers in oil and oil-related industries. Even with a business visa travel to and from Libya was not easy. Direct flights between London and Tripoli ended in 1986 when the British policewoman, Yvonne Fletcher, was shot dead by a Libyan from the upper floor of the Libyan Embassy in London. Then in 1992 when Gaddafi refused to hand over the Lockerbie suspects the UN imposed sanctions, international air links to Libya were stopped and the situation was exacerbated.

The choice of routes to reach Tripoli was between the more-favoured route by air and road via Tunisia, or that by air from London to Malta followed by the ferry crossing notorious for delays, bad weather and overcrowding. My air tickets and visa arrangements dictated that I travelled through Malta.

I was innocent (or was it ignorant?) of a great deal of the politics and indeed of the political upheavals that had taken place or were in progress at the time that I signed a contract to teach English in Libya. I was soon to find out that the early1990s marked the high point of the Libyan people's discontent and Libya had entered one of the most turbulent periods in the history of the revolution.

Desert Rose

Released from the thrumming heart
of the Sahara, the Ghibli's hot breath scours
pavements where dark men brewing tea crouch
and mutter. Rumours of the attempted coup

glow like hot coals. It is said that Skanska,*
the only oasis in this desert, has been raided.
Raped wine vats gape like cavities
from trees uprooted in a gale. The owner's

under house arrest. Her gunrunning days
for Gaddafi erased. They say, her partner's
revolutionary ways have been paid for
in blood. Today, I slipped past the guard

into Skanska. Only the pregnant camel stirred.
She sifted through rotting fruit,
stared blankly. At my feet
a severed sheep's head buzzed with flies.

Sleek and alert as a desert rat
Gaddafi moves camp from day to day.
The media's strangled silence gurgles.
Still I write postcards as if you receive them.

Only a desert rose can survive this heat,
the abrasive murmuring wind.
They've had my passport for two months now.
I've heard the borders are closed.

* Skanska: private club

Tripoli and Beyond

Land of Surprises

Just then Kate noticed the burnt-out carcass of a car dumped at the roadside. Unaware of the stringent rules about the use of cameras, she opened the window and clicked the shutter. Almost immediately a grey Peugeot saloon pulled alongside. A casually dressed middle-aged Libyan leaned out and jabbed his finger at us.

"Pull over! I want to ask you some questions," he ordered in polished English.

"Quick!" James urged, "the lights are changing. Tell Phil before he drives off!"

Gerry hopped out and ran to the car ahead while we parked on some rough ground at the side of the road.

"I'm from Central Intelligence. You've been stopped for suspicious behaviour," the man explained. "Give me the camera!" he ordered, turning to Kate.

At that moment Phil arrived and wanted to know what was going on.

"I was testing my camera," Kate added inventively. "The batteries haven't been working." The Libyan was unimpressed.

"Give me the camera," he repeated, taking it from her. "Now, you must come for questioning."

"Hang on!" Phil demanded. "Where's your identification?"

"I was off duty," he replied tersely, a faint flush darkening his sallow skin. "I'm from Central Intelligence. You've no right to question me!"

"Take the film but not the camera," suggested Phil. With that the Libyan flicked open the back of the camera and started pulling at the film. "Here, give it to me!" Phil said authoritatively, taking it from the Libyan and closing it. "As you can see, one photograph only has been taken," he added, displaying the roll number. With that he rattled off thirty-five shots of the pavement, rewound the film, removed it from the cassette, pulled it free and handed it over. After a brief silence the Libyan exploded.

"Who are you? Where do you work?" he demanded. Learning that Phil was the manager of a multi-national oil company he was taken off-guard. Clearly, if he pushed things too far he could be in trouble himself. "Get away from here immediately," he threatened. "This has nothing to do with you. I'll have you arrested! I'm taking these people for questioning."

At this point Phil shrugged his shoulders and returned to his vehicle. Minutes later, having been escorted to a checkpoint a few hundred metres along the road, we found ourselves surrounded by police cars. Then more vehicles arrived, complete with blaring sirens and flashing blue lights. Before we could work out a plausible alibi, the security officer strode over and opened the car door.

"We know you work for the CIA," he announced. "You're under arrest!"

* * *

Looking back over the past few weeks it was possible to see how a succession of signs, warnings and incidents led to the moment of arrest. In fact, the only way to avoid direct confrontation with security would have been dumb acceptance of the regulations that governed life in Libya; to have led a life restricted to work and the limited pleasures of the compound. This was not my plan.

From the moment I arrived at Malta's ferry port for the last leg of the journey to Tripoli, the five-star recruitment procedures I had received in London plummeted. After waiting for two hours to get my visa stamped and a further three hours queuing to board in direct sun – forty-three degrees in the shade – I was beginning to see why regular travellers avoided this route. It also provided ample time for the voices of friends and family to take control. "A year in Libya! You must be out of your mind!" Now, facing a night-crossing of six hours with 600 passengers, where free services meant no services apart from one scheduled meal in a dining room with seating for 200, I was beginning to agree.

As the outline of Malta receded, deterred by the length and breadth of the queue for the dining room, I turned my attention to reserving a cabin for the night. Libyan bureaucracy did not cater for advance reservations and a night of comparative comfort and privacy was a priority. Following the directions of a fellow traveller, I finally arrived at the hatch serving as an office and for one glorious smug moment found myself first in line and alone. Then the hatch opened and smugness and body space disappeared. Form filling, visa and passport checking and bureaucratic overdrive in increasing temperatures and diminishing elbow room followed.

I made the dining room for the third and final sitting in time for a plate of cold spaghetti, chips and bread; they ran out of fish on the second round. Tables cluttered with liberally distributed remnants of food and packaging from previous sittings and chairs strewn about the floor contributed to the general chaos. A straggle of late diners gradually thinned, leaving an extended Libyan family at the far end eating in silence. It was while I was toying with cold spaghetti and regretting that I'd given up the opportunity to live and work teaching English in Dubai in preference for a post in Libya, that I first noticed what had been shouting at me from the walls: bright green posters adorned with slogans proclaiming the principles of the September Revolution. Retrieving my notebook from my backpack I furtively began copying: 'Everlasting loyalty to the breakers of chains and the destroyers of frontiers' and the more chilling reminder: 'Committees Everywhere'.

Minutes later I retreated to my cabin and collapsed in the coffin-shaped bunk. In spite of the frustrations, now that we were on our way, I felt a growing sense of anticipation verging on excitement. I had recently returned from five years overseas, teaching English in Singapore and Brunei, and had taken full advantage of the locations to explore places 'off the tourist-trails' in Asia. This was to be my first landfall in Africa and the fulfilment of a dream. I reminded myself that the reason for accepting a teaching position in Libya was the opportunity it would provide for travel.

My reasoning was that a residency came with the job and would be a passport to travel in a fascinating country that remained achingly empty and waiting to be explored. I fixed my eyes on the porthole of swaying starlit sky and imagined climbing Saharan dunes; visiting ancient desert cities and the splendid Graeco-Roman settlements overlooking the Mediterranean Sea before finally succumbing to the dull drone of the engine and the luxury of heavy sleep.

The next thing I was aware of was an unceremonious hammering on my door. My first stage of panic – not knowing where I was – was superseded by the second stage. I was paranoiac about checking and rechecking all the entry documents ready for disembarking. I looked at my watch. Not only was it was well past the designated time for breakfast, even the third sitting would be over by now, but we were already in dock. Forgoing all but the basic toiletries, I hurriedly dressed and attempted to organise myself, all the while regretting that I'd missed a first view of the fabled white city from the sea along with the anticipation of arrival.

An hour later, on Libyan soil, I was standing on the perimeter of a jostling crowd of predominantly male nationals, struggling to identify and retrieve luggage from a huge mound. A huddle of females, swathed in cotton wraps from head to foot, watched the proceedings through small hand-held openings to one side of the face. Dressed in a mismatch of long, shirt-like, loose garments with ruffled low-crutch trousers underneath – the men were more noticeable for the variety of their head gear: lengths of material, some checkered and some plain, wound and tied into untidy heaps on the top of the head. The handful of Europeans I'd previously noticed while queuing to get on the ferry was nowhere to be seen.

As the crowd began to disperse and the mound of luggage thinned, I edged my way forward to rescue my two large, ancient and well-travelled suitcases crammed with sufficient clothes, books and personal effects for a year. I paused, looking about for some form of muscled or wheeled assistance, but it soon became obvious that neither luggage handlers nor trolleys were available. In the Libyan Jamahiriya (the state of the masses) every man was equal and it was every man and every woman for him and herself. Resolving to invest in luggage with wheels before my next trip, I dragged my cases through customs and watched as fellow passengers were greeted and the last disappeared.

Early as it was I could feel the sun's heat but not see it. The sky and air were a dull opaque yellow and my surroundings strangely monochrome. The scene before me was not unlike that of a faded sepia-tinted photograph of a deserted street, lined with grey concrete buildings, sad-looking trees, and littered with rubbish. Abandoned in climbing temperatures, I resorted to sitting like a refugee on my luggage on the sand-strewn pavement. The promised lift was not there. I had no contact numbers and no Libyan currency. Expectations from VIP recruitment procedures in London, like a glass of pure cold water, were now no more than a mirage.

Just minutes later a sand-encrusted minibus drew alongside and a young Libyan male, dressed in casual European-style open-neck shirt and grey trousers, emerged and without introducing himself asked my name and the title of the institution to which I'd been appointed. Checking my details on a list, he proffered his hand, not in greeting as I wrongly assumed, but for my passport. "For administration," he explained, sensing my reluctance to part with it. Flicking through the pages, he paused to glance from my face to the 'warts and all' photo-booth image on the last page, stuffed it into his pocket, lifted my luggage into the back of his vehicle and gestured for me to board. I did so with gnawing apprehension and a growing sense of finality. There was no turning back now.

Before the engine had started I was preoccupied with plans for weekend escapes. Malta was no longer viable. It would have to be west by road to Djerba Island in neighbouring Tunisia. Then it occurred to me that escape was going to be impossible! Without my passport and without an exit visa I was a prisoner in a country where the services of the British Consulate were reduced to one man and his assistant housed in a room at the back of the Italian Embassy.

I turned my attention to views through the sand-streaked windows: tumbled walls; rubble overlapping piles of sand and bricks; wooden scaffolding and partially constructed new buildings straddling and towering over the remains of old ones; litter and sand choking and spilling from gutters. It was like the aftermath of war and a remarkable contrast to the account of the fourteenth-century Arab traveller, Al Tijani:

'When we approached, we were blinded by the brilliant whiteness of the city from which the burning rays of the sun were reflected; I was convinced that rightly is Tripoli called the White City'. He also declared that he had never seen cleaner streets anywhere. A further description of Tripoli, written four centuries later by a Miss Tully, sister of Richard Tully, the British Consul, confirms Al Tijani's description. She too is struck by the extreme whiteness of the buildings as well as 'numerous palms planted in regular rows, and kept in the finest order'.

We turned off the main road into a side street and drew up at the gates to a compound surrounded by a high brick wall, topped by rusted metal stakes interwoven with barbed wire. I viewed the prison-camp surrounds and our progress through a military-type checkpoint as if from a distance, as if I were observing somebody else's life. Then I was handed a key and dropped off at one of a row of identical prefabricated bungalows lining both sides of a street. Reality took hold. I was alone. This was Gargaresh and for the next year this was home.

***

The garden of scrubby sand boasted a scattering of dusty oleanders, one date palm making a blob of shade, and at the back of the house some tenacious eucalyptus trees pressing against the bedroom window. Inside was shabby but habitable. Faded floral wallpaper and an equally faded sagging three-piece suite dominated the main living area. Sounding like overworked lawnmowers, antiquated wall-mounted air conditioners in rusting cages kept the place cool and overrode the cacophony of sounds from traffic competing for space on the adjacent main road. An initial inspection revealed primitive though operational plumbing. On the other hand, tangles of frayed wiring hanging from gaping wall sockets threatened electrocution just by thinking about touching them. Finally, the discovery of salt-flavoured tap water presented the toughest challenge so far.

I'd no sooner completed my inspection when there was a knock at the door. I was greeted by a welcome committee in the form of three expatriate female residents with smiling faces and bearing gifts of bottled water, tea, milk and a home-made fruit cake. Until that moment it hadn't occurred to me to check for food supplies or to think about where the next meal was coming from. Assurances from my visitors that the cupboards would be bare were soon confirmed.

The timing of the visit was perfect, and within minutes tea had been organised and we were exchanging horror stories and jokes about the problems of travel to and from Libya. A contender for the worst was an account of a ferry fully boarded and ready to leave for Malta when a storm broke. Although some travellers became seasick and food and drink supplies for the able-bodied catered for one meal only on the six-hour crossing, passports had been stamped therefore no one was allowed to disembark. Subsequently, to the horror and misery of those on board, the ferry remained in dock for twenty-four hours before setting off in turbulent seas.

The news added to my resolve to avoid further travel on the ferry to Malta at all costs and to follow the example of like minded expats who make their escape by road and air via Djerba Island. Finally, I was the eager recipient of advice about survival techniques. Most importantly, how to obtain drinking water from a lorry delivering weekly supplies to the compound and directions to a row of small Libyan shops and a dismal and under-stocked supermarket for daily provisions!

Pleasantries over, it was time for more serious issues to be raised. While two of my visitors disappeared to wash up and then left with promises of further opportunities to socialise,

Paula, the main spokeswoman, moved to perch beside me on the edge of the sofa. With her neat blonde bobbed hair, carefully manicured nails and trim figure she looked as if she were about to advise me on the protocol for new members joining a tennis club in Surrey. I was right about the tennis. She was the current ladies champion on the compound, but nothing she had to tell me could have been further from codes of behaviour in the Home Counties.

In fact, the meeting took on a bizarre air when in hushed tones and with the just detectable hint of satisfaction of those 'in the know' she launched into a catalogue of warnings, including tapped telephone lines, should I be fortunate enough to be allowed to make or receive calls, and interfered-with mail that could take anything from three months to three years to arrive anyway!

"Furthermore," she was insisting, "it's not safe to discuss anything except one's health or the weather, either in the house, which is sure to be bugged, on the telephone or in public places which are all serviced by spies from security."

"We're all prisoners here," Paula continued. "The security gates exist for two reasons. To keep us in and to keep friends, as well as intruders, out. Punishments are handed out by security; they depend on the mood of the particular guard."

"Punishments?" I repeated, images of handcuffs and cells rising before me.

"Things like no visitors or phone calls for a week – sometimes longer. No reasons. The most notorious guard, a wizened little man we've christened 'the Weasel', – a nasty piece of work – regularly refuses entry to any single Caucasian male between the ages of fourteen and sixty-four he takes a dislike to! The ultimate power of the guards," Paula added dramatically, "is in their absolute control of the telephone. From now on," she warned, "you'll be subject to their whims and to Libyan law."

Tiredness tinged with disbelief and the sensation of being a detached spectator was returning. Then becoming even more secretive, Paula looked over her shoulder and leaned towards me.

"The Leader – Gaddafi," she mouthed, "must never be mentioned by name. The Big Man, His Lordship, His Nibs. Never his name! Spies," she whispered. "Everywhere."

She was serious, I decided. She was deadly serious and she hadn't finished either. She was talking about delayed and non-payment of salary, especially before leave, should I be lucky enough to get my passport and an exit visa.

"Salaries before holidays," she explained, "are withheld to make sure one comes back afterwards. Why do you think we're still here?" she exclaimed before leaning forward and adding in hushed tones, "You'll need friends. There's a club. The Darts' Club. Plenty of supplies. Drink," she mouthed. "You'll meet the right people. Contacts," she added, winking one eye. With that she rose to her feet, delved into her handbag and produced an envelope. "Libyan dinars," she explained, pressing the envelope into my hands. "You may need them. Pay me back when they get round to giving you an advance."

Without waiting for a response, she tucked her hair behind her ears and let herself out.

I wandered into the kitchen, rechecking cupboards and drawers; nothing but crockery, cutlery and a range of saucepans. A cockroach ran from a rusting and empty small refrigerator and disappeared beneath it. I shuddered, wandered back into the living area and looked at my luggage. Unpacking would have to wait. I needed food, but more than that I needed to clear my head. Was the place really as crazy as Paula made out? I laughed aloud as if to reassure my throbbing head that it was all a joke, then putting the envelope of dinars into my shoulder bag, I made for the security gates. A guard with small beady eyes set in a crabbed, wrinkled face looked me over before making an impatient hand signal indicating that I could go. He, no doubt, was the Weasel. Turning left, as directed, I walked towards the main road and the local shops.

Rumour Has It!

Friday, 1st October 1993 was the deadline for Gaddafi to hand over those Libyans said to be responsible for the Lockerbie bombing. Nobody expected him to comply. On the contrary, his response to Western threats of immediate and tighter sanctions if the deadline was not met was one of schoolboy bravado: "We don't need the West!" In a display of childlike revenge, all communication with the outside world was stopped for twenty-four hours: the borders with Tunisia and Egypt were closed; the ferry boats to Malta were not running; telephone lines and cable TV had been cut off. The intention of this act of revenge was to impress the outside world. The world at large remained oblivious whereas we, 'the inmates', were hostages for the day.

Just days later, the place was thrumming with rumours about an aborted coup generating even more excitement and political paranoia. Concern and speculation about the effects on our daily lives, and indeed on our very lives, crept into every conversation. Tight control of the media meant that we relied on fragments of person-to-person information from a variety of sources which we pieced together, discarding and adding bits over a period of weeks. Ironically, the most reliable reports frequently came from information that has filtered overseas and is reported back on the elusive and crackling BBC World Service whose unauthorised radio waves escaped censorship but received Gaddafi's condemnation and accusations of British lies.

However, all too often, Libya – the centre of our universe – was not considered newsworthy and not mentioned. The problem of getting or giving information, exacerbated by fears of bugging and tapped telephone lines, meant that most exchanges took place in cars, which I learnt may well be bugged too, or in the open. Rumours of a failed attempt to overthrow Gaddafi by an armed attack on a military base where he was supposedly in residence were rife. A noticeable increase in police activity centred on roadblocks and the rounding-up of suspects were the only tangible evidence. The first whiff of news about the recent attempted coup arrived when it was discovered that Skanska, a private club, had been under attack. It was said that Jalloud, a military officer suspected of instigating the coup d'état, had been gunned down at the club and a former female gunrunner for Gaddafi was under house arrest.

The failed coup became a reality for me through my membership of Tripoli's British Sub-Aqua Club (BSAC). As soon as I discovered the existence of the club I joined, not so much for the quality of the dives which failed miserably to live up to my tropical baptism in the South China Sea, but for weekend visits to a variety of local beaches. For divers and non-divers alike, they provided opportunities to relax and socialise away from the restricted life on the compounds. As it happened, the divers used the facilities of Skanska to run training sessions for new recruits, involving the use of the swimming pool, and to house a compressor for filling tanks. Revived stories circulating about the club centred on a female expatriate said to have been a gunrunner for Gaddafi at the time of the 1969 September Revolution. As a reward for her services she was sold a partnership into the club on very favourable terms. Her partner, the allegedly murdered Jalloud, was said by some to be Gaddafi's second in command and by others to be his cousin.

The undisputed truth was that the club was backed and frequented by high-ranking Libyans and was the only place in Libya 'licensed' to sell alcohol. Apart from diplomats, who are exempt from such restrictions, the expatriate workforce relied on homebrews of varying quality to relieve the drought. Skanska's strong associations with Libya's revolutionary past had suddenly and dramatically been propelled into the present.

It so happened that it was my turn on the dive club's rota system to accompany James – a convivial Canadian and fellow BSAC member – on a visit to Skanska to refill the dive cylinders. I had had the good fortune to be paired with James on our weekly dives. Tall with a comfortable build – the sort of person that bear hugs were invented for – and endowed with an irreverent sense of humour at odds with the innocent expression on his youthful face, I was as comfortable with him on land as I was under water.

Nursing mixed feelings of unreality and adventure, I climbed into his BMW and we headed along the main road to Tripoli before turning right into a typical side street strewn with rubbish and rubble. Finally, we climbed a hill and drew up in front of a pair of rusty but solid, eight-foot high iron gates. A dark face looked out from the window of a guard hut, closely inspected James's pass and my proffered membership card and then disappeared. A bolt clanged and one side of the gates opened, giving us access to an expanse of overgrown wasteland.

There, in front of us, among a tangle of trees were three huge bronze Roman statues. The head and shoulders of a seated woman dressed in flowing robes disappeared into the branches of a eucalyptus tree while her feet remained buried in sand. Her left hand, holding an orb, stretched towards the standing ten-foot-high figure of a Roman soldier. Nearby, beneath the belly of a snarling female wolf, the infant forms of Romulus and Remus reached open-mouthed towards its huge teats.

"Genuine artefacts!" explained James. "You'll have to get used to neglect – everything – modern and ancient," he added, nosing the BMW towards another set of gates. "The double gates keep the club private – away from prying eyes. This is, or was, the playground of the powerful in a classless society where privilege is not supposed to exist."

A khaki-clad soldier, Kalashnikov slung across his shoulder, guarded the second set of gates. A pair of dark eyes slid over the car and focused on us. "*Salaam,*" James greeted the guard holding up his pass. There was no response, but the gate was opened and we passed through to an unexpected sweep of elegant green lawns. The gardens looked as if they had just been manicured: the sugar-almond blossoms of oleanders fresh and bright after recent rain; paths newly swept; the bronze figure of another seated, imperious Roman woman surrounded and shaded by the elegant fronds of pampas grasses. There was no sign of life. The tennis courts were silent, the pool deserted. Even the resident camel looked unnerved as she sifted through a wheelbarrow of rotting fruit.

James parked alongside a set of barns, one of which housed the compressor. Overawed by the oppressive heat and quiet, we hauled the cylinders into a tub of water and fitted them to the compressor without talking. The noise of the compressor bulldozed the silence. James disappeared into a small room reserved for the club's equipment. Alone, my imagination was fast at work. The act of preparing for the weekly dive as if nothing had changed on the very soil of a place which had recently been subject to violent change felt wrong. I moved a few paces to where through the twisted cones of sunshades lining the pool I could see a wing of the house. Like impenetrable mirrors, the windows held sunlight and reflections of the garden, making it impossible to see inside.

Mesmerised, I stared, wondering what it must feel like to be under house arrest; to know you can't leave. Without my passport I was unable to leave the country. House arrest was the next stage to bars – the total loss of freedom. What was she doing? Pacing to and fro? Going through the motions of routine? Or had she escaped through the secret underground tunnel rumoured to link the house to the coast?

Behind me a huge barn gaped in darkness. As my eyes adjusted outlines of machinery, neat piles of wood and a circle of stained wood-shavings on the floor took shape. There was a smell of oil and something more. I looked more closely at the stain. It looked like blood. It was blood. I was certain. Then from the shadowed recess of the barn I saw the whites of two eyes shining against black skin and glowing in the darkness. As I stared the outline of a man, dressed in military camouflage and leaning against the inner barn wall, took shape. A handgun bulged suggestively below his waist.

Rumours and stories, part of everyday life in Libya, concerned something distant and impersonal that went on around us and inconvenienced us but did not involve us. Even road checks were part of our daily routine. This was too close and too real. The man hadn't moved but was staring sullenly at me. I felt the skin on my scalp tighten. At the sound of a voice calling I spun round. Relieved to find it was James, I went to help load the cylinders.

"A soldier with a handgun – blood on the ground," I muttered. "The barn."

"Let's get the hell out!" he responded. We'd barely taken our seats and closed the doors before he started the engine and was nosing up the drive past the tethered camel. She shook a cloud of flies from her head and gazed at us blankly. Gates were unlocked and clanged shut behind us, bolts shot into place. My last image was of a severed sheep's head, swollen tongue lolling, lying among the rubbish on the verge outside the gate.

Once we'd joined the main road to Gargaresh the experience was already assuming a sense of unreality. My nervousness was further diffused when James recounted the gossip circling among the expat population about the female gunrunner being held under house arrest. Rumour had it that on a visit to a clairvoyant she had been advised that in order to live a long and successful life she must fulfil three conditions: firstly, she must give away all her money; secondly, she must take in and house a needy family; and thirdly, she could reverse the ageing process by drinking the milk of a pregnant camel.

"You're having me on!" I exclaimed.

"Absolutely not," James insisted. "And that's not all! Anxious to succeed she returned to the club, gave away the contents of the till, then to the chagrin of some members she took a poor family to live in one of the luxury cabins in the club's grounds. These cabins are reserved for the elite – used as temporary accommodation for new upmarket expatriate employees. Finally, she bought a pregnant camel. Apparently, the shortcuts in fulfilling the first condition have left her vulnerable to the vicissitudes of fortune and what's more," he insisted, "the camel's milk has had no noticeable effect on her appearance! But," he added, pausing for effect, "they say Our Leader is convinced of its aphrodisiac properties!"

"So I've heard. At least, I've heard about the aftermath. Audible flatulence! What about the camel? Is it *the* camel?"

"So they say!"

"It's a madhouse. Like living on the edge of sanity."

We had no sooner joined the freeway to make our way back to the compound when we saw a man standing at the roadside, frantically flagging us down. "Police check," James enlightened me. He pulled over alongside a small open-sided hut where a second man sat scratching his crotch and smoking. Assuming an air of nonchalance, James produced his identity cards and papers and got out of the car. The sharp-nosed policeman thumbed through the sheets, glancing at James from time to time. Finally, after returning the papers, he turned his attention to me. He stared long and hard before focusing on James and questioning him in Arabic. James's monosyllabic replies were part Arabic, part English. As the dialogue continued the policeman's rhetoric was increasing in speed and volume. I heard 'tourist' and presumed he was referring to me. Suddenly, he was standing at my open window.

"Marry?" he repeated over and over in a higher and higher tone.

"Marry! Marry!" he continued, demanding a response.

Unsure if this was an order, a manic proposal or interrogation I attempted to cover all contingencies by responding with a firm, "No."

"*Kalabsha! Kalabsha!*" he screamed, snatching at my hands through the open window and crossing one over the other at the wrists before holding them in a tight grip. Mesmerised partly by the pitch of his voice and partly by the globules of spit hanging like dewdrops from the ends of his drooping moustache, I suddenly became aware that James had taken up a position behind him and was trying to get my attention.

"Stay in the car!" he mouthed frantically. "Stay in the car!"

At that moment, attracted by the excitement, the second officer came to investigate. After exchanging a few sharp words with my assailant he pulled him away and flapped his hand at James, motioning him to go. Wasting no time James hopped in, turned the key and swung the BMW onto the highway. It flew like a dolphin between the traffic.

"Sorry," he apologised, throwing me forward as he swerved to miss the bumper of a car he was overtaking. "Can't hang about. The madman could change his mind!"

"What was he screaming?"

"Handcuffs! Believe it or not he wanted to arrest you! That's what he was doing with your hands – demonstrating using handcuffs to arrest you."

"What on earth for?"

"You're a single woman in a car with a male who is not a relative."

"What about you? Did he want to arrest you?"

"Come on. Get real!" James remonstrated. "This is no-woman's-land. Men aren't stoned for adultery. For all the Leader's pronouncements about discrimination against women being a flagrant act of oppression, it doesn't filter down to the people. Even if it did, their idea of discrimination doesn't match ours. This is what people fail to understand. Their values and ideals are not the same. I have a suggestion," he added. "Wear a ring. And next time say, yes."

"By the way," James continued, once we had put a kilometre or so between us and the checkpoint. "If it's any consolation, I'm told that the punishment for a woman caught travelling with a male she's neither married nor related to in Iran is on-the-spot flagellation!"

"Then Allah be praised we're not in Iran!"

"*Al Hamdulillah* – Praise be to Allah," responded James and we both laughed. Seconds later we sobered up. We were approaching another roadblock.

As we drew near, among the group of waiting cars we recognised some of our fellow expat residents from the compound. To my relief, James's muttered assurances that I had nothing to worry about as this appeared to be a run-of-the-mill road check set up purely to inconvenience expats turned out to be true. We slowly nudged towards the front of the queue to be subjected to nothing worse than a routine check of identity and car papers, peppered with the increasingly familiar verbal exchanges of '*salam*' (hello), '*shukran*' (thankyou) and '*ma'assalema*' (goodbye) before we were on the road again, heading for the security of our barbed-wire-encircled compounds.

In spite of James's reassurance that given the recent political upheavals the day's events were to be expected and to think no more of them, once I was on my own I was left with an uncomfortable feeling that somehow today we had stepped 'over the edge' into the insane world of political paranoia and that from now on we were destined to be players not onlookers!

The Splendour that Was Roman

Of Tripoli's surviving Roman remains the one not to be missed, and indeed the one I discovered is impossible to miss, is the four-sided Marcus Aurelius Arch. Faced in elaborately sculptured marble, believed to be the work of Greek masons, it stands where it was built in AD 163, glorious and imposing, on the intersection of two main streets and overlooking the harbour. Legend has it that as long as the arch remains standing the city will survive! Both have survived and benefited from extensive restoration by the Italians.

Standing before it, I was overawed by the size and magnificence of the arch as well as the remaining sculptured scenes: hand-cuffed Barbarians, garlanded cupids and naked winged Victories vied with images of Apollo and Minerva, the patron deities of the imperial city. Apollo driving a chariot drawn by winged griffins offset by the image of Minerva drawn by winged female sphinxes, both racing to assist the Roman armies against war-like desert tribes, was my favourite as much for its sense of urgency as for the depiction of male and female equality.

As part of a somewhat patchy and delayed orientation programme I had been invited to join a handful of new recruits on a trip to explore Tripoli's ancient past. In practical terms this meant we were picked up in a minibus from a prearranged meeting place near the compound, delivered to Green Square at the near heart of the city and abandoned for three hours. My concern was that since Gaddafi's assumption of power all texts written in English had been banned and that without either a guide or guidebook the visit would be nothing more than an uninformed sight-seeing tour. My last-minute appointment and departure for Libya had left me insufficient time for doing either detailed research or locating books.

Enquiries about where and how I could get hold of a guidebook had come to nothing until, once again, Paula came to my rescue and gave me a third-hand copy of Haynes's *Antiquities of Tripolitania*. This, she assured me, was the bible on Roman Libya. As Haynes and any other authority tell us, of the three cities of Roman Tripolitania: Sabratha, Leptis and Oea (Tripoli), Tripoli is the only one to have remained occupied until the present day.

The sense of the past captured by the scenes on the arch is both immediate and ongoing; the monument remains as a testimony not only to the former splendour and wealth of imperial Rome but to the failure of successive civilisations to come anywhere near to matching it. From Medieval times Spanish, Turkish, Arab and Italian invaders and settlers have all left their mark by demolishing sections of the Roman city and each other's in order to use the materials to build their own. The remains of the greater part of Roman Oea lie buried beneath these settlements.

Other surviving Roman artefacts include the remains of private villas containing mosaic floors and wall paintings in the old city as well as the remains of a large public building beneath my next port of call – the medieval castle. The former citadel, once the stronghold of the Christian Knights of Malta, finally fell to Ottoman forces, becoming the place where the Qaramanli dynasty held court until 1835. During the Italian occupation extensive restoration preceded the setting up of the first museum of ancient treasures recovered from the Graeco-Roman sites. Known as the Red Palace by the Arabs, the castle and its contents now claim to be the Jamahiriya (the state of the masses) Museum.

I must confess to not being an enthusiast of large, all-encompassing museums. There is something daunting about the size and morgue-like about rows of carefully labelled and organised exhibits kept behind barriers or glass that make me want to escape into the outside world. I'm more in favour of the immediacy of small on-site museums or information centres. However, even an 'in-the-wild' explorer like myself could not bypass this massive fortified citadel with its complex labyrinth of rooms, courtyards and passages serving as a storehouse for treasures from Libya's ancient past. As it was, time was not on my side either. I knew that the museum housed an impressive selection of Greek and Roman statues and mosaics as well as sections devoted to the Ottomans, but Paula had given me a list of 'diverse' places I hoped to see before meeting up with my fellow recruits at a Libyan coffee house near the pick-up point for the minibus. I looked at my watch – half an hour had passed already. I decided on a brief visit to the castle – my focus: the 'heart' of ancient Libya in the section devoted to prehistory.

An unexpected encounter with two Roman statues occupying niches in the entrance hall almost weakened my resolve; representing Rome's highest ideals of athleticism and the worship of deities, a portrait of an athlete tying a ribbon of victory round his brow and that of Apollo-Antinous (a copy of the Greek sun god, Apollo of Delphi) looked down on me from safe pedestals. Magnificent models of idealised manhood holding lifelike poses, their appeal was magnetic. Retrieved by the Italians from the sand-filled Hadriatic Baths at Leptis Magna, they were just two survivors among many Greek and Roman statues dismembered during Berber or Vandal attacks on the ancient cities. Many of the statues that survived the raids and were not safely buried under sand were ultimately destroyed by the Ottomans. Driven by Islamic disapproval of idolatry, Ottoman soldiers are said to have beheaded many of the statues that had escaped previous attacks.

As I made my way to the main hall, the focal point from where stairways and corridors to the exhibit rooms of the museum branch out, I became aware that a middle-aged man dressed in jeans topped by a leather jerkin was following close on my heels. I'd first noticed him standing alongside a potted palm just inside the reception area while I was purchasing my ticket. Wearing dark glasses, keeping just a few metres behind and stopping when I stopped in an inept Inspector-Clouseau manner, he brought to mind Paula's warning of 'spies everywhere'. I could only imagine that he was from security, and since I appeared to be the lone visitor I was also the sole object of his attention. To make matters worse, the polished, unused feel to the place made me want to walk on tiptoe, almost as if the sound of my footsteps was disturbing the resurrected past. Pausing to inspect a huge map on the wall, I located the position of the rooms devoted to prehistoric Libya and, with my shadow in tow, headed somewhat nervously for an encounter with some of Libya's ancient treasures.

From Greek and Roman sculptures to pin men armed with spears standing astride a two-wheeled chariot pulled by four horses! I was looking at a cast copy of rock art discovered in Wadi Zigza in the Fezzan and experiencing a buzz of excitement. The Fezzan, the stronghold of the powerful Garamantes tribe, was just one of Libya's far-flung places I hoped to explore. Before me a stylised portrait of two elegant sand-coloured giraffe, poised against a blue-green backdrop, took centre stage. From rock art to specimens of ancient man's universal tool – the flint – led me to the focus of my visit – the oldest skeleton to be found in Wadi Teshuinat in the Akakus Mountains.

Dating from 3,400 BC, the fragile skeleton, curled in a foetal position, not only fuelled my sense of wonder about the lives and beliefs of these distant ancestors but brought to mind a map I'd seen, showing the first humans fanning out from the heart of Africa to inhabit the furthest peninsulas, islands and continents of the world. This, I reminded myself, was one of mankind's distant forbears. Now, I was reassured. I'd taken the risk to live and work in Libya in order to satisfy my passion for exploring the landscape once lived in by people who were an integral part of it. If Haynes were my bible on Roman Libya then Herodotus' colourful histories blending myth, legend, rumour and reality were my bible on the people living in Libya before, during and after the Romans.

Bidding a silent farewell to the skeleton, I made brief eye contact with the dark glasses of my temporarily forgotten trailer, standing hands behind his back near the exit, and strode past. Hurrying down the castle steps in bright sunlight, I renewed my resolve to explore first-hand the even greater storehouses of ancient treasures and traces of the past to be found at their original desert and deserted sites just a few hours away by road or air.

Green was the colour of Gaddafi's Revolution and the entire square was once literally painted green and used for his rallies. Formerly the Piazza Italia, complete with Romanesque statues and flowing fountains, it had been a social hub alive with street cafés and music. I took the opportunity to photograph the few remaining works of Roman art: the lovely bronze sea-horse fountain and two columns next to the citadel capped respectively by a ship representing Tripoli and a rearing horse – a symbol of Libyan independence – the latter replacing the original sculpture of a she-wolf representing Rome.

On this day, the square was an empty soulless place littered with rubbish and used for anti-West rallies and as a bus and taxi station. Similarly neglected were the avenues of Italian-built apartments; once an elegant winter resort of white buildings that radiated south and west out of the old city along ancient camel tracks. The framework of the city is still there and it didn't require much imagination to see that with an army of organised workers, supplies of bricks and mortar and buckets of whitewash and paint it could be transformed to become the 'White City' once again.

Standing on the site of the original Roman settlement, the medieval walled city remains the beating heart of Tripoli. It is here that ancient and modern worlds stand side by side, collapse and rise again, phoenix-like from ashes and rubble. I followed a narrow passageway between buttressed walls and cave-like entrances to *funduqs* (hotels) – the hallmark of the ancient souk where guildsmen once gathered and produced and sold pottery, metalwork, clothing and jewellery. Once, it was not only a hub for local people but a meeting place where merchants brought and traded goods and slaves from the Saharan caravan routes. Today, the partially restored souk, inhabited and run largely by immigrants from Africa and Egypt, had a low-key feel to it. Shrouded local women picking through fruit, vegetables and spices and a straggle of expats browsing among local crafts including a range of ornate coffee pots, leather goods and hand-woven rugs, shawls and wall hangings ensured that business was ticking over.

After independence, in 1951, traditional families wasted no time in moving from the cavern-like dwellings of the souk into modern homes with running water and sanitation, vacated by departing Italians. Meanwhile, immigrant workers were equally quick to move into the abandoned souk and take advantage of Gaddafi's 'squatters-rights' policy of a house belonging to the occupant. Old Libyan families had no option than to abandon their former homes to the immigrants with the result that motivation for upkeep disappeared and the neglected souks fell into disrepair.

Added to this, Gaddafi's disastrous policy to replace all private enterprise with public supermarkets resulted in the forced closure of all local shops, including those in the souk. Ironically, in the long run, the economic effects were so bad and discontent so high that the policy was rescinded. The souk has gradually been restored but not to its former glory. Narrow streets were marked by potholes and rubbish; tangles of wiring and vines clung to and held together the cracked walls of buildings on either side. Nevertheless, among the cheap hotels and immigrant cafés it was possible to get a sense of the past from the rich carpeted walls of arched enclaves. Here, where old men, hunched over *shisha* pipes, play chess and backgammon and the aroma of coffee and spices fills the air, rugs and bags predominantly woven in a mix of burnt orange, deep red, white and black hang from ceilings and walls. Crowded with sacks of spices, heaps of woollen capes, robes, leather sandals, coffee pots and heavy, pendant Berber jewellery, floor space too is at a premium.

I spent an enjoyable time exploring and bargaining with friendly vendors – who given the lack of tourists made the most of the opportunity to show off their wares and sell at cut-down prices. My favourite purchases: two pen and ink drawings of street scenes showing cloaked figures in narrow passageways with buttressed walls, spanned by great arches; and secondly, a hand-woven bag in bright red and orange wool, studded with the traditional emblem of white stylised gazelles, that along with geometric patterns are a popular motif on carpets and bags.

I paused to examine Paula's hand-drawn plan marked with places of interest not covered by Haynes's exclusively pre-Islamic maps and headed out of the souk, past the ornate and elaborately carved Qaramanli Mosque with its distinctive Ottoman-style octagonal minaret towards a smaller and ancient counterpart, the Naga Mosque. Said to date from AD 912, the mosque's very appeal comes not only from its age but its simplicity and complete lack of symmetry. It has a charm of its own. Dozens of small brick-built domes, reminiscent of an over-large egg box, form the roof. Add to the unique roof structure an assortment of Roman columns in the sanctuary – the result is unadulterated character and a satisfying ascetic simplicity.

It is this simplicity of style that is so lacking in the ostentatious stucco designs and pointy minarets of the Ottoman mosques that dominate the city. Although one cannot but be impressed by the great size and ornate splendour of the mosques, it is as if the departure from the simplicity of form inherited from the pre-Islamic architecture of the ecclesiastical Byzantine period parallels a departure from the sense of spirituality it should suggest. For authenticity and character the Naga Mosque had my vote for the all-out winner.

The Ottoman legacy of mosques in Tripoli is supplemented by equally impressive palaces, harems and fine residences. Restoration in progress of buildings in the medina included the eighteenth-century Qaramanli residence which later housed the British Consulate. The archaeologist H. S. Cowper gives the following description of the consulate where he was a guest for several weeks in 1896 during the time of his secret explorations: 'This fine old house is said to be the largest residential building in Tripoli, and its great square, blooming with flowers which are the daily care of the mistress of the house, has always been to me, and is indeed in reality, a true oasis in the noisy squalor of the surrounding streets'.

The approach was unchanged. I followed a narrow,

squalid street alongside crumbling, adjoining buildings with overhanging balconies in various stages of collapse that posed as much danger to pedestrians as to users. The entrance to the former consulate, from a sandy track just wide enough for two camels to pass, ended before a massive, studded wooden door. On the other side I entered a world of cool, recently restored elegance: the marble floor of a courtyard no longer blooming with flowers but framed by recently restored, elegant white columns was overlooked by an arcaded gallery on the second floor and latticed windows surrounded by decorative blue-green marble tiles on the lower level.

At this time the former consulate, in the final stages of restoration, was empty. Nevertheless, standing in slanting sunlight, the ambience was evocative of the tinkle of ice against glass, refined laughter and the rustle of silk. I reminded myself that there was a great deal more to life in Tripoli than polite chit-chat over cocktails. It was in this very house that Miss Tully, sister of the then British Consul, Richard Tully, recorded details of a darker and more dangerous side of life. Her narrative accounts of day-to-day living covering the ten years of her stay (1783–93) provide fascinating detail about the great plague of 1785 that killed a quarter of the inhabitants of Tripoli; intimate details of the Pasha of Tripoli's interfamily conflicts and assassinations; as well as heartfelt and distressing eye-witness accounts of the arrival of slave caravans from the Sahara.

To one side, a door led into converted stables. The entire length of the outer wall consisted of huge archways filled by double doors through which horses once clattered. Under the low palm beams of the ceiling there was a tangible atmosphere of energy and warmth.

With the distinct feeling that I had experienced a brush with the past, I made my way from the former English Consulate Street to the shell of the Church of Santa Maria degli Angeli. In the Byzantine period Christianity spread not only along the coastal strip but was also propagated among tribesmen in the south. Haynes records the discovery of the remains of three fifth-century churches, equipped with new baptistries containing cruciform fonts of Byzantine type, in the interior of Tripolitania. Current long-term residents remember the days when congregations spilled from the doors of this now sadly neglected Catholic church after Sunday services.

On this day, awaiting the fulfilment of promises of reconstruction, the building remained derelict. Close at hand were the remains of a former Ottoman prison where Christians awaiting ransom were held captive until the right price could be negotiated for their release. Today, a moth-eaten and badly scarred camel tied to a post and a hawk roosting on the windowsill of the ruined building were the only signs of life in the deserted, rubble-strewn square. A sense of loss and aloneness suddenly overcame me – so much so that even the dull sound of my footsteps on the sand-strewn path was unnerving as I hurried back to the main square.

Every place and every nation keep memorials to the past but this was my first face-to-face encounter with a memorial to an enemy. Or was it? I was standing alongside the remains of the original Italian Embassy. Bombed in 1943, after the Italians retreated, the tumble of ruins remains where it fell. One school of thought has it that the piles of grey rubble have been left as a monument and testimony to the Libyan people's deep-seated resentment towards their most hated coloniser. On the other hand, there are those who believe that leaving the debris is no more than a symptom of an African malaise. Anything that is destroyed, ruined or broken is left that way. Just as burnt-out cars are left to rust at the roadside so bomb-site rubble is left because no one gets round to clearing them up! Whatever the reason, fifty years is a long time for the ruins to lie in waste.

A more recent addition to the outdoor museums of bombed buildings in Tripoli is the remains of Gaddafi's residency, hit in 1986 by one of President Ronald Reagan's squadron of jets sent to bomb Tripoli and kill him. The American raid, said to be in retaliation for the disputed Libyan bombing of a Berlin discotheque in which two American servicemen died, failed to eliminate Gaddafi but did kill up to 100 innocent people, including his year-old adopted daughter and some students from the International Oil Companies School. To commemorate the loss of lives the school was renamed the College of the United States Aggression Martyrs. This highly charged and somewhat bizarre title is nevertheless a more effective reminder of the attack on the people of Libya than the remaining heap of rubble. In the political arena the impact of the 1986 bombing had the effect of fuelling an increase of anti-American feeling and a renewing of patriotic fervour. In the long term it strengthened Gaddafi's position of power.

The crazy mix of ancient ruins, bombsites, dereliction and beautifully restored colonial buildings continued. This time it was a partially restored Turkish harem! From the second floor of an arcaded gallery I looked down on a courtyard heady with perfume from beds of red and white petunias. Said to be similar in design to the twin harem courts reserved for the women of the Qaramanli regents at their castle residence, the living quarters and boudoirs of the women occupied the second and third floors. Traditional rectangles of mosaic Arabic tiles, predominantly in blues, greens and yellows decorated the walls and floors. It was in the late eighteenth century during the reign of Ali Qaramanli that Libya was sinking into one of its periods of decline. Towards the end of Ali's life the French consul wrote: 'He rules, but is not obeyed. Shut up in his harem ... he builds nothing, repairs nothing, lets all collapse'.

Two centuries later these comments did not seem entirely out of place.

Has Anyone Seen Bruce?

Once again, James and his BMW came to my rescue – this time providing the opportunity to visit the largest, best preserved and restored of Libya's Roman cities: Leptis Magna. We formed a small party with Gerry and Phil – two of his colleagues – and at the last minute were joined by Kate, a recent expat arrival. A linguist and translator for an oil company, Kate had been wooed by a cleverly presented job description. Totally disenchanted with life in Libya, she was delighted to have the opportunity to escape the confines of the compound and join us on our expedition.

It so happened that the weekend of our intended visit was the weekend given as a deadline by the United Nations for Gaddafi to hand over the Lockerbie suspects. Nobody expected him to comply. He didn't and tighter sanctions were imposed. There were rumours of an organised anti-West rally in Green Square but since we were heading east out of Tripoli we didn't believe it was necessary to change our plans. Armed with cameras and a picnic lunch we set off in a small and joyous convoy heading for the freeway out of the city. As we slowed down and waited to turn onto a main road the burnt-out carcass of a car dumped at the roadside caught Kate's eye: a typical street image of Tripoli for her album. Unaware of the stringent rules about the use of cameras except at designated tourist sites, she opened the window and took the shot. Almost immediately a grey Peugeot saloon pulled alongside us. A casually dressed middle-aged Libyan leaned out and jabbed his finger at us.

"Pull over! I want to ask you some questions," he ordered in polished English.

"Quick!" James urged, "the lights are changing. Tell Phil before he drives off!"

Gerry hopped out and ran to warn Phil while we parked on some rough ground at the side of the road. The Libyan, dressed in grey slacks and an open-necked shirt with rolled-up sleeves, was waiting.

"I'm from Central Intelligence. You've been stopped for suspicious behaviour," he explained. "Give me the camera!" he ordered, turning to Kate.

At that moment Phil arrived and wanted to know what was going on.

"I was testing my camera," Kate added inventively. "The batteries haven't been working." The Libyan was unimpressed.

"Give me the camera," he repeated, taking it from her. "Now, you must come for questioning."

"Hang on!" Phil demanded. "Where's your identification?"

"I was off duty," he replied tersely, a faint flush darkening his sallow skin. "I'm from Central Intelligence. You've no right to question me!"

"Take the film but not the camera," suggested Phil. With that the Libyan flicked open the back of the camera and started pulling at the film. "Here, give it to me!" Phil said authoritatively, taking it from the Libyan and closing it. "As you can see, one photograph only has been taken," he added, displaying the roll number. With that he rattled off thirty-five shots of the pavement, rewound the film, removed it from the cassette, pulled it free and handed it over. After a brief silence the Libyan exploded.

"Who are you? Where do you work?" he demanded. Learning that Phil was the manager of a multi-national oil company, he was taken off-guard. Clearly, if he pushed things too far he could be in trouble himself. "Get away from here immediately," he threatened. "This has nothing to do with you. I'll have you arrested! I'm taking these people for questioning."

Even Phil knew that although this meant leaving us to deal with a tricky situation that he had set in motion it was time to disappear. Getting rid of Phil put the security agent back in control. He instructed us to follow his car. Minutes later we found ourselves parked at a police checkpoint surrounded by police cars and officials.

We were left sitting and wondering while telephones thrummed, and reports and consultations took place in a buzz of excitement. Minutes later in a blaze of blue lights and blaring sirens two more cars of plain-clothes men arrived and joined the furore.

Then the officer strode over, leaned on the open car window and announced, "We know you work for the CIA. You are under arrest. We are taking you to Central Intelligence for questioning."

My immediate thoughts were that this was a joke – we'd all laugh at the mistake, shake hands and be free to go, but as he continued with a combination of naive questioning and illogical accusations I realised he was serious. He was focusing on James, the nature of his work, the oil companies he worked for and had worked for and the time he'd spent in the field. He was so obsessed with linking James to a character called Bruce that, no matter how many times James denied knowledge of anyone called Bruce, he was mindlessly persistent, asking again and again: "Do you know Bruce?"

Meanwhile, Kate's protestations of innocence had failed. Hyped up by news of the sanctions, the Libyans were convinced they had discovered a group of Western spies and like a pack of hounds excited by the scent of fox they were baying for blood.

A plain-clothes detective instructed Gerry to get out of the BMW and into a nearby Suzuki jeep. His flushed face, almost matching his auburn hair and beard, indicated his alarm. The detective then got into the front passenger seat beside James. As we headed off into the traffic I turned from time to time, anxious to keep Gerry's mop of hair – just visible over the open top of the jeep – in view.

Since our car was in the lead, James had to rely on the neurotic and impatient gestures of the accompanying detective for directions. He spoke virtually no English but kept repeating, "Film, film," with the tone and speed of bullets fired from an automatic rifle while alternately thrusting his crooked right hand towards Kate for the film and knocking it against the front windscreen to direct James. Meanwhile, James was demonstrating considerable skill in following his sudden and erratic hand movements and dodging Libyan drivers attempting to overtake us on both sides. Finally, when Kate handed the detective the empty carton and pointed to the officer in the following car he became sullen but silent.

***

"About as imposing as you'd expect!" muttered James as he locked the car. We had been directed into a parking area in front of a drab two-storey concrete building housing the headquarters of Central Intelligence and were waiting for Gerry to join us. Once assembled, we silently followed our arresting officer to an unmanned reception area and through swing doors into a stone corridor lined with grey mould-stained walls. Our guide motioned to us to sit on a wooden bench opposite a small room. Through the half-open door I could make out a bucket under a filthy cracked sink and a gas ring with a black old-fashioned kettle on it. The place reeked of decay, urine and strong coffee. James's sotto voce comment that it was like a scene from *Midnight Express* was a chilling reminder of how vulnerable we were in the hands of these agitated people. Angry with the West, we had given them a focus for their suspicions and resentment.

Kate was the first victim. We watched as she was led into a room a few metres down the corridor from where we were sitting. Next, James was asked to hand over his car keys. As the minutes ticked away we thought about things we had left in the car that could be considered incriminating. Since we had planned to visit Leptis Magna, we each had a camera – then Gerry remembered that he'd tucked a map of Libya and some American dollars inside his camera case. Both maps and foreign currency were forbidden in Libya. To make matters worse, I suddenly remembered my copy of *The Guardian* smuggled in recently by a colleague. A ban of foreign newspapers had been imposed some months ago. Before we had time for further contemplation it was my turn to face interrogation.

I was escorted to join Kate in a small office, the walls lined with shelves untidily stacked with files and papers. A closed shutter covering the only window increased the seedy appearance of the room. A large fly was circumnavigating a naked light bulb dangling from frayed wires over the head of a stocky man with receding hair. Wearing the prerequisite sunglasses and leather jerkin of security, he was seated behind a large wooden desk with a folder of loose sheets spread before him. Seated on his left, our arresting officer was of a slight build and had clean-shaven, sharp features; thinning short hair plus the pregnant bulge at his waistline suggested middle age. The pair were conferring together in muted tones. I exchanged glances with Kate who was sitting upright in a sagging chair with wooden arms. A deep flush suffused her face and neck.

The officer looked up and motioned to me to sit in a well-worn, winged armchair next to Kate. He explained that his compatriot, who held the rank of captain, would ask the questions but since he spoke no English he would act as interpreter.

"Like your friend," he added, staring fixedly at Kate and referring to her job as a translator.

Then with the focus centred on me a series of questions ranging from work to personal details and interests were asked, responded to and translated. The abject simplicity of the questions and ludicrous attempts to incriminate put the whole affair on the level of a farce worthy of John Cleese. At the same time, arrests and imprisonments of innocent people on spurious espionage charges in other Arab countries – notably Beirut – were flashing through my mind. The English lecturer Brian Keenan and the journalist John McCarthy had been arrested in Beirut, interrogated, imprisoned and tortured over a number of years. They were as innocent as I was – as we all were. I tortured myself by wondering if this was how it started for them.

As if my interrogator were reading my mind, or I his, his next thrust was to accuse me of being connected with a former English teacher from the university in Tripoli, who had been deported for spying.

"This spy," he was saying, "was called Michael and he was a

very good teacher of English. What is more," he added, "Michael was a friend of the journalist John McCarthy and both were spies in Beirut."

With a tight and thudding heart I listened as the tangled web of involvement was spun around me. Next he was informing me that Terry Waite was connected with these two spies and it was after he had been in Libya to seek the release of British spies that the Americans dropped bombs on Tripoli.

The tedious and unremitting process of translating from Arabic to English and English to Arabic continued. The captain had done his on-the-spot homework. Accusations of being in league with known or invented spies had progressed to spying for companies near to our home bases in England. My current home was in Essex, therefore, I was accused of being planted as a spy for Marconi, who operated near Chelmsford! Then the heat was off me and on Kate. It was like a board game where they had a map and a list of clues and points were awarded for conclusions, no matter how tenuous or illogical.

James and Gerry, first interviewed separately in a different room, now joined us. Two wooden upright chairs were added for them. Once seated, we formed a tight semicircle facing our interrogators. A repeated pattern used for attempting to incriminate the guys was to link them with previous suspects working for oil companies. The ploy to trap James involved changing from the earlier repetition of "Do you know Bruce?" to "How long have you known Bruce?" to which his unfailing reply was: "I don't know Bruce!" Surnames were not used for spies that we were supposed to know or be connected with. Finally, we were told that Bruce, a spy for Schlumberger, had been deported.

It was Kate's turn again. It transpired that a former translator from the company where she was employed had been discovered to be a spy. What's more, we were told that this suspect, who was called Margaret, voted Conservative. Being together created a sense of bravado. The assumption that being called Margaret was synonymous with voting Conservative, like having blond hair or using a camera were synonymous with being a spy, sent a ripple of amusement between us. A fleeting smile crossed James's face. I caught his eye with near-fatal results. Repressed internal laughter in the form of vibrations in the pit of my stomach was threatening to rise and become vocal. Avoiding eye contact, I concentrated on muscle-clenching techniques and holding my breath before finally managing to convert a splutter into a cough. Then keeping my eyes averted, I blew my nose and practised deep breathing.

Meanwhile, Kate who had picked up on Margaret Thatcher's unpopularity – spawned by her support for Ronald Reagan's bombing of Tripoli and Benghazi – succeeded in diverting attention from me by denouncing Thatcherism and eulogising on the qualities of socialism – but not for long. The officer was stating that he'd seen a similar photograph to the incriminating one she had taken that day in *The Guardian* newspaper in England. I hadn't yet opened my copy of *The Guardian* and had no idea what he was referring to but wondered if they suspected that we worked for or sold stories and photographs to *The Guardian*? The mood and tone continued to swing between farce and fear – fear and farce.

The sensitive issue of the dive group's use of the raided club was resurrected. James confessed that he'd seen police on duty at the club but said he didn't know why. He denied any knowledge of the attempted coup. Although only James and I were active members of the club, it seemed that diving was considered to be the incriminating link between the four of us. James and my recent visit to Skanska, where the attack and murder of those suspected of the planned coup had taken place, increased the case against us and led to further accusations of espionage activities, involving looking for and knowing the whereabouts of Libyan submarines. The game playing continued. Determined to catch us out, they were waiting for the wrong answer. Innocent as we were, it was a game with uncertain consequences.

Finally, we were informed that there had been an attempt to overthrow the government by a group of Islamic fundamentalists from Algeria who were backed by Canadians. James and Gerry were just two of many Canadians who had replaced the out-of-favour Americans working in the oil industry. This time I avoided eye contact with James. It was the logic of the 'Mad Hatter's Tea Party'. Nevertheless, they made the rules and handed out the punishments. We had no choice but to play along as submissively as possible. After 'suspicious' behaviour, I had been warned that an arrogant manner or giving the impression of criticising or mocking anything to do with Libya were considered the most serious offences.

I thought of demanding the right to contact the British Vice-Consul for help. Then I remembered a story about a British man jailed in Tripoli for suspicious behaviour: he'd been walking along carrying a camera. The story repeated is that he was tall and good-looking with blond hair and this contributed to his downfall: his appearance distinguished him from the crowd. His camera had been smashed and he was jailed. An appeal was made to the Vice-Consul for help. A secretary answered. He was too busy. Someone would ring back. No one did.

Some months ago I may have dismissed this story as ridiculous and the stuff of Evelyn Waugh or a Graham Greene novel. After a few weeks in Libya I had begun to realise that life here was exactly that, and Greene would have found plenty of material for 'Our Man in Tripoli'! Canadian representation in Libya, in a back room at the Dutch Embassy, was about as impressive and comforting as British representation at the back of the Italian Embassy. We were on our own.

Then a volte-face. Three hours after our arrival at headquarters we were told that we were to be released. The officer admitted that he had received a radio message that morning warning him about four Yugoslavian spies that had been hanging around the People's Congress and that he'd already been tailing us with this in mind when Kate was seen taking *the* photograph. He admitted that two blond heads in the back of the car had caught his attention. The logic of blond hair and Yugoslavian spies had been confirmed by the suspicious act of taking a photograph! However, the officer confessed that now they believed that we were not spies after all and we were free to go.

The mood had changed from aggression to one of

uncomfortable cosiness. We were offered coffee, sweet, black and thick, and served in cups that Gerry muttered he'd seen being sluiced out in a bucket of filthy of water under the sink. We didn't dare refuse. The officer was making overtures towards Kate and me in the vein of 'women found him too aggressive but he didn't know what we thought?' We made non-committal noises. Then jotting his telephone number on a piece of paper, he handed it to Kate – in case we should need it! His promise that he would pay visits to us at our places of work to make sure we were getting along all right was a warning of what was in store. As we sipped the poisonous brew the officer returned James's remote-control car key. "Like 007," he said as he handed it to him. There was no suggestion of a smile.

We knew that we were not free but that from this day on we would be under surveillance. The plot they had failed to discover through interrogation, they believed would be uncovered by setting us loose to give ourselves away. Feeling decidedly low-key, we headed back to James's place to telephone Phil and have our picnic lunch. Although Phil had lost interest in the expedition we decided that in spite of lost time, the two-hour drive to Leptis and a diminished appetite for sightseeing, since we had declared that that was our intention, it would be in our own interest to continue. Given our new status we were certain that we would be tailed.

One of the points raised over lunch was a grievance that perhaps Phil had provided fuel for their anger by destroying what had been an innocent film, empty apart from the image of the burnt-out car, which would have been exposed anyway when the camera was first opened. James defended Phil on the grounds that he was experienced in dealing with locals and that, in their present mood, it was not beyond them to have kept the camera and finished the film with suitably incriminating photographs of the port or military installations thus placing them in a strong position to press charges for their own propaganda purposes.

"My thoughts exactly," Gerry confirmed. "The CIA is enemy number one. If they believe we work for the CIA they will go to any lengths to get us! It's pretty obvious they do believe it. After all they have more than enough incriminating evidence by their standards – American dollars, cameras, a map, a newspaper. People here are behind bars for less. Make no mistake. They'll watch us like hawks, hoping no doubt, that by letting us out we'll lead them to the centre of our plot!"

Our silent response said it all. Kate's final act of remorse before we left was to discard her camera and declare that as long as she was in Libya she'd never take another photograph.

***

The episode at Central Intelligence had left us short of time, but James's estimate that he should be able to complete the drive along the relatively modern freeway in less than two hours was accurate. We arrived at 3.30 p.m., giving us just two hours until the gates were officially shut. Apart from one car tucked into a far corner the place appeared utterly deserted and for one minute we feared closed. On further investigation we were relieved to find the gateway into the reception area open. The office was unmanned but a visitors' book with pen attached had been left conveniently on the shelf in front of the closed office window.

"So we are expected!" James remarked, taking the lead and signing his name. "We did the right thing. I'm convinced of it."

We followed suit, further congratulated ourselves on our decision to continue with the visit and, given the absence of any official services, appointed James as our guide. He had visited Leptis on several occasions and was aware of the immense size and layout of the place and the best route to take us on a whirlwind tour. Noticeably and unusually edgy, he was anxious to keep us moving and later confessed that throughout the visit he'd been haunted by an image of the gates clanging shut, imprisoning us in the ruins for the night.

Without other visitors the place felt dauntingly empty. To my racing imagination the ring of our footsteps over the flagstone street became the echo of the footsteps of the last departing Romans. With this image in mind I followed James along the tree-lined avenue to a flight of stone steps leading to a life-size bronze statue of the Emperor Septimius Severus, one hand extended in a gesture of giving. The gesture was appropriate for the emperor was a giving person. Born in Leptis in AD 146, he grew up there and although he became Emperor of Rome, ruling from AD 193–211, he did not forget his African roots and undertook huge programmes of work at Leptis. In AD 202 he returned to embellish his native city with splendid public buildings, strengthen the frontier desert garrisons and safeguard the farmland area on which Leptis depended for its commerce and trade.

His achievements were impressive. In fact, everything about the world of ancient Rome is impressive – from their conquests, civilisations and artwork to their decadence and barbaric cruelty. In Roman terms 'triumphal' best describes what was before us. Leptis Magna is a masterpiece of triumph from the magnificent four-fronted triumphal arch, marking the start of Triumphal Street, to the city itself. Even the order is triumphal; the city's imposing rectangular buildings stand shoulder to shoulder in perfect symmetry.

Reminiscent of the Marcus Aurelius Arch in Tripoli, the Severan Arch, built to commemorate the visit of Septimius to his native town, stands guard at the entrance to the city. Neither the remains of wooden scaffolding crowding the central arch nor the absence of marble surface panels could detract from the grandeur. The remaining panels of sculptured relief included the beautiful and tactile naked winged Victories, holding crowns and palm leaves and flying above the natural curves of the arch, as well as mythical figures amidst vines and acanthus scrolls. Missing sections and sculptures– including the *hauts-reliefs* of Septimius Severus are held in Tripoli's Castle Museum.

From the seventeenth to the nineteenth centuries it became both lucrative and fashionable to ship artefacts from the Graeco-Roman sites to Europe. Literally hundreds of columns half-buried in sand and left lying about the sites by the Arabs were excavated and transported, notably to France and England where they were used to enhance the palaces of Louis XIV at Versailles and Paris and to create an elegant ruin for George IV at Windsor Castle. The British Museum houses a variety of treasures taken for 'safe keeping' while others ended up in private houses and gardens. I stumbled upon one recently in the garden of a stately home in Dorset. An obelisk, taken from Leptis Magna by a British naval officer and shipped to England, stands in the garden of his former mansion at Kingston Lacey. Its size and weight are such that it is reputed to have needed five horse-drawn gun carriages to drag it from Poole Harbour to its present position.

As I followed James along Colonnaded Street, running through the heart of the abandoned city, I was contemplating the failure of the invading Arabs to recognise the splendour of the magnificent cities left by the Greeks and Romans – abandoning them to be buried under desert sands. Centuries later what had been of no consequence or interest to the Arabs for literally hundreds of years became a gold mine to the Italians. Thanks to the extensive excavations undertaken during the Italian era, some of the best sculptures and mosaics are safe in the museum and great sections of the ancient cities, including the Hadriatic Baths that we were now approaching, have been uncovered and partially restored.

A vast, column-lined, rectangular sports hall flanked by a complex of rooms, including a marble swimming pool, a gymnasium as well as hot, cold, tepid and steam baths, stretched before us. Momentarily caught up in admiring frescoes of men hunting cheetah and lions, I looked up to see James beckoning me to follow him. I stood for a moment, taking in the scene before us of a row of adjoining marble lavatory seats running the length of three walls. Privacy was not something of concern to the Romans and was certainly not a feature of the public lavatories! Luxury was.

The marble surrounds were in near perfect condition. I chose a central position and sat down. The distance on each side was just right for holding a conversation with either neighbour. The sheer size, grandeur and technological expertise of the place, including drainage channels under the marble seating, made our so-called civilised modern world pale by comparison and put to shame the filthy, mosquito-ridden holes in the ground serving as toilets at Libya's Central Intelligence that I'd been forced by necessity to use that morning.

"Cool, isn't it?" James asked, sitting alongside me. "Imagine taking a pew and indulging in the local gossip!"

"What about politics or intrigue?"

"Touché!" he replied, looking at his watch. "Unfortunately, we haven't time," he added, taking my hand and pulling me to my feet. "Our next coup will have to be planned on the move!"

We caught up with Kate, sombrely trailing Gerry who every so often stopped, his head buried in his guidebook, and continued along Colonnaded Street which connects the Baths with the Harbour and skirts the Severan Forum, our next stop. If the Baths were outstanding for size and grandeur the Forum was breathtaking for the beauty of its sculptured artwork. My eyes skirted the colonnaded porticoes and rested on the remains of a temple at the southern end. Before me great limestone arches linked a series of columns – set between the arches were carved marble Medusa and Nereid medallions. Each haunting face: lips pursed, cheeks full-blown, brows anxiously creased, caught in the act of blowing evil to the sea. It was a photographer's dream and my camera was working overtime.

Then James was guiding us to sculptured scenes on the Severan Pilasters: Dionysiac naked figures and scenes in vine and acanthus scrolls with animals springing from rosettes. I was in a lost world. I paused and looked up to see James standing in Justinian's pulpit – erected when he converted the temple into a basilica in the fourth century – next, he was hurriedly disappearing round a corner in a scene not unlike that from a speeded-up film of ant-like figures scurrying between climbing columns. Imposing, splendid, monumental, magnificent – words were inadequate to describe what was before us. It was like attempting to describe the Taj Mahal or a Namibian sunset without resorting to tourist brochure clichés. Impossible. You have to be there. You have to experience it for yourself!

Finally, we bypassed the market and arrived at the theatre. The vast semicircular auditorium encompassed the curved orchestra area and linked on either side with the rectangular stage. Staircases divided the seating into zones; niches provided pedestals for missing statues and secret corridors, with pop-up holes like rabbits' burrows and providing entrances and exits for actors as well as access to and from the streets. On each side of the stage stood a life-size naked male statue of the Dioscuri – the twin sons of the nymph Leda and Jupiter (Zeus). Apart from severed extremities their sensuous and well-proportioned forms have survived the centuries. More fortunate than many of their contemporaries from Sabratha that suffered attacks by Vandals or were beheaded by fanatical Muslim soldiers, they have succeeded in keeping their heads. During the Ottoman period bored Turkish soldiers are said to have played a part in further destruction of the statues by idly lopping off any remaining extremities.

Suddenly James appeared, posing as a statue on an empty pedestal at the foot of the auditorium. On the grounds that he wasn't prepared to risk arrest or the loss of his extremities, he refused to accept Gerry's challenge to remove his clothes to make his Grecian pose more convincing. Then leaping into action, he led us up the stairway to the very top of the auditorium.

Diminutive and mesmerised by the sheer size of the theatre, we gazed through distant lines of incomplete and broken columns across unexcavated land and beyond to the deep blue backdrop of the Mediterranean Sea. It was the time for contemplation and brushing up on history. Gerry reminded us that during the disintegration of Roman Africa Leptis suffered Berber raids and Vandal incursions leading to destruction and neglect. Then following partial restoration, after the Byzantine period, man deserted Leptis Magna and nature took control, burying the ancient cities. The Trajan Basilica and Forum were yet to be uncovered. It was both sobering and gratifying to know that so much more of Leptis, as well as of the remaining Graeco-Roman sites remain buried and preserved under desert sand.

As the others made their way towards the exit, pausing to change the film in my camera, I suddenly became aware of long shadows, emptiness and intense silence. To be here without busloads of tourists and all the commercial paraphernalia that accompanies tourism was like a dream. But now that I was alone, memories of this morning's interrogation surfaced and the palpable silence became unnerving. I put away the used film, loaded the next into my camera and turned.

My heart leapt into cardiovascular mode! An old man dressed in a Roman tunic and cape stood right before me. His shabby outfit was creased, as if it had just been pulled from the bottom of a dressing-up box. He had crinkly grey hair, sharp currant eyes and was unshaven. I reasoned that he must be a security guard. Or was he a security agent? Rumours that had recently filtered from the embassies of attacks on two French women at the site made me fear for my safety. He was gesturing and jabbering in Arabic.

"I don't understand," I replied. "English. *Inglesse*!" I added, backing away as if this were sufficient explanation for my response. I kept my eyes fixed on his as if outstaring a wild animal. He was making no attempt to follow but still jabbering and gesticulating. I half-turned and, catching sight of an exit, spun and ran.

Heart still pumping overtime, I hurried along a passageway until I found myself in a flagstoned street between two arches. I checked behind me. Nothing. Then turning on the spot and reminding myself that the distant strip of sea was north, I headed in the opposite direction. Seconds later I saw the recognisable outline of the Severus Arch, and almost immediately spirals of smoke rising from Gerry's cigarette led me to where my fellow CIA conspirators were resting on a convenient half-tumbled wall. As I approached James peeled away from the group and waved. Feeling the wonderful lightness of relief, I strode towards them, stopping occasionally to take a backward shot of Triumphal Street, my imagination conjuring the grating rumble of chariot wheels and clatter of hooves on flagstones.

We'd no sooner left the site than James pointed out the route to the remains of the Circus and Amphitheatre, situated to the east of the harbour.

"Another occasion. When we've more time," he explained. "Still half-buried but the atmosphere's electric. Just being there gives me a thrill. The place echoes with the past – wild beasts, gladiators and, of course, chariot racing. Said to be on a par with the Coliseum in Rome. A must!"

Light was fading by the time we'd reached the main road to Tripoli. There was an air of elation, as if we'd achieved something that had nothing to do with the need to confirm our visit to satisfy Central Intelligence. The two hours at Leptis had been no more than an aperitif, but a potent one. The place yawned with unexplored treasures. James stopped to let Gerry buy a bag of ringed doughnuts and some cans of coke from a roadside stall. We tucked into them, bandying some of the most memorable lines from the morning's scenario between us as if from some well-known play. Variations of 'How long have you known Bruce?' were the most popular and, in our present mood, no matter how many times they were repeated, resulted in hilarity. Even Kate who'd been notably sombre throughout the visit joined in.

Just as everything was running smoothly the traffic started to slow. In true Libyan fashion blaring horns and vehicles nosing alongside from right and left continued until nothing could move. We debated whether it was a road-check or an accident, then remembered the anti-West rally in Green Square. This, James decided, was the cause of the jam. Then just as the traffic started moving, Gerry alerted us that we were being followed.

"A blue Fiat," he warned, "apart from us, it was the only vehicle parked at Leptis."

Suspecting that he was correct, James resolved to lose our pursuer. We were approaching a roundabout. Living up to the recently conferred 007 image, he wove between the traffic, circled the roundabout twice, then bypassing the jammed main exit to Tripoli, headed off along a minor road. After a few hundred metres the tarmac ended and the road became a sandy track. Nevertheless, James put his foot down and the BMW flew over the rutted surface, soaring over bumps, headlights searching the thickening darkness.

"I'll show them," he promised. "If it's games the bastards want – it's games we'll play."

"Take it easy, James," Gerry warned. "We're being followed,

but we may as well take it easy. We've nothing to lose. All we're doing is heading back. This way we'll end up in a ditch or get taken in again. Speeding makes it look as if we're on the run."

His voice expressed our shared concern but James was not in the mood for caution. The track had narrowed to a lane lined on one side by a rough stone wall while on the other a screen of trees blocked out the sky. Above the wall the sky was leaning over us, heavy with velvety darkness and fretted with stars. We were silent – immersed in our own thoughts. I could sense that Kate had sunk into her 'I'm never going to get out of this hell-hole' mood! Looking back, I saw only darkness. We were bouncing along, following our tilting and dipping headlights, through landscape that was opening up into scrubby desert.

"I haven't a clue where we are," announced the indomitable James, stretching and reaching for a cigarette, "but what the hell. We're on our own. We've half a packet of smokes, half a tank of gasoline, shades. Let's hit it!"

Ignoring Gerry's advice, he put his foot down hard and the vehicle soared and bounced over the pot-holed track until I was convinced she would grow wings and take off. Suddenly Kate was thrown out of her dark mood.

"Okay, James," she said, "you can slow down – there's nothing following and look, I can see a light. I can see lights!" she added with more animation than she'd shown on the entire trip.

As we drew nearer we realised we'd reached a small settlement or village. A row of shop houses lined the track then petered out as we reached a junction. A tarmac road crossed our path. There were, of course, no signposts.

"Right, I think," said James and, since no one questioned his judgement, set off again, headlights probing the darkness. All too soon we seemed to be in the same situation as before: the road had faded to a track and we were surrounded by low-lying scrubby vegetation.

"I'm pretty sure we're heading the wrong way." Gerry had rolled his window down and was leaning out backwards, gazing at the sky. "At least there's no cloud. Now, let me see, it should be ..."

"Intelligent fellow. No wonder they thought you were the stuff of CIA. Hang on!" James directed, "I'll stop then you can get out and stargaze properly."

"There!" Gerry exclaimed as he completed an on-the-spot circle. "The North Star. I was right. We should be heading that way – not south into the desert. We need to find the sea. We need north."

"Somebody's determined to give us a hard time," I said. "Somebody's got it in for us."

"Have you no faith?" replied the indefatigable James as he turned the car. "We've still got a quarter of a packet of smokes, a quarter of a tank of gasoline. We don't need shades. Let's hit it!"

We hit a ridge of compact earth and took off from the runway. James's optimism proved right. Once we'd retraced our route to the junction and headed north he began to recognise features of the landscape. Fifty kilometres later even the comparative newcomers to Libya recognised a group of pylons and then some high-rise buildings on the outskirts of Tripoli. With the end in sight we completed the journey with revived spirits. As we entered the compound the Weasel squinting through his half-open window caused a moment of disquiet. His penetrating eyes checked the faces in the car but he made no attempt to question us. It was impossible to tell if we were expected. James cruised through the lifted barrier, dropped the three of us off and set off for a dinner party engagement in a neighbouring compound. There was going to be no competition for the most entertaining after-dinner stories that evening!

Bronze statue of the emperor Septimius Severus: Leptis Magna

Triumphal arch dedicated to Septimius Severus

Medusa and Nereid medallions held between great limestone arches

Dionysiac figures on finely sculptured Severan Pilasters

The auditorium of the theatre against a backdrop of sea

Re-assembled columns form an elegant backdrop to the stage

The Morning After

The following day was a work day. The college where I was under contract to teach was unique in several ways. In the first place it catered for bilingual students of mixed European and Libyan parentage studying Cambridge overseas courses in preparation for attending university. My role was to teach English Literature to small classes of highly motivated pupils; highly motivated because their object was to obtain grades high enough to merit government grants to continue higher studies in the UK. This was a form of escape the students dreamt of. The college principal betrayed the presence of Italian blood in his veins from his habit of referring to me as 'Adriana'. The senior mistress, of English origin and the mainstay of the college, had lived with her Italian partner in Libya for many years and in spite of political upheavals and the deprivations suffered under the Gaddafi regime regarded Libya as her home.

The premises were pretty unique too! Housed in a former Italian villa, the building was old and run down with rooms primitively furnished with post-war single lidded desks, complete with inkwells and child-sized chairs; ancient badly scarred blackboards straddling pegged easels, complete with supplies of white chalk and filthy dusters. A further drawback suffered by the college was shared premises; two further institutions used the same building. One followed on our heels for the duration of the afternoon and another moved in for the evening. There was no library and no facilities or resources. Basic textbooks were ordered from the UK for each course and sold to individual pupils or recycled from those leaving at the end of each academic year.

The absence of books was the direct result of Gaddafi's policy of ridding the country of imperialistic influences by ordering the burning of all texts in English. A member of staff remembered the day that soldiers armed with Kalashnikovs tramped through the building, collecting all the books from the shelves before setting fire to them in the playground, watched by wide-eyed pupils. There were neither blinds nor curtains on the windows, neither was there air conditioning or heating. In summer we opened the windows and in winter, when temperatures could drop to near freezing, we kept warm by wearing several layers of clothes and fur-lined boots.

The main body of the staff, like the principal and students, was made up from a mix of Libyan and European members. The Libyan female contingent, forming the greater part of the workforce, was dominant in manner, numbers and build. Their ample forms were dressed in European-style tops and skirts, albeit dowdy in style and drab in colour with a less than stylish *hejab* (scarf) tied on the head. Since the only European clothes available in Libya were imported stock from Bulgaria on sale in the local supermarkets, their unstylish dress code was just as likely to be the result of lack of choice as lack of taste. The most highly ridiculed garments on display on the supermarket shelves were voluminous woollen knickers reaching from waist level to the knees! In retrospect they may well have been useful thermal aids for combating winter temperatures!

Female members of the college staff were the most liberated Libyan females I met! Response to any mention of the Leader or politics were more than likely to take the form of an irritated 'tut' or an indifferent shrug of the shoulders. They were not overzealous in the line of duty. On the odd occasion when a staff meeting was called after the morning session, one of them would track me down and remind me to respond to any suggestion made by the principal with: 'Yes. Yes.' This, it was explained, would keep the meeting short and then we'd all be free to go home. Who was I to argue?

***

The evening after our adventures at Central Intelligence Kate and I shared a bottle of home-made white wine. She was chain-smoking and more determined than ever to leave the country as soon as she could get her hands on her passport. In an effort to calm her, I was attempting to be philosophical and dismiss the interrogation as a crazy adventure – a one off – a mistake. After she left I had no problem falling asleep but woke in the night, my mind startlingly clear. By Libyan Intelligence standards my room was fermenting with subversive material. From the experience at Central Intelligence I knew that my written accounts of life and travels in Libya would be considered a criminal offence. If a photograph of a burnt-out car was sufficiently incriminating to have the four of us accused of working for the CIA and interrogated then I dared not think about the consequences of the discovery of my writing.

One of the most serious crimes in Libya, punishable by imprisonment, was criticism of the regime. The fact that security had raised Terry Waite's visit to negotiate the release of former hostages was playing on my mind – as were the fatuous but dangerous links with America's bomb attacks. I recalled hearing the story of one of the men who had been arrested and imprisoned when letters from colleagues he was taking home to deliver were intercepted and read by security. The crime: he was the bearer of comments that amounted to criticism of Libya! It had taken protracted visits by Terry Waite to secure his release. By comparison I feared that written accounts of my experiences since arriving in Libya would merit a firing squad.

In fact, paranoia about the transfer of so-called subversive material was such that the use of photocopying machines was forbidden unless the material had been vetted and the operation supervised by a Libyan. In addition, all fax or telephone messages out of the country had to go through security. Material that came in was heavily censored.

Many restrictions, not explained to new recruits before arrival, only become clear when the law is unwittingly broken. The use of cameras is the most obvious example. It was from the chance visit of a friend while I was working on my laptop that I learnt

I was breaking a serious law: the compulsory registration of typewriters and computers. In fact, without advance permission from the authorities private computers were forbidden! No one could believe that I'd walked into Libya with a laptop computer and printer in my hand luggage. As a CIA suspect it was too late to make a confession. Now I was faced with removing all incriminating material and hiding the laptop and printer.

I am no technological expert but there were some basic steps I could take to save my work. I decided to transfer detail from hard to floppy disks, hide these and get rid of all printed material. First I had to transfer the material then clear the hard disk. I looked at my watch. I had just one hour until it was time to leave for the college. Beginning to fulfil the role I'd been branded with, I set about my subversive activities until I believed I'd left no evidence. Then packing the laptop and printer into my dive-bag, I locked the bag and stowed it into the bottom of the wardrobe, closed and locked the door. Next, I put the keys in my briefcase and secreted the floppies into a side pocket. The final stage was to get rid of printed material.

I was in the habit of printing work in its final stages and then reading through it before making final adjustments. I flipped through the wad of pages. Fleeting memories of Kate's film and the imprisoned British hostages surfaced. It had to go! Taking half a dozen sheets at a time, I mechanically tore them into strips then across into squares, put the pieces into a plastic bag, tied the top of the bag into a knot and dropped it into the bin. Almost immediately I retrieved it. I couldn't leave it here or transfer it to the bin in the garden. The house was probably being watched. Security there would have warned security here. I thought about the toilet but the paper was thick and the plumbing unreliable. As a last resort, I squeezed the bag into my briefcase. My next plan was to deposit it anonymously somewhere en route to the college.

Minutes later, like a spy on the run, I was hurrying down the road. The black surly guard had replaced the Weasel. I nodded and ducked under the barrier, conscious of my bulging secret. The street outside was heaped with rubbish. There were no bins or facilities for disposal outside of the compound. Litter was dropped or dumped onto pavements and into gutters. Every so often someone set fire to the mounting piles. Some of the paper burnt, plastic smouldered and filled the air with dark smoke, solid substances cooked and rotted slowly. Blackened tins remained to be trampled, squashed by cars or kicked by youngsters. I couldn't drop my bag here. It would attract attention. A huddle of homeless Sudanese immigrants had collected outside the gates, hoping for casual work in the compound. One had set himself up with shoe-mending oddments to make a few dinars. Two boys stared from a doorway. A ragged child threw a piece of wood in my direction and ran off. The road was full of eyes.

I walked to the end, practising shallow breathing in an attempt to avoid inhaling foul odours from the river of sewage running down the side of the road. Workmen had filled a major outbreak with concrete and now it had found a new outlet. Next I turned my head to avoid looking at the remains of a run-over cat – its body flattened like a rug – but failed to eliminate the image of its open mouth and agonised expression stamped in my head. It floated before me. Once I reached the main street I flagged a taxi and sat wedged alongside two swarthy males, hugging my secret.

The hill leading to the college was once an upmarket Italian residential area of detached, walled villas. Today, although considerably run-down, the villas continued to be supplied with refuse bins lodged between mounds of rubble on the pavement outside. My plan was to deposit the bag and its contents in one of these bins. As soon as I'd left the taxi and started walking I knew it wouldn't work. As always my blonde hair attracted every pair of eyes. Men working overhead on a house froze and stared as if caught and cast in a flow of lava. A pair of youths, leaning against a wall, burned holes through me with their eyes. A car, crunching over piles of sand and rubble scattered across the road, slowed, tooting as it passed. What if I were being tailed? If I were to be picked up after dumping my bag of dismembered parts, and they too were picked up and pieced together, I would be handing them evidence. I had no choice but to carry my burden with me.

My students were immersed in a monthly test, leaving me time for marking essays and preparing for tomorrow's sessions, but the bulge in my suitcase was taking precedence over Hamlet's dilemma over his uncle's guilt. As soon as I got as far as dismissing my fears as crazy I remembered the madness of the accusations made against us. This was a crazy world. I decided that the only way was to set fire to the sheets. But where? It couldn't be in the garden behind the bungalow or in the bin, without smoke and detection. Burial was an alternative but once again detection was a possibility.

It wasn't until I was in the taxi on my way back to the compound that I devised a plan that might work. As soon as I was in the house I made for the kitchen. I was attempting to untie the knot on the plastic bag holding the torn sheets when a sharp knock on the door sent my heart racing. Dropping the bag under the sink, I kept perfectly still. It could be Kate but equally it could be security. If security were here to search and found the bag – the torn strips of paper would be guilt on a plate. I waited, holding my breath as if breathing would give me away and hoping whoever it was would go away. After several minutes of silence, I tiptoed to the corner of the lounge window. I could see no one. All was quiet and the street seemed deserted. I turned the key in the lock then, remembering that I hadn't checked to see if the house had been searched in my absence, made for the bedroom.

The wardrobe door was closed and secure just as I'd left it. Back in the kitchen I retrieved the plastic bag, struggled with shaking hands to untie the knot then, picking up the teapot, emptied the remains of the morning's tea into it. Two things happened. The surface of the print turned brown, smudged and ran, and the torn squares of paper clung together in a sodden mass. Satisfied with the irretrievable state of the pieces, I emptied the excess liquid into the sink, shook the contents together until they formed a pulpy mash and was retying the knot when a determined rapping on the door sent my heart racing again.

Thrusting the bundle under the sink once more and taking a deep breath, I walked to the door. Just as I was about to open it a voice called.

"Anyone at large?"

It was James. "Thank God," I whispered as I let him in and relocked the door. He listened in silence as my story tumbled out then responded in hushed tones.

"Sounds as if it's done for but I think you'll feel better with it gone. Why don't you give it to me – let me dispose of it? It's possible," he added, lowering his voice, "that we – the four of us – are on the bugging list. You'll know if you are," he added. "We'll speak more – on the next dive trip," he continued. "In the meantime – how about you give me the remains and put the kettle on? I'll stow the booty in my boot, so to speak."

As I followed his suggestions and watched him disappear with the remains I suddenly understood the true meaning of 'lifting a weight from the mind' and why there are so many expressions to describe the incredible 'lightness of relief' that now swept through me. It wasn't tea I needed. Taking a half-empty bottle of wine from the fridge and two tumblers from the cupboard, I filled them just in time to hand one to James as he came through the door. "To survival!" he said, smiling his approval and raising his glass.

Of Cabbages and Kings

'I cannot vouch for what I am about to tell you but only repeat what the Libyans say'.

Herodotus' words are my sentiments exactly for I too cannot vouch for the truth of what I tell you but only repeat what others in Libya say!

One of the methods of survival in Libya was getting together with other expats to share stories and experiences. This not only helped to reduce tension but more often than not was a source of entertainment. After-dinner conversations frequently gravitated to stories of Gaddafi's shortcomings. The more serious focused on the detrimental effects of his policies and actions on the people and country, and the more entertaining on rumours concerning his idiosyncrasies – primarily his obsession with being surrounded by beautiful, young females. The members of his modern-day harem, variously referred to by the media as 'the Nuns' or 'the Green Nuns', are said to have black belts in judo and are notorious for becoming involved in scuffles with security agents from other countries when protecting their Leader on trips abroad.

Expatriate residents were more in favour of the theory that they are a bunch of schoolgirls, trained in an academy that is the epitome of a girls' boarding school except that the lessons given are propaganda about their Leader and armed military parade-ground drills. A TV crew did get their cameras in once and made it clear that the girls hadn't a clue how to fire anything and that the whole affair is a charade. It is a military-style harem of schoolgirls, dressed as soldiers, who swear to lay down their lives for their Leader and are rumoured to have duties that extend beyond guarding his body. If the following eye-witness account of attempts to train schoolgirls to march is anything to go by then on the credibility front Gaddafi's female army has a long way to go!:

"Puce in the face the officer in charge was bellowing, 'Left! Right! Left! Right!' Even after weeks of practice some girls were moving their right legs, some their left and some were in-between. When he called, 'Halt!' some stopped, others carried on marching. It was like a take-off of *Dad's Army* – so bad or so good that I had to stuff something in my mouth to stop myself exploding with laughter."

In 1981, under the slogan 'The People under Arms', the latest phase of the revolution was launched. Schools and workplaces were to undergo military training in time for the parade to celebrate Gaddafi's twenty years in power on 1st September 1989 as well as ensuring that thousands of people would be ready for action, should the need arise! One of my colleagues, who witnessed the phase, recounted her experiences to me.

Gun training was compulsory – nobody could get a passport or visa without the final qualifying certificate. There were three guns to master: a pistol, a rifle and a Kalashnikov. Even housewives had to learn how to clean, load and fire guns. The final test was target practice. Trainees were taken to a military firing range and allowed fifteen shots. A local secondary school teacher returning from the test, waving her qualifying certificate, was asked her score.

"Nil," she replied. "I had to take the test not pass it."

Finally, to help pay for arming the nation a set amount of money was withdrawn from everyone's pay packet each month, including the expatriate workforce – enough, my informant said, to pay for a consignment of Kalashnikovs! Military personnel were sent into secondary schools to conduct compulsory assemblies to train pupils to march and teach them to handle guns. The boys took this training seriously, were anxious to please the officers in charge and passed with flying colours. On the other hand, training the girls proved to be more challenging:

"As a result of an inability or lack of desire to listen and concentrate the girls found marching in time impossible. I thought the officer in charge was going to burst a blood vessel in his neck. While the poor man was delivering instructions some of the girls were talking, some looking in the wrong direction while the more industrious students had notebooks with them and were revising for tests. If the officer came near they stuffed the books into their clothes.

"After training came the delivery of cadet uniforms for the parade. None fitted. The girls spent all morning swapping tops and bottoms with each other. Finally, they were told to take home what they'd got and make it fit. At that time tight trousers were fashionable, at least in Libya. The girls came back with skin-tight trousers and some of them had sewn flowers on their military hats. Others wore their *hejabs* (headscarves) underneath the hats. Next army boots were delivered – all one size, huge and laced halfway up the legs like paratroopers. These were rejected.

"When it came to the actual parade, to set off the tight trousers the girls wore high-heeled shoes. However, the best touch was provided by earrings – long, gold, dangling earrings swaying over the Russian Kalashnikovs strapped across their shoulders. Next to the girls, the most entertaining group in the parade were the 'human frogs' – Libya's deep-sea divers. Kitted in full diving gear, including fins, they demonstrated remarkable skill in marching backwards and surviving the heat!"

Another resident recalled watching the televised arrival of the King of Morocco who had been invited to attend the celebrations. It all began with Gaddafi and his bevy of female bodyguards waiting at the jetty to welcome the monarch who was arriving by boat. TV cameras were focused on the royal visitor as, immaculately dressed in a black suit, white shirt and black tie, he walked towards Gaddafi followed by his similarly attired bodyguards. The customary greetings of proffered noses were exchanged between the two leaders.

Then as Morocco's king climbed into the waiting car his personal bodyguards attempted to get in with him. However, Gaddafi's female attendants – backed up by his authentic macho-male military bodyguards – had other ideas. Pulling the king's men out of the way, they attempted to get in the car themselves. A fight broke out between the two factions. Gaddafi intervened by grabbing one of the king's guards by the scruff of the neck and hurling him into others who lost their balance and fell over. Residents, glued to TV screens at home, watched the unedited scenes in disbelief.

Today, the world at large is no longer surprised by Gaddafi's flamboyant and eccentric behaviour. The more pompous and conventional the venue or person he is meeting face to face, the more outrageous his behaviour is likely to be. Bedouin tents, camels and female bodyguards are all part of his roadshow.

When the BBC's World Affairs Editor, John Simpson – with camera-man in tow – arrived in Libya to conduct an interview he was expecting the full works. On the contrary, the designated venue was a windowless caravan in a military compound. When he was eventually permitted to transfer to the expected and preferred Bedouin tent he'd spotted nearby and Gaddafi finally turned up, instead of being kitted out in full Bedouin garb he was dressed in a Nelson Mandela-style Hawaiian shirt and an aged straw trilby worn sideways on. In spite of assertions to the contrary, the fact that Gaddafi didn't remove the hat and no one advised him to do so during the interview clearly upset John Simpson's attempts to maintain BBC respectability. In the cat-and-mouse entertainment of the scene it wasn't difficult to tell who was the cat. In fact, on this occasion, Gaddafi's game-playing and ability to confuse were given full rein.

It was not until the near end of the interview that Gaddafi made a surprise revelation. His casual declaration, that although the Lockerbie suspects were not guilty they could stand trial – the effective means of unblocking the entire issue of sanctions – was a major scoop. The question remains. Did Nelson Mandela's influence go deeper than his dress code? Was he instrumental in putting Gaddafi into a kissing frame of mind?

Game-playing and politics apart there was more to the interview than met the eye. The untimely flatulent effects of Gaddafi's love of camel's milk added yet another dimension to the interview. In his written account John Simpson admits that at the time he was unaware of the sound effects. However, picked up and recorded on the personal microphone pinned to Gaddafi's floral shirt, they were loud and clear on the recording. Now the bemused smile that had appeared on Gaddafi's face from time to time during the interview made sense! The 'breaking of wind' was audible in both the truncated version on the *Nine O'clock News* as well as on *Simpson's World*!

Meanwhile, back in the dark days of the sanctions a favourite story revived for newcomers was that of Gaddafi's uneventful ascent to power. The military coup was reported to be a 'walkover' that took place while the monarch, King Idris, was receiving medical treatment overseas. During his absence a group of military officers placed his nephew Crown Prince Hassan Rida al Sanusi under house arrest, abolished the monarchy and proclaimed the new Libyan Arab Republic. The pièce de résistance on show in the museum in Tripoli features a battered VW Beetle, from which Gaddafi stepped to take control. A far cry from images displayed around the country showing him as a dashing officer on a rearing horse, brandishing a sword and leading his country to freedom and independence! The reality is that it wasn't until January 1970, three months after the takeover of power, that he emerged from a group of young officers as leader. A disciple of Egypt's Abdel Nasser, Gaddafi's anti-Western policies were to have immediate and far-reaching effects.

The undisputed truth is that disillusionment at home from the failure of a number of Gaddafi's internal policies resulted in regular attempts to unseat him. His remarkable success rate for survival is attributed to the posting of numerous spies in public places, an elaborate system of house bugging and phone tapping plus tight control of the media and international communications. Most expatriates took this in their stride and were prepared to go for a walk or drive to discuss 'sensitive' issues, especially the latest rumours on the political front.

During this period of hyper-political activity there was no doubt about Gaddafi's fear for his safety. He was said to never sleep in the same place for more than one night and to travel in disguise. In all probability this is how he evaded Reagan's bombers. The lead story at the time was that, disguised as a woman, he travelled in a hearse while Gaddafi lookalikes travelled alongside in convoy!

Of more immediate concern to the expatriate community were horror stories about medical facilities in Libya. These included a lack of trained medical staff, out-of-date or unhygienic equipment and the deliberate infection of foreigners with the Aids virus. It wasn't until I had been in Libya for some weeks that I learnt about the obligatory initiation rites practised on new recruits: Libyan law demanded that every newcomer underwent a compulsory medical test. Previous recruits competed with their stories.

"Unbelievable! Didn't have to undress or remove jewellery."

"We were lined up and pushed one by one into a small booth just as we were."

"Machines didn't work. Staff continued pressing buttons as if they did!"

"No one spoke or read English. A woman seated at a desk shuffled through a pile of medical forms until she came to one with a vaguely matching photograph! I've suffered from an identity crisis ever since! What a farce!"

Reports of the compulsory tests for Aids were of a more serious nature, especially the account of an individual who suffered a needle forced into bone; the attacked arm subsequently turned black and blue from shoulder to wrist. In addition to personal suffering were fears concerning the sterility of needles and the validity of results. Although Libya was reputed to have highly sophisticated medical equipment they didn't have qualified staff with the necessary expertise to use it thus out-of-date and worn-out stock continued to be used. Rumour had it that without warning or explanation newcomers were rounded up, herded into a minibus and taken to a local clinic for chest X-rays and blood tests for Aids.

The five-star medical treatment I had received at a Harley Street clinic in preparation for the start of my contract in Libya included a chest X-ray and test for the Aids virus. I had to bring the results of these tests with me. When I intimated that on these grounds I was going to refuse further tests I was warned that this could result in reprisals – notably non-payment of salary and retained passport. "There is no choice!" I was told emphatically. In spite of this or, maybe because of this, I made up my mind. If and when I was summoned I would not comply, then I put it to the back of my mind.

So much time had gone by since my arrival that I convinced myself that I had escaped. Then just days later, during a coffee break at college, I received a message. A driver was coming to pick me up at 11 a.m. No reasons were given. My suspicions roused, I asked for an explanation only to have them confirmed. My destination was the local clinic. I explained to the administration staff that the authorities had my medical records including the results of a chest X-ray and blood test for Aids on file, further tests were unnecessary and a possible health hazard. I asked them to tell the driver I was not going.

Minutes later I was surrounded by a crowd of administrative and teaching staff. Various spokesmen and women took it in turns to cajole, plead, demand and threaten. Although I was beginning to fear being taken by force, I was adamant in my refusal to comply. Only when I tested the situation by defiantly spinning on my heels and walking away did they give up. From the corner of my eye I watched the principal throw his hands in the air and dismiss the driver.

It was through meeting and spending time with expatriates that had settled in Libya and made it their home as well as meeting and talking to ordinary Libyans like my teaching colleagues and local shopkeepers (many spoke good English) on a day-to-day basis that I was able to develop a more balanced view of Libyan people and their country. As in so many countries with policies thrust upon them by governments or self-appointed leaders it was the people who suffered. The average Libyan was friendly, resourceful and curious about the outside world. Bewildered by political upheavals and worn down by constant changes of policy resulting in growing poverty and estrangement from the outside world, they just wanted peace and to be free to get on with their lives. Others developed an incredible laissez-faire attitude to the events shaping their lives. Maybe this was the means of keeping one's sanity and the means of survival!

Footprints and Shadows

My first sighting of Sabratha's Roman Theatre was from the road while en route to a diving site west of Gargaresh. The image of the elegant curved frontage, rising from desert scrub not unlike a surrealistic painting, had stayed with me and I was determined to see it close up. However, apart from visits to local beaches with the diving group and one trip to Tripoli, opportunities for travel were eluding me. The tourist industry had closed down and most expats, advised by their companies not to travel, refused to leave the compounds except to go to work or the local shops. One long-term employee reminded me, "We're here to make money and save money and not to put ourselves in jeopardy."

It was a logic I could not identify with and which did not deter me from my determination to travel. Meanwhile, I found myself acting as a psychiatric consultant to Kate. She had not recovered from the interrogation and spent all her spare time sitting by an open window, smoking and planning ways of retrieving her passport. She invented deaths in her family; planned reporting its loss; considered stealing it; and finally, resorted to fantasies for escape that made the imaginings of Johnson's *Rasselas* trapped in the Happy Valley pale by comparison.

As the weeks passed and there was still no sign of the passport, Kate settled for a plan to escape at Christmas when, according to her job description, she would be issued with a visa and return ticket for an interim leave. With this idea in mind she started marking off days on the calendar and using her linguistic skills to stretch the minds of bored oil wives by teaching them French. Tired of the limitations of stuffing aubergines for the dinner party circuit and distilling wine, they were seeking culture and paying highly sought after black market American dollars for it.

Finally, she joined the Darts' Club and discovered the numbing effects of Flash, a potent brew smuggled in from Tunisia.

"Are you out of your mind?" was Kate's not unexpected reply when in desperation I asked her if she would accompany me on a trip to Sabratha. My fellow CIA suspects were not available. Sadly, James was nearing the end of his contract and had resolved to avoid any activity that could prevent his safe and speedy exit, while Gerry was out of the country on his annual leave. I was on my own. Without private transport the alternative mode of travel was in a 'People's Taxi'. Yellow and white ancient Peugeot estates with seating for eight but carrying up to ten, the taxis have set routes from which they do not deviate.

No matter where you lived the pick-up point for trips west was Tripoli. For residents in Gargaresh wanting to travel west, this involved catching a taxi on an eastbound route into the centre of Tripoli in order to get another one out which would pass by the starting point an hour or so later. It was pointless to expect logic! If you were prepared to put up with this inconvenience plus the discomfort of no air conditioning; cramped seating and two-door entry from the pavement side for three rows of seats; ash and butts from cigarettes made from a mixture of camel dung and weeds carpeting the floor space as well as asphyxiating smoke from the driver and assorted male Libyan passengers, the fare is set and cheap.

Even if I had to resort to using a People's Taxi to get to Sabratha and even if I had to travel alone, I was determined to visit the site. I set off for the pick-up point on the main road, fully prepared to spend the greater part of the day travelling Libyan-style and finished with a lasting memory of being pinned against the door by two overweight local women for the entire outward journey from Tripoli to Sabratha.

Unlike their female counterparts in neighbouring Arab countries where the all-encompassing chador and even the visor allow viewing for both eyes, Libyan women view the world with one eye. This is accomplished by holding the side of the *farashiya* – a drape covering the head and shoulders – across the face leaving an opening just large enough for one eye to be exposed.

Inconvenience apart, the serious consequence is reported to be a high incidence of blindness in one eye among older women. On the other hand, the number of overweight Libyan women has been accounted for by the Arab male's great liking for corpulent females. Apparently, this was as true for women in the past as it is for those of today – a point made beautifully clear by Miss Tully in one of her letters: 'ladies in Tripoli who think if they are not too fat to move without help, they cannot be strictly handsome'.

My travelling companions, like huge cones swathed in black *farishiyas* from head to toe, filled the seat and clutched at the material beneath their viewing holes with small plump fists.

It was a relief to finally escape from the heat and claustrophobia of the vehicle. Staggering into bright sunlight, I reassembled my limbs to find the outline of the theatre right before me. With Haynes's plan of the site in my hands I made for and then paused alongside the on-site museum. I had been warned that the museum would be closed and true enough there was no sign of life behind the firmly locked doors but it was a good spot to get my bearings. The main entrance to the imperial city was in a direct line leading north-westward to the Forum. I could make out distant, ordered lines of restored columns marking the outline of the Imperial City and the Christian Basilicas of the Byzantine period. Utterly deserted, the tumble of ruins and columns stretched into the distance on both sides and northwards towards a strip of blue melting into the horizon – the Mediterranean Sea.

Sabratha has a dramatic past. Originally a Phoenician settlement and trading post and a one-time Greek settlement, the city flourished under the Romans, becoming well known for its trade in grain, oil, gold, ivory, ebony, wild animals and slaves brought from Central Africa via the Fezzan and Ghadames. Its consequent dramatic and potted history includes severe damage from earthquakes and attacks by Austurian Berbers in the fourth century, consolidated by serious destruction under Vandal rule. Pillaged and left to decay, it was partially restored and fortified by the Byzantine Emperor Justinian. Used for a time as a military garrison by the Arabs after their conquest, it was finally abandoned to fast-encroaching desert sands.

Since I was on my own I resolved to take the advice of friends and restrict my visit to places within hailing or high-speed sprinting distance of the main road. I planned to make my way east, bypassing the theatre, and head towards the coast to the outlying site of the Temple of Isis. This way I could save Sabratha's pièce de résistance till last. It was also conveniently near the edge of the site and the exit road. With the stunning outline of the honey-coloured curved frontage of the theatre right before me, I walked towards it, my footsteps the only sound disturbing the absolute silence of this abandoned world. The belief that I was a lone visitor to this amazing Roman theatre and UNESCO World Heritage Site left me both excited and more than a little unnerved

My mission for both monuments was not so much historic as aesthetic. I wanted shots of skyward-climbing columns against a backdrop of sea as well as a selection of shots of the elegant tiers of arches and columns of the theatre so painstakingly reassembled by the Italians. Pausing once more to inspect the map, I identified the position of the temple by a line of columns visible to my right on the very edge of the sea.

A short cut across rough ground overgrown by low-lying green bushes seemed the best option. Before long the heat and glare from the overhead sun matched by flies, tumbles of walls and shrubs armed with wicked spikes had turned the route into an assault course, but I'd gone too far to turn back. I continued picking my way, unhooking lethal spikes from my skin and garments and wiping sweat from my eyes, until I was close enough to be in range for some distance shots: tantalising glimpses of sea between the columns of a courtyard that once surrounded the temple.

The shushing of waves, collapsing and retreating on the beach, was the only sound from the raised podium of the temple. I stood for a moment, marvelling in my solitude and the surroundings. It was here that the Italians discovered a fragmented statuette and dedicatory inscription in honour of Isis, enabling them to identify the temple dedicated to the worship of this fascinating goddess.

Egypt's influence on Libya infiltrated many aspects of life and the cult of Isis was no exception. An ancient Egyptian deity, her cult took various forms. One of the most popular is as the goddess of the cow-horn headdress; she is associated with the religious practices of revering the cow still practised by Hindus to this day. However, Isis, also revered as a mother goddess, has been equated with the Holy Virgin of Christianity and considered the deification of motherhood. With the acceptance of Christianity as the official religion of the Roman Empire in the fourth century BC the worship of Isis was banned. Many of her temples were destroyed or converted to Christianity. Most remarkably, surviving icons of Isis and Horus, her son, were renamed as the Madonna and Her Child. Indeed, in many of the earliest carvings, it is said that it is impossible to tell which pair they depict.

The mental leap from the Temple of Isis to the Roman theatre was aided by the return trek. This time I took the longer route west along the beach, skirting the crumbling remains of the Baths of Oceanus and two Christian Basilicas, until I reached the seaward end of the theatre complex. Relieved to escape from the heat, I stood for a moment, absorbing the shade, gulping the remains of warm bottled water and surveying the scene before me. Like everywhere on and around the site layers of sand covered the ground and every surface, collecting in nooks and crannies. When a breeze arose if you remained perfectly still you could sometimes hear the movement – not unlike the pattering of raindrops. Looking back, I could see the trail made by the neat outlines of my footprints. Soon they too would be erased.

Before me shadowed archways opened onto views of the auditorium and the three-storied gallery of marble columns, forming an imposing backdrop to the stage. The place was clothed in silence. Eyes searching the shadows, half-expecting to glimpse a figure in a toga; ears alert for a footfall or movement, I walked forwards scanning the remaining rows of empty seats to reassure myself that I was alone. Then a series of marble bas-reliefs framed in adjacent recesses between colonettes on the stage front took my attention. I moved closer to inspect the images ranging from various deities to scenes from everyday life. Mind and camera focused on a panel in the near centre depicting a libation – the pouring of wine as an offering to the gods – on the joined hands of the personification of Rome and Sabratha in the presence of soldiers. Alongside, a soldier waited with a handsome sacrificial bull.

Satisfied with my achievements and resolving to return to the site with a companion for further explorations, I retraced my steps towards the exit. On reaching the museum I turned, intending to take one final shot of the pale theatre walls slipping into shadow. Fingers poised on the case of my camera, I paused. A man was standing against the theatre wall. He was smoking – his hand held mid-air as if he too had been taken unawares.

We continued our long-distance gazing until, attempting to rationalise his presence, I turned, walking in the direction of the road. Dressed in dark trousers and an open-necked shirt with rolled-up sleeves, he could be either a curious local or a visitor. But, I reasoned, there was no nearby settlement; this guy was without tourist trappings and surely I would have been aware of another visitor. A guard from the museum was another option, but he would be in uniform and anyway the museum remained closed and unmanned. Security was the final possibility. Whatever the guy's purpose, it was the idea of his being there without my knowing it that made me uneasy. Where was he when I was inside the theatre? Gerry's words came back to me: "They'll watch us like hawks!" As if another sighting would answer my questions I stopped and turned once more. There was no sign of a man. No sign of life. Nothing but the outline of the theatre rising into the immense blue dome of sky: a memento mori – a gift to the Roman gods.

Outline of the Roman theatre rising from desert scrub: Sabratha

The temple of the Egyptian goddess Isis: Sabratha

Shadowed archways lead into the theatre

Painstakingly re-assembled gallery of marble columns

Bas relief depicting the personification of the union of Rome and Sabratha

Theatre walls bleached in bright sunlight

Tourism is Alive and Well!

'We are ready for tourists. Why aren't tourists coming to Libya?'

The expatriate community, who doubled as tourists when the occasion arose, could have answered the Libyan Tourist Board's rhetorical question at some length! Along with management and maintenance, tourism in Libya had long since fallen by the wayside. That the company was advertising its readiness for business came as a surprise.

As a result of the strangling effects of twenty-four years of post-revolutionary government on commercial enterprise, plus a fall in oil prices, the authorities were persuaded to loosen their reins and encourage new ways of creating capital. Libya has more than its fair share of treasures from the past to entice tourists, but just as it was decided to open the doors sanctions were imposed, making getting into the country difficult and the attitude towards Westerners less than friendly. To make matters worse, kidnapping and even shooting of tourists by Islamic fundamentalists in neighbouring Egypt and Algeria had been in the news.

The first hint that the tourist office in Tripoli was alive and well and ready for action was the trip advertised in the local paper. Under normal circumstances I avoid organised tours. Being herded in a group reminds me of school outings and I prefer to have the freedom to make independent choices about when and where and for how long when travelling. But circumstances were far from normal and opportunities to explore Libya were few. The highlight of this trip was a visit to one of the second-century Roman villas strung along the coastline, formerly used to accommodate wealthy Romans. It was this opportunity that made up my mind.

One cold, dark December morning a hunched figure could be seen leaving the compound, picking her way through rubbish-strewn streets to the meeting point. There, I joined a huddle of fellow early risers wrapped in scarves and woolly hats or zipped into padded jackets. Early mornings are the most miserable part of Libyan winter days. Two hours ahead of GMT, they are dark and cold. Conversely, by midday temperatures can reach seventy degrees. Two hours later the sun was up, we were still waiting and I was having dark thoughts about Libyan tourism and planning to leave when two shining new minibuses arrived.

The first stop on our excursion was the city of Misrata. Some 250 kilometres east of Tripoli, the city is known for its Italian-style open squares, wide tree-lined streets and residents with a reputation for being highly organised and with good heads for business. The main attraction for tourists is the quality of locally made textiles and carpets. We were heading for a modern carpet factory before being let loose to bargain for a carpet in the local souk.

It was the weekend and not only were we late starting but the vehicles had to be run in, adding extra time to the journey. When we finally arrived it was to find the factory closed. Nevertheless, we were herded through a side door and along a corridor to a neon-lit room where a row of girls was seated and motionless behind machine-operated looms. Dressed mafia-style in dark glasses and black leather jerkins, a huddle of men waited to one side. Suddenly, both the girls and the men launched into action. Then it became clear. Armed with a battery of cameras, the men were here to film tourists watching local girls operate the machinery. We were hurriedly placed into strategic positions while the filmmakers, poised with fingers on triggers, zoomed in. The tourist board was in full swing, promoting their trips in a documentary to be shown on Libya's equivalent of the *Six O'clock News*!

By the time the filming was over and we reached the souk it was 1.30 p.m. Shutters were down and shops were closed.

Fortunately, one enthusiastic and business-like shopkeeper, eager to make some money, opened up and commanded excellent sales of his carpets at much lower prices than those available in the souk in Tripoli. Meanwhile, my stomach was reminding me that an arrangement for lunch at a distant hotel was well overdue. The urgency to eat sent some members of the group on the prowl for *schwarmers* (slices of meat from a leg of lamb on a rotating spit, wrapped in Arabic bread) or camel sandwiches. For the rest of us, left waiting and nursing our hunger pangs, the sun was up and there was no shade.

The designated place for lunch was at a hotel reputed to be the place where Gaddafi was residing when he composed the celebrated ideologies printed in his *Green Book*. Back on the minibus, overcome by warmth and tiredness, hunger pangs gave way to sleep. An hour or so later I was awakened by the sound of wheels crunching on gravel. We were crawling up the driveway to a large country house, surrounded by trees and bright flowering shrubs. Magnificent fuchsia and bougainvillaea exploded in riots of orange, red and purple. We followed our guide up a flight of stone steps through double wooden doors leading into a large open reception area from which a further set of double doors led into the dining room. Long tables had been set in preparation for lunch: spicy Libyan soup followed by couscous and bottles of cold water to quell our thirsts.

Hunger abated, I considered the scene that had inspired Gaddafi: wide windows stretched across the back of the room, providing panoramic views across lawns and carefully tended flower gardens and beyond to a range of gently undulating dunes and in the distance the sea. A memorable if overdramatic slogan came to mind: 'The era of the masses which approaches at a rapid pace following the era of the republics influences the feelings and dazzles the eyes'.

From what I had learnt about the Libyan people so far during my stay I knew that such inflated and abstract sentiments have been smothered by the sands of time long since. In fact, sand is the one thing you can be certain of in Libya. It drifts across streets, smothers drains, transforms everything in its path into ghostly apparitions until successive layers bury man's mightiest civilisations. When the hot sand-laden Ghibli blows from the Sahara it fills the pores of your skin, stings your eyes and creeps into your lungs. It is then that the practicalities of the camels' closed nostrils and thick fringe of lashes and desert-dwelling Tuareg's elaborate wrap-around turban-cum-veil can be seen. When the Ghibli blows, a *tagulmust*, or a substitute, is a must!

Now, with no wind and the sun dipping below the horizon, revived by our late luncheon, we finally set off to find what should have been the focus of our trip: a visit to the second-century Roman Villa Silin that centuries ago had been swallowed and buried in sand. Completely buried, discovered and recovered by French archaeologists in the 1960s, it was thought to be one of several strung along the coast, owned and lived in by wealthy Romans stationed at Leptis Magna or Tripoli. For the greater part of a thirty-minute ride we bounced along an intermittent sandy track through the heart of desert scrubland covered by thorn bushes: a hostile environment inhabited by wild dogs, snakes and lizards. At one point there was a clear and magnificent view across dunes interspersed with heady palms to a line of hills sprayed red across the summits by fiery sky.

The outline of the villa, silhouetted against deepening sky, appearing and disappearing as we climbed and then descended a ridge of sand on our final approach, caused a stir of excitement. Then it was before us – a solid, squat fort with a small domed roof designed to withstand attacks from marauding tribes as well as the erosive powers of the sea, crashing onto rocks below in explosions of luminescent spray.

Emerging from the minibus, we were confronted by a pair of eight-foot wrought-iron gates. The guide rattled the chain holding the pair together. After some reciprocal chain rattling on the other side the gates were pulled open, revealing an unshaven, fierce-looking character dressed in a Roman tunic and cloak, looking as if he were about to take part in an amateur production of *Julius Caesar*. There was an uncanny resemblance to the character I'd encountered at Leptis. So much so that I wondered if he were the same person transported from site to site when a handful of tourists were expected? Not for the first time in Libya I felt as if I were taking part in a weird dream.

He led us to a courtyard in front of the villa, flanked by stone sidewalks. The floor was covered with remarkable mosaics of hunting scenes. The guide did nothing to prevent visitors tramping across the mosaics yet insisted, "No flashlights," for those of us with cameras. Unfortunately, by now the great bronze disk of sun had slipped behind the dunes and the last remnants of evening's magical light were sliding away. Excitement tempered by frustration, I focused my camera on an intriguing mosaic detailing a scene depicting two short, fat, near-naked men wearing loincloths and brass helmets and carrying two bamboo sticks in each hand. Surrounded by huge bell-shaped flowers, one was being pursued by a crocodile while the other was looking fearfully over his shoulder.

By the time we entered the villa it was too dark to see anything and frustration gave way to farce. There was no lighting of any form. All we could do was stumble from room to room with occasional glimpses of wall frescoes from a hand-held cigarette lighter or match in a scene that would have done justice not to a dream but to a clip from a Peter Sellers' film.

***

Inspired by the success (by their standards) of the trip to Villa Silin, the Libyan Tourist Board was offering a more ambitious outing to Waw al Namus, the crater of an extinct volcano deep in the heart of the Sahara. This journey, to one of the most remote places on earth, was especially challenging for the lack of notable life-saving oases en route. With the Libyan Tourist Board in charge it was not an expedition for the faint-hearted!

Sabha, the capital of the Fezzan province and just one hour's flight south of Tripoli, was the starting point for the over-sand adventure. Two sand-sprayed four-wheel-drive vehicles, each with a Libyan driver speaking minimal English, were ready and waiting for our arrival at Sabha Airport. Jean Paul, a French resident and the only one of the eight expatriates travelling to speak Arabic, organised the luggage and the party between the two vehicles. While I joined Jean Paul and two of his compatriots in one vehicle, a Canadian couple and a British couple got together in the second. Finally, the small convoy set off on the 400-kilometre drive across desert plains towards the overnight stop at a former military camp en route to our destination.

Averaging over 100 kilometres an hour, the vehicles lurched and bounced across a desolate lunar landscape through whirling clouds of dust that reduced visibility to nil; as we hurtled through the vast no-man's-land on the extremity of the Great Sand Sea the sensation was not unlike riding a bucking bronco in a miniature globe where nothing existed beyond an encircling bowl of flying sand. Clouds of dust seeped into the vehicle, gritting the eyes, nose, mouth and filling the pores of the skin – no place or object was sacred or sand-free. There were no seats belts to rein us in or offer some respite against the vehicle's negligible suspension! Fortunate to have a window seat and a strap to hang on to I could protect my joints from some of the jarring and my head from hammering against the roof! Overcome by a dull resignation I lost count of the hours then, as darkness began to close in, Khalid (our driver) pointed to some lights in the distance. "Hotel," he called.

Fixing my eyes on the lights, I watched them grow brighter until they shone as enticingly as a jewelled palace on the top of a hill. Imagination apart, we were approaching a military checkpoint and desert outpost once occupied by the Italians. It was located near the oasis of Waw al Kabir (Big Crater), one of several volcanic outcrops in the Libyan basalt plateau, including that of our final destination, Waw al Namus (Crater of Mosquitoes). Close up the hotel was no jewelled palace, neither was it an hotel but an officers' mess in a run-down military base. The kindest way to describe the accommodation was basic and the plumbing non-operational. Delighted to be stationary at last with the smell of food in the air; a row of beds to collapse on and bottled water to drink; even the lack of plumbing didn't disturb us. ''Since the secret of plumbing hasn't yet been cracked in Tripoli we can hardly expect running water in the desert!" was one intrepid traveller's response.

The next day, joined by a pick-up truck carrying radio equipment and a live sheep to be slaughtered for dinner, we set off on the final stage of our journey. The three drivers started in a convoy but very soon spread out and were racing abreast across a desolate plain of sand and gravel, each vehicle surrounded by its own whirling dust cloud. Gradually, the distance between the vehicles increased.

Approximately one hour later the pick-up was no longer in sight. Jean Paul, an experienced desert traveller, was becoming increasingly concerned about the dangers facing the group. Finally, alerting Khalid he insisted that he caught up with the remaining vehicle and signalled to the driver to stop. As soon as this was achieved he ordered the two men to make radio contact with the pick-up. It was then discovered that although the convoy had been issued with radio sets for each vehicle the entire outfit, along with food, water and fuel were in the missing pick-up. We were out of contact!

Scrambling to the top of a sand dune, the chastened Khalid stood hands shielding his eyes, a lone figure silhouetted against an ocean of sand, scanning the horizon for the lost vehicle. There was no sign. Once again Jean Paul took control and insisted that the drivers turn back towards Waw al Kabir. Although retracing our steps, he reasoned that we would be near a settlement and a petrol station in the event of breaking down. There was nothing but desert en route to Waw al Namus. It was unanimously agreed that to continue would be madness.

The drivers doubled back, this time at the reduced speed of fifty kilometres an hour to conserve fuel and improve visibility. Finally, we came upon the pick-up parked alongside a rusting petrol trailer belonging to a nearby government farm on the outskirts of Waw al Kabir. The unconcerned driver had made a detour to get extra fuel and was in conversation with a young Sudanese farmhand who had appeared from the direction of a shabby Portakabin to take full advantage of the opportunity to do business. At this point it was decided to top up the fuel in all the tanks. There was one problem. The petrol was stored in large plastic containers but there was no funnel. This did not faze Khalid. Cigarette hanging from his lower lip, he unscrewed the cap to the tank and cupped his hands round the opening while instructing the young man to pour.

"*Allez!*" Jean Paul yelled. "Get out!" he ordered, signalling to the group to vacate the vehicles; muttering about 'crazy bastards' and 'incompetent fools', he proceeded to herd us towards the scant shade of an acacia.

Once the operation was complete and we were back on the track to Waw al Namus the drivers made up for lost time, careering like whirling dervishes through flying sand but this time keeping each other in sight. Sunk in a semi-comatose reverie, I came to at the sound of Khalid's voice. "Volcano!" he was repeating, gesturing into the distance where the outline of a rounded hill was growing on the horizon. To my dazed imagination it resembled the swollen dome of a Byzantine basilica. Meanwhile, gravelled plains had given way to giant paving slabs of smooth grey rock while sand-coated jagged ridges interspersed with grey speckled hillocks were scattered around us.

"I've been having grave doubts," Jean Paul confessed. "But it looks as if we're almost there."

At times the going was as smooth as driving over a newly made road, then the jigsaw of loose slabs was jumping and attacking the undercarriage, unnerving the passengers if not the driver. Focused on reaching the crater, Khalid was making no concessions in speed to accommodate the challenging surface. The final approach across a plain of dark cindery stones gave way to deeper sand and then an increase in gradient until the growling engine juddered to a standstill. The drivers got out and lit cigarettes; the passengers tumbled out, unfolding cramped limbs. Beneath our feet the golden desert sand was coated in coarse black volcanic grit.

We had come to a halt halfway up a steep incline. From the top there was a perfect view across a vast arena of darkened sand some several kilometres wide. From its very heart rose the majestic form of the volcano's striated golden dome; at its feet the waters of a lake mirrored the deep blue of the sky. The entire spectacle was held in the wide embrace of an ashen collar of sand. My under-the-breath "Wow!" of amazement was followed by a succession of exclamations of wonder, then a profound silence. Just standing on the edge of this lost world was an out-of-time and out-of-place experience!

While it is not difficult to imagine a mountain peak erupting, spitting fire and blowing its top, here in this silent desert wilderness the very idea of an underground force stirring and raising its fiery head before erupting in a massive firework display, witnessed only by distant stars, was mind blowing!

While the energetic Canadian couple set off to climb the volcano my fellow Brits were content to rest on the rim, recover from the ride and photograph the scene from afar. I joined forces with the French brigade who planned to make it to the oasis and take advantage of the lake to cool off. Overheated and covered in a film of sweat-streaked sand, I could think of nothing better than a refreshing dip. Tentatively edging and then involuntarily racing down the steep inside slope, we then set off at a more dignified pace towards an inviting grove of heady date palms that together with beds of reeds and bulrushes skirted the lake.

"It's just one of three that circle the cone," Jean Paul enlightened us. "The volcano's been extinct for some 5,000 years, yet the water in one lake is said to be warm."

Hoping it wasn't the case with the one we were approaching, I continued to nurse heady images of cooling off in its waters. As we neared the oasis the air became noticeably heavy and moist, the ground swampy and thick with tangles of bull rushes and reeds. Sheltering in the shade of a clump of palms we paused, dabbing sweating brows and gulping warm bottled water. Not a breath of air. Nothing stirred. The place was steamy with humid heat and lifeless. Or was it? *"Regardez! Regardez* the water!" an excited voice cried. At first glance the surface appeared opaque. On closer inspection it was quite literally swarming with mosquitoes. A stabbing pain on my neck quashed any doubts and then the air was alive with the blood-seekers' shrill vengeful tones. We truly had arrived at Waw al Namus: Crater of Mosquitoes!

"*Mon Dieu!*" and a series of war cries against the increasing barrage of attacks on exposed limbs followed by an authoritarian, "*Allons!*" heralded a hasty retreat. With the sun below the crater's rim it was not a place to swim or spend time after dark!

The first pin pricks of stars in a dome of pale lilac sky and a welcoming breeze greeted us as we crested the ridge. Sundowners organised by my compatriots – even without ice – while watching the dome sink into darkness and the smudged figures of the intrepid Canadians making their way towards us were a perfect ending to our adventures. Just then the drivers too came into view. They had trekked to the oasis to gather wood for a fire. The sight of their laden figures followed by the pathetic bleating of the captive sheep reminded us that there was a throat to be cut, a fire to be built and a barbecue to be held under the stars.

Ghadames

Do-it-yourself Tourism

After a brief interlude the tourist department had once again gone into hibernation. It was do-it-yourself tourism or nothing. My solo visit to Sabratha reinforced the need to find a like-minded companion to explore further afield. Finally, I decided to accept Paula's invitation to spend an evening at the Darts' Club. This, she assured me, was the most likely place to meet someone as intent on travel as I was. Weekly meetings were held on a rotation basis at the houses of committee members and the next was to take place at a nearby compound adjoining the beach, called Friendship Village.

"It has to be American. Only Americans could christen a compound in Libya with such a name, or anywhere else for that matter!"

"Originally, it was," Paula confirmed, steering me between rows of terraced sandstone villas with peeling paint, mould growing up the walls and shutters hanging from broken hinges. "Believe it or not, it was quite upmarket in Esso days. In fact, Gargaresh was once an American stronghold with a range of intercontinental restaurants and trendy shops in the main street while the beach was a hive of activity: water sports, cafés – the lot!"

Looking at the current slum conditions of the compound and from my experiences of life in Libya so far, although I could understand some of the reasons for people being drawn to live and work in Libya I found it difficult to understand what kept them, sometimes for a working lifetime. As we walked, Paula enlightened me about the 'Golden Handcuff Syndrome': the addictive stashing away of tax-free savings that takes hold so that one is never ready to leave.

"There's nothing to spend it on so saving is easy," she explained. "Then there are those who become distanced from the real world – psychologically as well as physically. Many find it impossible to settle when they go back. John, our host for the evening, is nearing retirement and has lived here for decades. That's his house," she said, pointing to the end of a nearby terrace. "Tim and I are of the same ilk. At first we couldn't wait to get out. Then without realising, it grew on us. Coming up for ten years now. Saving for a retreat in the European sun. Security!" she warned, suddenly lowering her voice and drawing my attention to the outline of a guard. The ubiquitous Kalashnikov slung across his shoulder, he was smoking and leaning against the only working and dimly lit lamp post on the compound.

"We'll make a detour. This way!" she continued, guiding me across the street. "Don't want to lead our friend to a den of iniquity! The most notorious recruits," she added in a low voice, "are those running away from something. A recent classic example – a fifty-plus woman escaping the wrath of her second husband. He discovered she was having an affair with his son! She knew he wouldn't pursue her to Libya! Used to seek solace in booze at the Darts' Club. Under the influence, she confided that she was engaged to be married to the son and that he was holed up in a flat in London waiting for her return!"

"Sounds like pure tabloid. Is she still here?" I asked, intrigued at the prospect of meeting such a celebrity.

"Long gone. Did a runner at the first opportunity. The Libyan deterrent of withholding salary doesn't stop those determined to leave. Once they can get their hands on their passports they take off!! On another occasion, the same lady was being escorted home after a heavy drinking session when both she and her escort were picked up by armed guards. When they reached her house, Tony – her escort – was instructed to wait in the vehicle. He said that both guards went in with her and were gone for so long he was convinced they were having their way with her. Tony's still here, should you be interested in a firsthand account!"

We had walked the length of the compound before making a loop and finally were following a sandy passage leading to the back entrance of John's house. Inside the place was buzzing with voices and the entire dimly lit lounge area bathed in a haze of smoke. Small groups were gathered round a makeshift bar while to one side the darts enthusiasts were in full swing! Knowing my intention was not to play darts, Paula steered me towards the bar where a lanky British male was leaning on the counter and cradling a tankard of beer in his huge hand.

He turned to greet us with a lop-sided smile. He had a rather crumpled appearance, giving the impression that he'd just stepped out of a tumble drier, but his manner was friendly and easy. A glass of home-made sparkling white wine in my hand, I learned that he had already visited some Roman sites including Sabratha and was eager to explore the desert. Just minutes later, after exchanging stories, Simon announced that he had a contact who could get return air tickets to the ancient desert city of Ghadames – an oasis settlement some 640 kilometres south-west of Tripoli.

As I assured Simon that I was prepared to risk the well-publicised dangers of flying to get to the sand-mud desert city, I could feel a bulb of excitement growing inside. He was offering to organise the air tickets and promised to get in touch with me as soon as he had secured them.

***

A weekend in the desert was on the horizon. I tempered my excitement by reminding myself that this was Libya and nothing was certain. Getting hold of air tickets was one problem – the safety of flying in Libya was another. For a start there were no international flights and the remaining aircraft, used for internal flights, were suffering from lack of maintenance and parts. Prior to the renewed sanctions, which took effect from the 1st December, French airline staff had serviced Libyan aircraft. The difficulty of getting replacement parts since the first sanctions imposed in 1991 added to the dangers of flying.

In fact, stories about the problems of flying were rife. In December 1992 one of Libya's eight Boeings crashed. All the passengers and crew were lost although the pilot and co-pilot had miraculously survived. Since the sanctions, French service engineers had been withdrawn and the dangers of flying in Libya had increased to such an extent that some oil companies had undertaken great road-building projects across the desert and now used road transport only into the desert sites. At that time, six of the original eight Boeings were in use. Guesstimates have it that number seven was being used for spare parts! Most individuals weren't prepared to risk flying. If I want to do something badly enough I ignore danger. Simon, I was to learn, behaved as if danger didn't exist.

Simon paid his contact for tickets and we waited for two weeks. Then the day before we expected to leave our money was returned. No tickets and no reasons. Simon believed that we would be able to purchase them ourselves at an airline office on our way to the airport. Nobody else did. In fact, long-term expatriate residents, including members of the Darts' Club, were full of gloom and doom warnings and ultimatums. We remained steadfast.

There had been storms for several days and the morning we were due to leave I woke to no electricity and no running water, though a deluge was falling outside. My head was alive with warnings: Simon's impracticability; the dangers of flying; the weather; reports of recent murders of tourists near the Algerian border: Ghadames is within sight of the border; the problems of getting hold of tickets exacerbated as a result of restrictions imposed on expatriates since the sanctions. Finally, there was my CIA status. Although by now I was convinced that we wouldn't get away, I decided to leave it to fate. If we got tickets and the flight, we'd go. In preparation I'd locked away my forbidden possessions: laptop, printer, disks and American dollars. One thing was certain, Simon would be waiting for me. I got up by candlelight, packed my bag and set off into the gloom of a dark February morning.

The arrangement was that Simon's driver would to take us to an airline office to purchase our tickets and then drop us at the airport. The odds were against us: the weather was not on our side, phones weren't working and the driver was forty minutes late. By the time we set off we should have been checking in at the airport. I had convinced myself that it wasn't going to happen. Simon was unnervingly silent. It was still raining heavily. The streets were flooded. Swirling fetid water was filling the clogged drains with even more litter and sand. Then, in the way that life has of suddenly changing direction, we found ourselves at the airline office with tickets in our hands. Moments later, whooping with joy and congratulating ourselves, we were heading for the airport.

Halfway there and still jubilant we faced a volt-face. The driver decided he didn't want to take us – the ten-kilometre journey was too far. His long, unshaven face, dissatisfied expression and unkempt appearance did not inspire confidence. I could feel bottled-up frustration and mild hysteria rising and started remonstrating and pleading: "We'll miss the flight – you can't dump us here in the rain!"

Simon remained stolidly calm. "Heading in the right direction," he muttered.

Then on a major roundabout on the outskirts of Tripoli the driver slowed down and kept his hand on the horn to get the attention of a taxi driver about to overtake us. Amidst screeching brakes both vehicles pulled over to the side of the road. Simon leapt out. Ankle deep in flood water he was bargaining with the taxi driver. Water dripping from his nose and chin, he signalled to me to get out. We transferred our baggage through the downpour and skidding traffic into the taxi.

Half an hour later we were at the wrong (international) airport. Fifteen minutes later we were at the right (domestic) airport. Fortunately, flight times are not take-off times in Libya but subject to the will of Allah and today Allah was on our side. With mixed feelings of elation and trepidation, I once again abandoned myself to fate, trailed Simon through the grey space serving as a departure lounge and joined the body of Libyan males surging towards the waiting aircraft.

The plane was not one of the remaining and dreaded Boeing 727s but, according to Simon, one of the less-can-go-wrong variety – a twin-engine Fokker F27. It sounded like a tractor and taxied along and round overgrown airstrips for so long I thought that the entire journey was to be overland. Then with a sudden surge of speed, an increase in noise and the sight of huge wheels lifting and folding like the legs of an enormous grasshopper, I was convinced. We were airborne.

There were no safety instructions or seat belts, never mind such luxuries as lifejackets and oxygen masks. Neither were there any restrictions on smoking. As soon as we took off, the body of Libyan passengers lit up, filling the cabin with a whirling noxious haze. Services on the one-and-a-half-hour flight included a boiled sweet at take-off and, a few minutes later, a drink. The air steward carried a tray of plastic cups half filled with tepid water, tea bags and a bowl of sugar. The alternative refreshment was Coke. I passed on the refreshments and turned my attention to the view

The cushion of heavy cloud that had obscured the fertile coastal plain gradually dispersed and I was looking down on the vertical edge of a vast red plateau – the frayed edges looking as if they had been nibbled by a huge monster. As we moved further south, the red wasteland was traced by dried-up water courses lined by trees – tiny black blobs like the markings on an exquisitely drawn map. Simon's long legs stretched towards the aisle. His eyes were closed and his face wore the expression of a contented cat. Laughter lines radiated from his eyes and the corners of his lips tip-tilted in the expression of an eternal optimist. Over six feet tall with a moth-eaten haircut he was as easily distinguishable in a crowd as a tourist or a spy as I was with my blonde hair.

Minutes later, a young fresh-faced Libyan, dressed in a spotlessly clean white *jalabiya* (loose, full-length garment) and a brown woollen cape casually draped about his shoulders, came forward to take the spare seat next to us. Simon opened his eyes, withdrew and folded his legs into the space in front of him.

Introducing himself as Abu Bakr, the Libyan informed us that he had been born and grew up in Ghadames and now ran the tourist office. He offered his services as a guide. Our exchanged glances indicated that we both suspected that security was on our trail. We had been warned. Like expatriates, tour guides in Libya have a dual role. While we double up as tourists – they double up as security agents. As soon as he retreated we exchanged sotto voce comments.

''What do you think?'' Simon asked.

"We've been earmarked.''

"Travelling with a CIA agent is a risky business!"

"But interesting?"

"Certainly not dull."

"At least we've a guide."

"Native of Ghadames."

"Sounds okay to me."

"Sounds good."

"At least we know where we are, if you see what I mean?"

"I agree," Simon concluded. "Let's make the most of it!"

An hour later, under a pale sun looking as fragile as a glass globe, we landed on a desert airstrip surrounded by mile upon mile of red sand capped by endless blue sky. Two elongated, flat-topped hills, standing above the arid plain, were the only focus on which the eyes could rest. The airport, a square featureless concrete building, consisted of one main room with a counter, a weighing machine and a row of orange plastic chairs. Baggage was delivered outside from the back of a vehicle, rather like a cement mixer disgorging its contents. Abu Bakr was waiting and had organised a lift for the ten-kilometre drive to the only hotel in Ghadames. Simon gave a discreet thumbs-up sign. The smile on his lips said it all.

Kiss the Hand You Cannot Sever

An Arab legend would have us believe that in the seventh century AD when the Arab conqueror, Okba Ibn Nafi, arrived at Ghadames, exhausted from the heat, his mare pawed the earth with her hoof and a spring gushed from that very spot. Spring of the Mare: Ain al Faras. This was the name given to the hotel.

Wheels crunching over the forecourt, we drew up to a row of dusty palms standing guard against terracotta walls. Built by the Italians over half a century ago, the hotel boasted traditional features of Saharan architecture including sand-based brickwork with a pattern of open triangles along the top of the walls. During the Italian era Sophia Loren is reputed to have stayed at the hotel and more recently, in the days before Libya was boycotted, Mark Thatcher while taking part in the Paris–Dakar Car Rally. More importantly, the hotel is literally on the very doorstep of the ancient city.

Inside the building was dark, shabby and cold. An even darker lounge attached to the reception area was crowded with sagging velour armchairs, all peopled by Libyan males wearing drab robes and long lengths of material bandaged about their heads. Rapid eye movement from and back to a mammoth television mounted on a table in one corner, the only indication of interest in our presence, made it difficult to tell if the reaction was one of indifference or antagonism. The room stank of full ashtrays and was dominated by strident tones issuing from the black and white speckled screen. MEALS FOR REQUEST, printed in large letters on a placard, drew our attention to an otherwise empty reception counter. Eventually, one of the slouched figures rose from his armchair, stubbed out a half-smoked cigarette and made his way unceremoniously towards us. We swapped employment cards for keys and waited while our details were painstakingly jotted into a book.

The hotel formed a quadrangle round a courtyard as shabby and neglected as the building. Withered vines hung from a broken trellis; a dry fountain was spewing litter; an hibiscus with crumpled red blooms was the only near-living thing in the flowerbeds. Even the hardy date palms looked bedraggled. On either side of a central pathway, fallen plastic tables and chairs were carelessly strewn over a lawn of sandy hillocks. I followed a track leading behind the trellis to number thirty-nine, wracking my brains for some explanation of the significance of the number. If there were no other visitors, why was I out here on a limb in number thirty-nine? All I could come up with was John Buchan's thriller and our lives as shades of the adventures of a man on the run. We weren't exactly on the run, I consoled myself, though the sense of being pursued was never far away. Simon was heading to the opposite side. A rather extreme form of gender separation, I presumed.

Cold inhabited the room – penetrating and tactile. There were three narrow beds. Each had a hard foam pillow, a thin sheet over the mattress and one folded blanket. Settling on the central bed as the most draughtproof, I helped myself to additional blankets. Above my head hung an ancient air conditioner boxed in a rusty cage; electric points had been rudely inserted in walls yellow with age while a switch, hanging from a hole in the wall, operated an ugly strip light that straddled the ceiling. It looked wholly unsafe.

I crossed the stone floor, tracing a sour smell to the adjoining bathroom and tested the plumbing: tepid water spluttered then trickled from taps but failed to operate in the bidet or toilet. A plastic bucket, standing on the floor, was on offer for 'do-it-yourself' flushing. There were no plugs in the basin or bath. Sophia Loren here! It was impossible to imagine. Although winter and near freezing it was warmer outside in the last light of the pale swollen sun. I picked up my camera. Evening light was a good time to get some shots.

Pausing in the courtyard to lean against a pillar in slanting sunlight, I saw Simon striding towards me.

"Not exactly the Ritz," I greeted him.

"Not exactly."

"Verging on squalid, I'd say."

"At least cold keeps germs at bay."

"At least we're here."

"Feels great."

"Feels like adventure."

"Worth the risk."

"Worth ignoring born-again pessimists."

"Let's go then. This way!" Simon directed, gesturing grandly to the start of a track just a few metres from the hotel.

I followed in his wake, eventually arriving at an open space which looked down on the oasis –the starting point for the settlement at Ghadames – a city so ancient that historians believe it was inhabited by Neolithic man 4,000 years ago. Natural springs are found in oases throughout the desert regions of Libya. Settlements like Ghadames have grown up around them and caravan routes have used them as stopping points since pre-Roman times. The Greek geographer Strabo likens North Africa to a leopard's skin, its habitable areas being scattered like spots over a background of waterless desert.

Herodotus frequently draws attention to the diurnal and seasonal changes in water temperature so characteristic of desert springs as well as to their whereabouts, for without their sweet water life and travel could not exist. Ghadames existed because of the availability of underground water. Walled-in and with no visible surface water, banks of sand sloped to a circle of palms, grasses and shrubs, hinting at its underground presence. The outer sections of the city fanned out between a series of passages running between high sand-mud walls from which I estimated it would have been possible to see over from the back of a camel. A distinctive feature of the architecture was rows of bricks, in the shape of fat tiles, placed side by side along the tops of walls like books on a shelf. They ran across open land, divided by a network of low walls into overgrown silent enclosures that once held crops and animals.

A narrow passageway led to an open area circled by tiers of steps: the market and meeting place for travellers and merchants, their camels packed with ivory, gold, ostrich feathers, slaves and wild animals, before the last stage of the long journey north to the Mediterranean. We climbed the steps to a central point from where we looked down on the square. In the absolute silence it was not difficult to imagine the tinkle of caravan bells as the long procession of camels arriving from Niger or Chad shuffled to a standstill. Above this the excitement of traders' greetings and bargaining overriding the stench of fear of shackled slaves and caged animals destined for the arenas of Libya's Roman cities as well as for the magnificent city of Rome itself.

Now, in the deserted quiet, disturbed only by our own footsteps, we rejoined the pathway passing a fort with high walls punctuated by randomly placed tiny square holes serving as windows. Traditional raised cornerstones, believed by local people to keep ghosts away, marked the top corners of the highest buildings and turrets. Ahead of us the outline of a tower and the small dome of a mosque glared white against cerulean sky; sunlight painted one side of the buildings gold and cast long shadows on the other. A dove was cooing. Cameras clicked and whirred.

A sandy passage led through an archway and into an open courtyard: a daytime suntrap with a series of arched niches cut into the walls, providing comfortable windproof seating. On one side was the entrance to the mosque and on the other the entrance to the men's living quarters. An arcaded portico led into a maze of tunnels that connect and interconnect the ground floor rooms of the entire city: the male preserve, as dark and intricate as a network of rabbits' burrows.

We felt our way through the thick darkness of a tunnel, occasionally coming across sudden gaps in the wall where more passages fed off to right and left. Ahead, a shaft of light guided us to the next courtyard. By the time we emerged from the underworld, as mysterious as any one of Italo Calvino's

Invisible Cities, the sun had slipped out of sight. Brilliant stars were sprayed across the sky. The air tingled with the frost of a desert night.

Back at the hotel we made for the bar. There was a choice of stewed, sweet tea or coffee thick enough to keep a spoon upright. I settled for syrupy tea. The morgue-cold dining room adjoining the bar was furnished with a stained floral carpet and small tables covered with plastic cloths. Too late we discovered the importance of the 'Meals for Request' notice at reception. We hadn't requested meals, therefore, no food was available. There was no standing on ceremony here! At that moment, our security agent-cum-guide, now in the guise of a guardian angel, glided up and offered to take us to a local Tuareg café in the village. Simon winked. We were realising the benefits of our self-appointed escort.

The café was rustic, filled with small wooden tables and crowded with men all wearing the distinctive swathed headgear of the legendary nomadic Berber warriors of the Sahara, the Tuareg. Outstanding for their long robes, embroidered sheaths for their weapons and swift Mehari camels, the Tuareg are especially recognisable by the *tagulmust* – the long strip of cotton cloth which they wrap round their heads, necks, chest, chin, and face up to the eyes to protect them from sand-laden desert winds.

The Tuareg reputation of being the fierce guardians of the Sahara has been substantiated by the accounts of a number of early explorers. The nineteenth-century traveller and scholar Heinrich Barth on his travels from northern Cameroon to Mali was not alone in so fearing them that he: 'had been obliged to adopt the character of a Mohammedan, in order to traverse with some degree of safety the country of the Tawarek [Tuareg], and to enter the town of Timbuktu'. More recently the Tuareg in Libya gave the colonial French in Algeria a hard time by conducting countless raids over the border.

In spite of their fearsome reputation the atmosphere in the café was informal and friendly. Although no attempts were made to communicate verbally, eye contact, smiles and body

language were warm and we both felt unexpectedly at ease
– something we had not experienced in the environs of Tripoli
or indeed in the hotel! Dressed in their traditional long robes
topped by windcheaters and with the casually wrapped and
knotted *tagulmusts* on their heads, they appeared both charming
and rakish. We joined them in a palatable meal of couscous
served with chicken legs and Arabic bread.

At nine o'clock the next morning the sun was shining, the
air tinged with frost and the hotel dead. I was standing in the
reception area, dreaming of an enormous pot of tea, when
the manager appeared. I reminded him that we had ordered
breakfast.

"Ramadan," was his brusque explanation. Then, in response
to my stunned silence, "Arabs don't eat!"

His dead-pan expression confirmed my fear and answered my
silent reply: We're not Arabs. There were indeed no concessions
for tourists. Dismayed, I realised that the first sliver of the new
moon heralding the start of the month of fasting must have
been sighted last night. The remains of snacks I'd packed for
the journey would have to suffice until sundown this evening.
This in turn jolted my memory and the Meals for Request notice!
We'd have to order now for the evening meal. With this in mind
I set off to find Simon.

At ten o'clock precisely, as he had promised, Abu Bakr arrived
wearing the lugubrious expression adopted by Arab males
when fasting. Nevertheless, he looked handsome in his long
striped *jalabiya* and woollen cape. After his customary "Hallo
how are you fine?" greeting he led us along the track we'd taken
last evening into the old city. As we walked he explained that
his family had moved out in 1979 and that by 1984 every family
from the old city had to evacuate – an estimated 8,000 people
were rehoused in the new town.

It is rumoured that, fearing that the old city was a place of
intrigue and impossible to watch, 'the Powers' authorised
the building of a new and modern housing complex for the
inhabitants and directed the complete evacuation of the old

settlement. The reluctance of some families to move was still evident. As if the city were still alive, we were passed by a constant stream of people: a boy carrying a goat; two elderly men wrapped in cream *baracans* (cloaks) out for a stroll in the sun; an old couple: the woman bent over by the weight of a bundle of dried grass tied across her back while her husband strolled unencumbered at her side. She was pulling at the end of her striped *farashiya* attempt to hide her entire face. An old man, carrying a walking stick, moved briskly along the passage as if he had business to attend to.

"Old men like to come back," Abu Bakr explained. "Visit home. Pray at mosque."

In an open courtyard near the entrance to the 'underground' houses two old men were sitting in the sun. One, wearing a large pair of modern spectacles, looked especially vulnerable and caught between two worlds.

"*Bonjour*," his companion called. "*Ca va?*" adding yet another dimension to the mixture of time, place and cultures.

Abu Bakr's clean-shaven, oval face was as expressionless as the tone he adopted to describe the everyday customs and way of his former life. His one reference to the distant past: "Before Arab two different tribe live in city," was left tantalisingly in mid-air. Only when we pressed him did he satisfy our curiosity by explaining that two main tribes once lived in the city, the Bani Wazid and his people, the Bani Walid. While the Bani Wazid lived in three separate but interconnecting sections of the city his tribe, he confided, occupied four. The main square was for all the people. The Tuareg, he explained, were newcomers to Ghadames. It wasn't until recent years that some of them gave up their nomadic lifestyles and set up homes in new quarters to the east of the city

With its natural supplies of fresh spring water and growing opportunities as a trading centre, Ghadames would have been a convenient place for Berber tribal groups to gravitate to and set up permanent homes. Strategically located at the most northern point of the Tuareg domain, Ghadames became a vital last stop of the trans-Saharan caravans en route to the Mediterranean; it was here that the highest prices for slaves were paid in the local market. Then in the eighteenth and nineteenth centuries when the trade in slaves was in decline the Tuareg changed course from slave traders to slave owners. They enslaved black Africans as their servants to tend their livestock and gardens and to perform domestic duties in their homes.

It is said that to this day, home to the majority of the Tuareg remains within the limitless reaches of the Sahara. Fiercely independent, they describe themselves as 'Noble and Free'; they recognise no boundaries, obey no laws. Political tensions of the mid-1990s, that ended when cease-fires were signed with Niger and Mali, had reignited. The Tuareg took up arms and the kissing stopped when an increase in cattle tax was imposed. The invisible boundaries of their territory, where the Sahel meets the green fields and villages of settled agriculturalist Bantu, are where age-old hostilities take place. At times of severe drought the Tuareg gravitate towards the Niger to water and feed their herds and find food for themselves. This is when the hatred between the Tuareg and the sedentary people flares; denied freedom of access to fertile watered lands north of the river, the Tuareg not only burn villages and steal livestock but enslave the people.

On his travels through Mali the Polish writer and foreign correspondent Ryskard Kapuscinski asked a man from Mopti where he could meet the Tuareg; the guy looked at him with pity and disbelief; Kapuscinski was taken to see the remains of a Mali fishing village destroyed recently by the Tuareg. Local people, he was told, regard the Tuareg as the terrorists of the Sahara.

In spite of the 1971 law abolishing slavery in Mali members of the Bella tribe remain as 'slaves' to the Tuareg in all but name. When asked why, the Bella's response is the response of a number of African tribes when questioned about why they continue with controversial or brutal customs: It is tradition; it is our culture; or it has always been this way. On her visit to Timbuktu in 2001 the indomitable solo traveller Kira Salak paid a Tuareg master for the freedom of two of his female slaves.

We followed Abu Bakr into one of the tunnels into the city. As our eyes grew accustomed to the thick darkness he stopped to point to one of the heavy palm wood doors where a row of small strips of leather had been nailed to the surface. "Each time a man travel he nail leather to door," Ali enlightened us. "This way he tell friend and neighbour he go away."

That the pieces of tell-tale leather remained in place gave a sense of immediacy to the recent past as well as a sense of loss. Built long before designs were committed to paper each door differed in some way from its neighbour – the very asymmetry of the designs remains part of the attraction. From time to time we emerged from the interconnecting tunnels into the bright sunlight of a courtyard – one was once the marketplace, another led to an Islamic school. This, Abu Bakr believed, was the first school in Ghadames.

It is possible that at one time a Christian school may have existed in the city. Among their converts to Catholicism the Byzantines included the people of Cydamae (Ghadames). In fact, between the fourth and fifth centuries Ghadames, an episcopate under the Byzantine Empire, was served by four bishops. Columns, capitals and pieces of masonry used in the mosque have been identified as the remains taken from the former Christian basilica.

Though nominally Muslim the Tuareg retain many pre-Islamic rights and customs, including that of insisting that the men wear veils while the women remain unveiled! Claims of their former Christian beliefs have been supported by the importance of the symbol of the cross in their culture, notably in their jewellery: the Agadez Cross; on their swords and shields and in the unique design of the saddle: a circular seat which rests on a V-shaped frame. While the back end of the frame is marked by a finger-like point, the upward curving front is fashioned into the shape of a cross. We had the good fortune to see one close up, propped on a wall, the distinct form of the cross silhouetted like a crucifix against the sky. The question remains: was the conversion of the Tuareg to Islam the result of Kissing the Hand to avoid death or slavery at the hands of proselytizing, sword-wielding Arabs?

A fascinating pen and ink drawing shows Barth's Tuareg guide holding a crucifix in his hand while sitting aloft a camel draped with a cloth marked with a cross as distinctive as those worn by Crusaders. In fact, Barth thought the word Tuareg came from the Arabic: *tereku dinihum*, meaning 'they changed their religion'. All intriguing stuff! That change in religious belief went hand in hand with a fanatical intolerance towards 'unbelievers' is undisputed.

Catholic missionaries from the Society of White Fathers in Algeria, established in Tripoli and Ghadames from 1878–81, planned to set up further missions in West Africa, travelling via Ghat into Niger and the Sudan. The story told is that in December 1881 three White Fathers set off from Ghadames, accompanied by five Tuareg guides. Before reaching Ghat they were assassinated by the Tuareg. They were not alone in receiving this fate at the hands of the Tuareg. The Scottish explorer Gordon Laing was just one of a number of European explorers to suffer a similar fate for refusing to renounce his Christian faith and convert to Islam. It was literally more than a traveller's life was worth to refuse their 'favours' as escorts through the desert. Barth was one of the few travellers who discovered that the Tuareg's religious fervour diminished and he could put them in a kissing mood when he offered them a substantial portion of his expedition goods!

Just minutes later, Abu Bakr was in conversation with an Algerian who was hiding in an empty room. Learning that he had no passport, he left the man to his own devices. It was a jolt into the present and an uncomfortable reminder of the closeness to the border of the former French colony and the current spate of Islamic fundamentalist violence against foreigners.

We left the courtyard and joined a passageway where we heard, then saw a fast-running stream of water fed by a natural fresh-water spring: the legendary Spring of the Mare. Water from this spring, once used to irrigate the fields of the oasis and now channelled to the houses of the new town, is said to be warm in winter and cold in summer. Abu Bakr invited me to test it. Hand-warm and perfectly clear, it explained the one luxury available at the hotel – warm tap water.

Finally, we entered another tunnel. Stopping in front of a large palm wood door, Abu Bakr handed Simon a metal key some six inches long. "Place for women. Men downstair. Women upstair. Open door!" he instructed.

"Feels wrong," Simon muttered, "like breaking and entering a nunnery."

The key clunked, the door creaked as it opened on to a darkened stone stairway. Once Ali had locked us in we followed him up the steps, emerging onto a middle floor used as the main living area. Although deliberately set up as a museum it was impressive. Red was the dominant colour – in the rugs and cushions covering the floors; lengths of material draped across walls and in the traditional three triangle designs painted on walls and over cupboards; two small doors opened onto recesses in the wall. Rows of small brass dishes and brass-framed mirrors decorated the walls. Light coming from the only window – an opening in the roof – reflected off the white walls and refracted from the mirrors illuminating the room.

At one end, behind a curtain, was the marriage bed furnished with especially rich rugs and embroidered bolster covers while two more areas where the women and children slept were divided off by curtains. When boys reached the age of twelve or thirteen they moved downstairs to live with the men.

A set of wooden steps led up to a small and austere room reserved for the grandfather. Apart from a bed, his only comfort was a large copy of the Quran lying open on a stand. Men, it seemed, spent the final days of their lives in the upper storeys, their needs attended to by the women.

A second flight of stairs led to rooms for storing food, washing and cooking. In the kitchen there were two deep oval stone hollows for kneading bread. Baking and cooking were done over fires made from the thick stems of palm fronds and laid in hollows between a row of small stone domes on which cooking utensils were balanced. Colourful food covers, like huge conical straw hats, adorned the walls. The largest specimen was placed over a huge couscous pot. Pointing to a sealed opening in a wall, Abu Bakr explained it was a place to store grain.

* Abu Bakr

"First fill with grain. Then fire burn oxygen and cover put on. Grain stay good till winter."

Nearby, a second hole, which plummeted to ground level, was used as a chute for waste.

Finally, we were standing on the flat interconnecting rooftop of the city. Here, on the top levels of the building, the women could meet and talk together. Just as the men's passages interconnected beneath, so the rooftops provided the women with access to all the upper roofs and upper storeys of the houses in the city. In his expressionless monotone, Abu Bakr was telling us that women were allowed down twice each day, morning and evening, when the men were at prayer in the mosque, to get water for washing and cooking.

"Before prayer finish they come back," he added.

Simon and I exchanged glances. "You mean," queried Simon, "except to get water the women were not allowed downstairs, not allowed to walk outside."

"They have roof," Abu Bakr persisted. Then conceded, "Sometime – women walk with husband."

Silenced by his phlegmatic response, we followed him down the stairs into the sunlight. The feeling of sand beneath my feet, sunlight streaming through passages leading to the oasis and the freedom to walk through them took on an entirely new perspective.

The use of courtyards, enabling each extended family group – male, female, young and old – to have its own safe meeting places for recreation and relaxation – a long-established Eastern tradition – did not explain the extreme form of gender separation practised in Ghadames. The origins and reasons remained unclear. Had the arrival of Islam and its insistence on gender separation been taken to an extreme in Ghadames? Or were the women of this labyrinthine city being protected from slave traders and invading foreign armies? Whatever the origin, that the practice continued over the centuries and was brought to an end less than ten years ago, only when the old city was evacuated, was difficult to come to terms with.

I was still contemplating the plight of the women of Ghadames when on our way back to the hotel we passed two local females. Completely wrapped in striped cotton *farashiyas,* they held the ends across their faces, each revealing one eye in a neat triangular gap. It was difficult not to apply western judgements and feel terrible compassion for these women who, released from a lifetime of restriction to the rooftops of the city less than ten years ago, were now restricted to viewing the outside world with one eye. It was also a sobering reminder that centuries of oppression were going to take more than a handful of decades to overcome.

***

Sandra and Eric, two Swiss adventurers currently staying with Swiss Embassy friends in Tripoli, joined us in the afternoon. Just one more advantage enjoyed by embassy staff was the freedom to organise visas for friends and family to visit them in Libya.

''Sounds like pure punishment,'' was Simon's response when he learnt the couple had travelled 640 kilometres along a desert track by bus to reach Ghadames.

"We were told that to fly was tantamount to a death wish!"

"I've heard the buses aren't much safer."

"A nightmare night ride," Sandra confirmed. "Long, rough and smoke filled. I daren't think about the return!"

"I don't want to add to your misery but there's no food till sundown. Ramadan is upon us. No concessions for tourists.''

"Now, we can help on that one. Our friends in Tripoli were prepared and have set us up with a picnic. We'll be happy to share."

While we helped demolish supplies of Arabic bread, houmos, chicken legs and salad, we discovered the plans for the afternoon's run to a desert lake and a Roman fort. First stop was Lake Tumin – a salt lake in the desert, once important for the supply of rushes used for the walls and roofs of desert homes.

With Abu Bakr as our guide and a Tuareg driver, swathed in a romantic *tagulmust* and looking as at home behind the wheel of the ancient Land Cruiser as he would have done on a camel, we set off into the desert. There was an air of elation and expectation as we approached the red plain of Hamada al Hamra; known and feared as an area of impenetrable desolation, it was a region crossed by the Roman armies in expeditions against the warring Garamantes tribe. Then the tarmac road we'd been following disappeared beneath drifting sand and a line of miniature rippled dunes and we were heading west across a featureless gravel plain.

Following ruts, rather like those left by tractors across previously sodden but now baked fields, our route was taking us on a course running parallel to the foot of a low-lying escarpment some fifty metres on our left. The surface of the great plain, dotted with boulders, was becoming increasingly white with crusted salt – as if there had been a light fall of snow or a hoar frost. Finally, a line of shrubs marked an underground watercourse, then a flash of blue.

"Did you see that?" Sandra called hopefully. "Looked like water."

In the distance I too caught a glimpse of what could have been a mirrored patch of sky reflected in the waters of a lake. Held between a break in a ring of trees, it appeared to be cradled in the centre of a small hill straight ahead of us. However, distances are as deceptive in the desert as at sea and the seemingly endless jarring and trundling over stony desert to reach our goal took so long that I feared what we had seen was no more than a mirage or wishful thinking. Finally, the vehicle did slow and we drew to a standstill at the foot of a hill.

Out of the vehicle we had our first experience of trudging through deep, soft sand to reach the top of the ridge circling the lakes. The effort of the sinking and lifting of feet reminded me of trudging through snow with similar feelings of anticipation and getting nowhere very fast. Then we were standing on the crest, overlooking three interconnecting lakes cupped in a hollow. Some 100 metres wide, the lakes were protected by a ring of shrubs, trees and rushes that grew from the soft hills of sand surrounding it. The main, central lake, said to reach to a depth of thirty-five metres, reflected the blue of the sky and fed two shallow interconnecting pools on either side from overflow channels. Crouching on the shoreline, I gazed through crystal-clear water to plants with waving fronds growing two to three metres down the vertical sides. The centre remained a deep impenetrable green.

"People use rush for house, mat, basket, shoe – many thing. After dark they afraid," Abu Bakr explained. "Believe strange creature live in water. People not come after dark."

A small Roman castle was next on our itinerary. Along with several larger forts established in the second century its purpose was to help deal with attacks from desert tribes in an attempt to bring the pre-desert firmly within the Empire. We were trundling west across the same red, featureless desert with occasional patches of scrub and salt, marking the dry remains of a water course, and straight into the eye of the fast-descending sun. Low winter sunlight dazzled and burned through the windows, hinting at its full summer power when temperatures reached well over fifty degrees in the shade. Suddenly, the desert-red, camouflaged castle capping a small hill rose before us like a sleepy dinosaur.

As soon as we were at a standstill Abu Bakr was out of the vehicle, striding towards a well at the foot of the hill and pointing to the entrance to a tunnel alongside it. "Secret way to castle," he explained.

On hands and knees Simon was peering into a semi-collapsed opening not unlike an entrance to a fox's lair. His head and shoulders disappeared briefly before he reluctantly backed out, rubbing sand from his hair and giving up on an impulse to reach the castle through the tunnel. From where we were standing at the foot of the hill, the perfectly camouflaged sand-coloured stones of the castle walls appeared to grow out of and be part of the mound it capped.

Buffeted by strong winds, we scrambled up and involuntarily slithered down a steep, winding path, slippery with loose sand and stones until breathless and eager we were hauling each other up the stone ramparts of the remaining curtain wall which once circled the castle.

Positioning ourselves along the western ramparts, we enjoyed panoramic views to a row of magnificent dunes. From this vantage point the strategic importance of Ghadames became clear. Poised like eagles in the safety of their aerie, the Romans had clear views across uninterrupted miles of stony desert plains. The approach of caravans with their precious loads or invading tribes from any direction could be seen long before they arrived. Not only did the castle's location give the Romans an excellent vantage point for detecting any movement or approach across the flat red plains surrounding the castle and across to the Algerian border – it also enabled them to impose taxes and control trade at this strategic position.

Haynes tells us that occasional coalitions of tribes fought against the Romans and that in AD 547 three great tribes, each ruled by kings: the Ifuraces, the Garamantes of the Fezzan and the Nasamones from Syrte, attacked the Tripolitanian coast before launching a surprise attack on the Byzantines, who had followed them into the desert, inflicting a severe defeat on them.

The Romans weren't the only invaders to be resisted by indigenous people. Although contemporary Libyan Arabs prefer to see their predecessors as fraternal settlers warmly welcomed by local people when they arrived in Libya, the reality is very different. Haynes states that Arab invaders were strongly resisted by indigenous tribes: 'great Berber tribal groups of medieval Tripolitania emerge: the Nefusa and Houara, who were later to contend bitterly with the Arabs for the possession of their country'.

Driven into the Jabal by invading Arabs, the Berber people developed troglodyte dwellings into defensive citadels. Although eventually abandoned – some not until the 1970s when families continued to return to escape the extreme heat of summer – the recognisable ruins of these Berber strongholds stand on the peaks of the Jabal to this day. As late as 1911, when the Italians arrived in Libya, tribal resistance to invaders was such that it took the Italians three years to gain a foothold in Ghadames. When they finally arrived, such was their love of the ancient city that they treated the Ghadamsia with great sympathy and built the hotel,

Ain al Faras, on its very doorstep. Today, the surrounding desert was an empty wasteland. Pointing to a gap in a row of trees growing in front of the distant line of dunes and using his hand as a marker, Abu Bakr indicated: "Algeria left: Tunisia right."

Leaving the castle, we turned south across the plain, the sun now drilling a hole through my window. There were an increasing number of shrubs and the occasional oasis, marked by a clump of palms, like islands in an ocean. Ahead of us stretched the meandering alluvial plain of a former river, wide enough to have been a great delta or a vast lake. Occasional sheets of white flashed like tin foil. It seemed as if with just a slight rise in the water table great stretches of the desert could be transformed into an inland sea or vast lake. One minute we were crossing flat ground and the next we were climbing a hillock of compact sand to find ourselves at the foothills of a line of awe-inspiring dunes. The low sun cast deep shadows, emphasising the beauty and perfect symmetry of the huge crescent curves.

We soon discovered that there's nothing like dune climbing to take your breath away. Feet and legs disappearing under us as soft sand gave and rolled away, we trudged breathless but joyful to a perfect knife-edge. The line defining the crest separated the two sides of the dune – one as smooth as milk – the other rippled like the held surface of a wind-blown lake. It was the absolute silence and sense of eternity that held us motionless. Lifted by a breeze, a veil of powdered sand drifted, rested and took off again.

.

A walled sandy passage leads into the heart of the desert city of Ghadames

Entrance into a maze of tunnels interconnecting the men's living quarters

The outline of a tower and dome of a mosque

A decorated stairway leads to the women's rooftop quarters

Lake Tumin: a lake in the desert renowned for growing rushes

*Visitors at the foot of the ruins of a small Roman fort:
Qasr al Ghul (Castle of the Ghost)*

Climbing Saharan dunes: a dream realised

Pointed cornerstones on the rooftops are said to keep evil spirits away:
Ghadames

The Fezzan

Everything You Can Imagine – Everything You Can't Imagine

Back in Tripoli I was discovering that fasting Libyans do even less work than usual, are more dangerous on the roads, are more bad tempered and behave with increasing animosity towards those of us who are not Arab and not fasting. The greatest drawback to their ill humour was not being able to make international calls thereby ensuring that we were out of touch with our families. The frustration came from knowing the facility was there and although we were willing to pay for it we were being denied it for churlish reasons. There was no direct-dialling facility on the compound – all calls, local and long distance, had to go through security. Whether or not the call was connected depended entirely on the mood of the guard on duty. As the weeks of fasting went by moods became patently worse.

As Ramadan entered its fourth week my frustration was increasing. I had not received or been able to make one long-distance call. To attempt to do so one had to go to the security building and fill in all the details on a form, then return to one's accommodation and wait for the guard to make the connection. Since the start of Ramadan, every time I went to place a call the guard told me to come back later. This was followed by a variety of delaying tactics: he was too busy – come back in an hour – he was praying – all the lines to England were busy – he was asleep – and so on for three frustrating weeks. I had been warned that any person showing signs of anger or frustration was in danger of never making or receiving another call, Ramadan or not. One way of surviving was by adopting a polite face-to-face manner, meanwhile muttering 'poisonous bastard' and similar terms of endearment under the breath. During Ramadan the Weasel and his accomplice had been renamed 'the Two Hitlers'.

This was not my first overseas posting but it was my first experience of being completely out of contact. Although I knew that my family's concern would be heightened by my silence and my sense of frustration was growing, there was nothing I could do. Once again, the bizarre warnings I'd received on my arrival were proving to be horribly true.

In spite of the dangers and frustrations of travel in Libya, I was haunted by memories of the seductive and timeless beauty of the desert and determined to return. Simon was equally as enthusiastic. This time our plan was a desert safari along the trans-Saharan caravan route through Wadi al Hayat in the Fezzan. Located between Sabha and Ghat, the wadi is home to the remains of the ancient citadel and royal cemetery of the Garamantes, one of Libya's most powerful tribes. It was also the starting point for locating some of the oldest rock art in the region.

Eid al Fitr, the holiday to celebrate the end of Ramadan was the next opportunity to escape. Since, once again, the date depended on the first sighting of the new moon it was difficult to make precise arrangements in advance. This meant resorting to the *Insh'a allah* (God willing) syndrome. It was my turn to organise air tickets. We decided on an approximate date for the start of the trip and I set about attempting the impossible. After two weeks of taking People's Taxis into the tourist office in Tripoli I got no further than being assured that a representative from the equivalent tourist office in Sabha would meet us at the airport, take us to a hotel and organise a driver and four-wheel drive to take us through Wadi al Hayat to the distant Tuareg outpost of Ghat.

"Ali Saleem will telephone you," the agent in Tripoli assured me. "I have given him your number."

Although I had no faith in receiving a telephone call I consoled myself that, at least, I had a name. With the help of a Libyan colleague I attempted to make direct contact with the elusive Ali Saleem by telephone from work over several days without success. All we could do was work out the date of the new moon, pray for clear skies, book our flights to Sabha and *Insh'a allah* take it from there.

The success of our trip to Ghadames had roused considerable interest. A variety of people were keen to join us on our new venture, including a couple who had lived in Libya for up to twenty years and never travelled beyond Tripoli and its environs. However, as the day for departure drew near and we had no definite bookings we were down to two recruits: Henry, a dark-haired, blue-eyed Anglo-Indian who had the distinct advantage of being fluent in Arabic, and Gerry – one of the original four CIA suspects.

Since the interrogation Gerry's attendance at evening classes, where he was studying classical Arabic, had increased suspicions of his CIA status and put him under further scrutiny. After all, there could be only one reason for studying Arabic! Not only had he been followed to his place of study but the security officer shadowing him got into the back of the same taxi, got out with him and followed him to the very door of the classroom. Worthy of a degree in subtlety! A couple of days later the security department at his place of work informed him that Central Intelligence had been making enquiries about the nature of his work. Surprise, surprise! By now we were accustomed to our role as suspects and to being watched. We could either stay on the compound doing time or get on with exploring a fascinating country we were growing to love.

***

Finally, tickets in our hands, we were at Tripoli's International Airport and preparing to board one of the remaining, and notorious, Boeing 727s to Sabha. On this occasion, it was to be the start of a journey to explore the chain of oases crossing the Fezzan. One section of the departure lounge had been taken over by a crowd of brightly dressed local women and children on their way to celebrate the Eid that heralds the end of fasting with families and friends in Sabha. We decided that their sombre demeanour, which contrasted with their celebratory outfits, was probably fuelled either by fear of flying or by fasting which would continue until the first sliver of the new moon was sighted.

As soon as the gates opened the party of females came to life and surged forward. Taking advantage of the only privilege afforded to women in Libya, that of boarding first, I hurried after them. This privilege, I learned, was not in the interests of chivalry but to prevent male passengers taking advantage of the crowded conditions to assault female passengers! Since everyone is equal in SPLAJ – the Socialist People's Libyan Arab Jamahiriya – no seats are allocated in advance thus, in our female roles, we were able to board first without being molested and clear of the free-for-all demonstrated by the crowd of silent males once they were released from restraining barriers.

The now familiar portrait of the late-middle-aged colonel depicted as a young and dashing officer astride a rearing stallion, brandishing a sword and leading his country to independence, greeted our arrival. It was a solemn reminder that Sabha was the place where in 1977 Gaddafi declared: 'the dawn of the era of the masses' and gave birth to the Jamahiriya. The walls of the departure lounge, covered in rousing slogans from his *Green Book*, exposed some of the Leader's questionable policies.

'Anyone who enters this house is the occupant' loomed on the wall ahead.

"If all else fails," Gerry muttered, "we can spend the night here! On the other hand," he added, gesturing to the wall behind us: 'Everything you can imagine – Everything you can't imagine'. "Now that promises to cover all contingencies!"

Meanwhile, Simon and Henry had located our baggage and since there was no sign of anyone from the tourist board waiting to greet us we headed outside to scout for a taxi.

We didn't have to look far but followed Simon to a row of waiting clapped-out saloon cars. We squeezed into the first in line and were on our way before discovering that our driver was demanding exorbitant rates. We had made the mistake of failing to negotiate the fare before we set off, but by now we had more immediate concerns. Rattling as if it were about to fall apart, the vehicle was straddling the centre of the road and dodging from side to side to avoid collisions with oncoming or overtaking vehicles.

Within minutes a police car, blue lights flashing, was driving alongside and escorting us to the roadside. Fearing security was on our tail and a speedy end to our expedition, we were relieved to discover that it was the driver and not us who was under scrutiny. After confiscating his papers, the police instructed him to deliver us to the tourist office in town before reporting to the police station.

The excitement was such that we almost lost the opportunity to glimpse en route the one landmark that Sabha was famous for – its Italian fort. Taken by the French in 1943 and used as a base for the Third Saharan Company of the Foreign Legion, it was now a local military base. Its grey stone walls and turrets could be viewed in passing but were definitely out of bounds for photographers!

When we finally arrived at the Tourist Board's new and near-empty premises it was to discover that we were not expected, no arrangements had been made for our trip and the one guarantee I thought we could be sure of – the tour organiser, Ali Saleem – was not available. In fact, introductions and explanations for our visit were met with blank looks. 'Everything you can imagine – Everything you can't imagine' came to mind!

Dressed in a traditional full-length white robe with a red and white checkered scarf tucked rakishly over a headband and behind his ears, the agent on duty reminded us that it was the weekend of the Eid and no one would be prepared to leave family celebrations to take us into the desert. His hawk-like features and bored, arrogant manner did not inspire confidence, but there were no other options and this was not the time to back off. I could feel my blood pressure rising.

"The tourist board in Tripoli promised that Ali Saleem would organise a driver for us. Do you know him? Can't you contact him?" I pleaded.

Finally, irked by our presence rather than inspired by altruistic concern, the agent made a few telephone calls and located a colleague who promised to try to find the owner of a four-wheel drive who would take us to the desert city of Ghat. Then he made arrangements for a taxi to take us to the hotel and instructed us to wait there.

Later that evening we were introduced to Emad, a local farmer who owned a Toyota Land Cruiser. He spoke no English, owned no camping gear and was demanding double the expected rate. But, we reasoned, he was a farmer willing to accommodate us over the Eid and it was fair enough that it had to be financially worthwhile for him.

The alternative was to spend four days in Sabha – a concrete city in the desert – or risk taking the late afternoon flight to Ghat. This would mean giving up the drive through Wadi al Hayat, the main purpose of our trip. What's more, we'd heard a rumour that the hotel in Ghat had burnt down last year and we had no way of knowing if we'd either find accommodation or secure a guide when we arrived there. Trying to get information about Sabha while in Tripoli, or Ghat while in Sabha, was as difficult as making contact with another planet. We decided to cut our losses and arranged for Emad to pick us up for an early start to drive the 575 kilometres to Ghat the next morning.

At nine storeys, the Al Fateha Hotel, or new hotel, appeared to be the highest building in Sabha. From my top-floor balcony I could make out the perimeter of the city and where it ended the great stretch of desert reaching to the horizon. Once composed of three separate oases' settlements the city was now a modern sprawling urban centre marked by minarets, water towers and clumps of green. I reminded myself that due south was Chad.

During the war with Chad over the Uzu Strip, Gaddafi channelled support to insurgents and indiscriminately armed local people – handing out machine guns, Kalashnikovs and handguns – ostensibly to protect themselves against the French who were fighting with the people from Chad. Robbery and violence in Sabha were said to be commonplace. In the courtyard below, huddles of local men, standing or crouching on their haunches, gave the place an air of intrigue. It was not a good holiday venue!

However, beyond the perimeter of the city lay the gateway to the start of our journey through the vast east–west corridor of oases, steeped in the history of the Garamantes tribe. Herodotus makes a number of colourful references to the more extreme warlike practices of the Garamantes, but in this instance highlights their role as highly successful farmers: 'who spread soil over the salt to grow seed in'.

In fact, the farming practices of the Garamantes were not restricted to spreading soil over salt. Geological activities of lifting and faulting in the area have resulted in bringing supplies of underground fossil reserves of water close to the surface, creating a series of oases and opportunities for successful farming. Taking full advantage of this, the Garamantes are reputed to have set up a sophisticated system of underground water tunnels for irrigating crops which is still in use to this day. Tomorrow our journey would take us from Sabha to Ghat through this chain of oases.

A chill in the air sent me back to my room in search of a sweater. Compared to our experiences so far, the hotel was remarkably comfortable and tasteful in both design and furnishings. Pale blue walls and a deeper blue, picked up in the curtains and paintings, had a calming effect. On closer inspection the fittings were suffering from the lack of maintenance symptomatic of life in Libya: a sliding wardrobe door fell off when I tried to open it; there were no hangers; the bar-fridge was not working and housed an empty water bottle and the prerequisite cockroach. I shut the door firmly before the intruder could escape. There was, however, the ultimate luxury: a shower with warm water and, what is more, the bed was not only comfortable but made up with two clean cotton sheets.

Finally, in spite of it being Friday and Ramadan, we were served an evening meal of chicken, houmos, Arabic bread and salad. The air of civility was a marked improvement on that experienced at the hotel in Ghadames.

***

On the dot of 7.30 the following morning Emad, our farmer driver, was waiting in the hotel's forecourt. Wearing a full-length white robe, gathered and embroidered like a smock across the front of his chest, and a length of white material wound about his head, the first impression was that of a shepherd from a nativity scene. Happily he was not accompanied by a flock of sheep or even a herd of camels but seated behind the wheel of a highly polished and upmarket Toyota Land Cruiser. For travel in Libya, this was luxury indeed! We set off in the direction of Ghat along a graded road – a euphemism for a rutted track worn by other travellers – following the ancient caravan trail linking the main desert settlements of the Fezzan.

At last we were in the former territory of the fierce warrior tribe whose hunting exploits were not confined to local wildlife but, as Herodotus tells us, extended to the use of horse-drawn chariots to hunt and capture the much maligned Ethiopian troglodytes: 'The Garamantes hunt the Ethiopian troglodytes in four-horse chariots, for these troglodytes are exceedingly swift of foot – more so than any people of whom we have any information. They eat snakes and lizards and other reptiles and speak a language like no other, but squeak like bats'.

It was the discovery of the prehistoric artwork of the Garamantes in the Fezzan that first provided clues about their lives and their highly sophisticated if barbaric hunting techniques. Their numerous rock paintings in a flat, childlike style depict matchstick men wielding weapons and standing astride two-wheeled chariots drawn by three or four horses.

Now with Henry as our interpreter, my copy of Haynes, giving details about the site but no indication of its whereabouts, and information gleaned by word-of-mouth we headed for Garama (Germa) the ancient capital of the Garamantes' dynasty. Their commercial empire, which stretched south to Lake Chad, is marked by the rock drawings of the horse-drawn chariots with which they ruled the Fezzan. The warrior tribe, said to have invaded the central Sahara from the north, winning battles over pastoral people with their chariots and superior metal weapons, also conducted successful raids against the Romans.

Such was the threat posed by the Garamantes that in 19 BC the Roman proconsul, Cornelius Balbus, led an army of 20,000 men across the inhospitable stony wastes of the great Hamada al Hamra in an attempt to conquer them. Finally, in order to pacify the warring tribe the proconsul formed a trading alliance with them. In return for manufactured goods the Garamantes brought slaves, gold dust, ivory, ostrich plumes and wild beasts from sub-Saharan Africa. Haynes tells us that, following many ferocious raids and attacks on the Romans, the king of the Garamantes finally joined forces with them on slave-raiding expeditions.

Contrary to our hopes we learnt that Emad professed to have no knowledge of the sites we were hoping to find. He made it clear to Henry that his definitive role was to drive us to Ghat. His inscrutable expression gave no hint of what was going on in his head. In spite of this news and in spite of the lack of maps or any other aids, filled with the enthusiasm of raw adventurers, we settled for keeping a lookout for any sign of an ancient settlement.

We were well into our journey when Henry, shouting triumphantly, pointed ahead to the remains of mud-sand walls, rising from among sand hills at the side of the wadi. Under his directions Emad followed a track north of the main route, taking us to the outer perimeter walls that once surrounded and defended the ancient capital. Centre stage, abandoned to the heat of desert skies and spread over a wide expanse of flat ground, was a complex of iron railway tracks, trucks and pulleys – the remnants of equipment used by the Italians during their 1930s' excavations. We wandered across the deserted tracks. The artefacts, left in position as if the workers expected to return the following day, remained as solid yet ghostly reminders of the Italian presence. The effect was strangely sobering.

Nearby, a huge unearthed square, marked by stone slabs, lay before us like the preface to a locked book. Some of its secrets, revealed by excavation work in the 1960s, include the foundations of a temple and stonework dating back to the first century AD. These were still intact. Other finds, taken to the museum for safe keeping, included Roman pottery and some fine glassware, confirming both the influence and intertrading between the Romans and the Garamantes.

Beyond the temple, the roofless remnants of the settlement sprawled across hummocky ground. We climbed to where the remains of the former *kasbah* (castle) – a sagging tower – stood on the highest land. From the top we had uninterrupted views over the site and across the wadi to where the powerful tribesmen had driven their horse-drawn chariots. It was here that the Roman armies joined forces with the Garamantes on expeditions deep into the wilderness to capture slaves and wild animals. After marching due south for four months they reached 'an Aethiopian country called Agysimba, where the rhinocerus congregates'.

The intriguing image of congregating rhinoceros apart, the noise and clamour of the assembling Roman armies and gathering of warlike Garamantes was reason enough for the naming of the Wadi al Ajal: 'at the appointed time', i.e. the hour of death! Reminiscent of *The Valleys of the Assassins*, explored by Freya Stark in 1930s' Persia – it too was a highly dangerous place to travel through. Now, the Romans and the Garamantes are long departed and the 100-mile-long chain of fertile oases has lost its original evocative name for the more euphemistic: Wadi al Hayat, or Valley of Life.

From our elevated position we could also make out the shape and size of the abandoned city – the labyrinth of passages and rooms and intricate network of walls, diminishing in room size towards the perimeter where the animals were penned. Once an impressive fortified settlement, surrounded by a moat with towers and high walls, it is now crumbling and sinking back into the earth. Our own silence, overpowered by a greater compelling silence, was suddenly broken by a crescendo of shrilling cicadas.

Enthusiasm fuelled by our discovery, we set our sights on finding the cemetery of the royal Garamantes. Haynes tells us that kings, who were probably elected, and could perhaps be deposed by an assembly of tribal elders, ruled the two great Libyan tribes, the Garamantes and the Nasamones. Italian excavations at Garama discovered that the Garamantes' funeral rituals and cult of the dead were elaborate – corpses of rulers were buried in two-step pyramidal tombs and supplied with rich trappings for the afterlife. The royal cemetery was our next objective but once again we were relying on second- and even third-hand information to find the site.

"If what I was told is correct, the tombs are further west – off the main track and beneath an escarpment at the far side of the wadi," Henry insisted. "Slow down. Drive slowly!" he instructed Emad. "Then if you guys keep your eyes peeled for upright stones we should find them."

Groves of date palms and tamarisk trees, fringing irrigated fields, obscured the view from time to time, but generally the vegetation was low-lying and we were hopeful that with five pairs of eyes on the lookout we would be able to see ten-foot-high obelisks from the track. Then out of the blue a new tarmac road cut straight across the wadi ahead of us and continued up onto an adjoining hillside.

Fearing that we had missed the site, Simon took control, directing Emad to follow the road. Climbing steeply between a dramatic chasm bulldozed through the rock walls of an escarpment, it led to the summit of a plateau. It was a perfect lookout platform, providing panoramic views across the oasis, but there was no sign of the cemetery.

"Probably a new oil company road – one of many being built – used by oil companies to avoid the increasing dangers of flying in Libya," Henry surmised.

What we didn't know at the time was that this very road provided a short cut across the Messak Settafet (Black Plateau) towards a premier site for viewing prehistoric Tuareg rock carvings. Ignorant that we were turning our backs on some of the best rock art in the Fezzan and minds bent on our mission to find the tombs, we retraced our route into the wadi and had just started heading west again when Gerry sighted a stone obelisk on the far side of the road.

Emad drew up before a dilapidated wooden gate that opened to an area about the size of a football pitch. The entire site was marked at regular intervals by mounds of sand not unlike rows of sagging termite mounds – each indicated the position of a grave. Half a dozen had been uncovered and reassembled; others in the early stages of restoration had toppled obelisks lying alongside while the majority of the graves remained buried.

Close up, each brick-built pyramid, some ten feet in height, was centrally placed on a twelve-foot-square platform of sand bricks marking a grave. Once, they must have been pretty impressive. Today, wandering between the fallen and partially restored obelisks, the sense of excavation and work in progress suddenly abandoned was apparent once more. It was a bleak, exposed site remarkable for what we had learnt from Haynes's writings about the lives of this formidable tribe and the elaborate care they took of the dead as well as for the wonders that still remained unearthed.

Italian archaeologists revealed that funeral rites and the cult of the dead were linked with the same preoccupation of the afterlife as practised by the Egyptians. Further discoveries by the Italians of calcined bones and other remains tell of sacrificial meals given to the dead at the time of the burial. In addition, a number of tombs were provided with stone offering tables on which the dead man's family could continue to place regular offerings of food and drink after closing the tomb. Other offerings, including small obelisks, crudely shaped horns or hands of stone, are thought to have been the adopted symbols of the funeral cults of people the Garamantes traded with. Horns were borrowed from the Egyptians and their sun god, Horus; obelisks were borrowed from the Carthaginian cult of Tanit – the goddess of Carthage. Finally, the discovery of Roman lamps, pottery and glass vessels, ranging in date from the late first to the fourth century, was a clear indication of both the trade and exchange of cultural ideas that had taken place.

Just as the Garamantes grew more powerful through their trading alliance with the Romans so they faded from history when the Roman Empire receded. The cemetery, like the remains of the city, was overshadowed by an air of desertion – an aching emptiness.

***

By late afternoon we had reached Serdeles, a settlement amidst fertile farmland and at the meeting place with the road from Ghadames. At this strategic position, overlooking the junction of routes to Sabha, Ghat and Ghadames, the Italians built a splendid grey stone fort. On this day, surrounded by fields of deep green, it was an impressive farm, watered by high-powered irrigation sprinklers.

Emad pulled over for five minutes' rest and to give us a chance to stretch our legs. Sunlight filtered through the feathery fronds of a grove of casuarinas where a chorus of doves sang their international song. The scene and a sudden whiff of Henry's Gitane cigarette took me back to a vineyard in France. In my mind's eye I saw the hillside before us clothed in vineyards during the Italian occupation.

"I'd give my soul for a glass of chilled white wine," I confessed to Simon.

"Dream on!" he sympathised before adding, "An ice-cold beer would go down well!"

Nursing our thirsts, we made our way back to the vehicle for the last leg of our journey. As shadows lengthened and deepened we headed across a swirling blue-white hallucinatory river of dried salt towards the Akakus range where strange and dramatic silhouettes of rock hills reached some 500 metres against the sky. We reached the foothills of the mountains at sunset and Emad stopped to break his fast – his first meal since before dawn this morning. Henry explained what he had learned about the region from Emad – primarily that the highest mountain, known as Jabal Idinen, or Mountain of the Spirits, was feared by local people who believed it was inhabited by evil spirits. When talking to Emad and reporting back to us, Henry's thin and studious face, capped by a head of straight dark hair, came alive.

Just now, in failing light, you didn't need much imagination to conjure the outlines of gothic castles and a group of cloaked Titans watching from the top of impenetrable walls. The mood and place were apt for storytelling and, as it happened, a confession. Henry explained that he was something of a petroglyph maniac, and it was the possibility of seeing rock art in this region that had persuaded him to overcome ten years of caution and join us on the trip. He then proceeded to recount the following story of Heinrich Barth, the first European explorer to record the presence of ancient rock art of the region.

"While exploring in these very mountains, Barth decided to climb Mount Idinen. He succeeded in reaching the summit but was so exhausted and thirsty that by the time he'd made the descent he had drunk all his water. He then lost his way and finally collapsed, losing consciousness. When he came to, in a desperate attempt to ward off dehydration, he resorted to cutting a vein in his wrist and sucking his blood. Remarkably, he survived and later recounted in his diary his unique technique for survival."

"More upmarket than drinking one's urine, I suspect," Simon volunteered, swiftly changing the mood and leading to a debate on the pros and cons of drinking blood and needing a knife, or urine and needing a container in order to stay alive.

"If you're severely dehydrated there's a good chance you'll be out of urine and as a last resort a sharp stone will serve as a knife!" Henry responded. "How do you think ancient people managed without knives?" he added before launching back into story mode and explaining that in his diary Barth admitted that he knew that sucking his blood would not have been enough to save him. "In fact," Henry continued, "his life was saved by a Tuareg tribesman who had spotted his footprints in the sand – a member of the very tribe he had previously feared. This time," Henry explained, "the Tuareg in question was his guide and his protector."

I was familiar with the story – Barth is one of my most admired explorers. An 'Unsung Hero' he journeyed for five years through the Sahara, keeping a diary in which he described his adventures in the desert. Even when his two travelling companions died from fever he continued his explorations to Timbuktu alone before eventually returning to Europe unrecognised. At the time no one celebrated the unique feat he had accomplished. Saddened and worn out by the hardships of his solitary journeys through the Sahara, he died not understanding the human imagination incapable of appreciating the frontiers he had travelled to alone.

By the time Henry had finished his story the sun was down and a half-moon had risen, bathing the mountains in silvery light. Meanwhile, Emad had quietly withdrawn and was waiting patiently behind the wheel of his Land Cruiser, his expression as inscrutable as ever. Fully in the mood for adventure and putting bets on whether or not rumours that the hotel in Ghat had been destroyed by fire were true or false, we clambered into the vehicle for the last leg of the journey.

Our relief on finding that the sandstone hotel was still standing was tempered by the discovery that the building was in complete darkness. There were no lights and no sign of life. Remembering that it was Ramadan and the staff would be eating their first meal of the day, we followed Emad in search of food for ourselves. Before long the smell of roasting chicken lured us down a sandy lane to a small café where, seated round a rickety table beneath the widespread branches of a thorny acacia, we were soon tucking into spiced soup, chicken and salad.

Back at the hotel nothing had changed. The place was cast in darkness and utterly silent. We had no blankets or bedding and the thought of a night sitting upright in the vehicle did not appeal. Finally, some desperate banging on the door brought a response. We heard a bolt slide and the door creaked open, revealing a ghost-like figure in a long white robe. From an exchange between the robed figure, Emad and Henry we learnt that there had been a fire and since then the hotel had been without electricity. Nevertheless, we were invited to stay and handed candles to find our way to cell-like rooms strung along a stone corridor. There was warm spring water from metal showerheads in concrete cubicles but flushing the loo was of the usual bucket and 'do-it-yourself' variety.

My monastic cell contained a single bed with a lumpy mattress, a pillow and two sheets. Anticipating a cold night, I pulled on my tracksuit. Stretched out on my narrow bed I had a perfect view of a star-crusted sky framed by a small window. Alone and immersed in the profound silence of a desert night I succumbed to immense feelings of contentment. The fact that we had travelled through the legendary Wadi al Ajal, explored the remains of the Garamantes' fortified city and royal burial place and arrived at the distant outpost of Ghat was enough. Tomorrow was tomorrow and part of the excitement was the uncertainty of what it would bring. 'Everything you can imagine – Everything you can't imagine' was fast becoming my motto!

The crumbling remains of the Garamantian Citadel: Garama

Garmantian pyramidal tombs in the royal cemetery: al Hatya

The dramatic outline of the Jabal Idinen, 'Mountain of the Spirits'

From Oasis to Oasis

The next morning Ghat's local telegraph system was in full swing. Before we had signed out of the hotel, Mustafa, a local Tuareg tour operator, was waiting for us. Taller than the average Tuareg, he was dressed in the traditional white gown over low-crutch trousers, his turban wound carelessly round his head with the veil looped under his chin! His small hooked nose, closely set eyes and drooping moustache gave him the appearance of an affable villain while his fast-talking salesmanship and enthusiasm indicated a greater business acumen than I had met anywhere in Libya so far.

Finally, we settled for a guide, some bedding and a two-day excursion through the Tanezzuft Hills and Dunes north-west of Ghat with a promise of a visit to caves with rock carvings. Satisfied with his success, Mustafa directed us to a nearby café where we could get breakfast of coffee and bread before the start of our trip, giving him time to locate a guide and finalise preparations.

This was everything and more than we dared hope for. We knew that the prehistoric Tuareg hunter-gatherers and herders used the numerous rock shelters and grottoes of the Akakus Mountains for their homes as well as for their paintings and rock carvings. Their artwork features a wide range of narrative scenes from everyday life as well as images of wild creatures, including elephant, giraffe and rhinoceros, from over 4,000 years ago when the region was wetter and forested.

The caves we were going to visit were north of Ghat in the lower reaches of the Akakus. Here, Henry believed, we were more likely to come upon images of herders and domestic cattle from the pastoral era – nevertheless, they were part of the extensive outdoor gallery of Berber artwork that we had dreamed of finding.

Before we set off we decided to make a quick tour of the remains of the ancient city and Tuareg stronghold of Ghat – literally across the road from Mustafa's office. Some eighty kilometres from Djanet over the border in Algeria, Ghat lies in the Wadi Tanezzuft between the two adjoining mountainous regions – the Libyan Akakus to the east and the Algerian Tassili-n-Ajjer and Ahaggar Massif to the west. Together with the Tibesti Mountains south of the Fezzan they form the great Saharan Plateau. Composed of largely extinct volcanoes and pinnacles of naked rock, the tallest peaks of the Ahaggar Massif reach to almost 10,000 feet. Herodotus states that here is a mountain of great height called Atlas, the peak of which is always in cloud and which the native people, known as Atlantes, believe supports the sky. These people, he tells us, 'are said to eat no living creature and never to dream'.

Strategically positioned on the trans-Saharan caravan route from Niger to Ahaggar and from Ahaggar to the Mediterranean, Ghat became a Tuareg stronghold. The ancient walled city's interconnecting passages, compact and shoulder to shoulder, followed the contours of the hill, providing a cool and safe retreat. Lacking the solidity of Ghadames, sections of the walls and a number of the adjoining dwellings collapsed after a major flood in the 1960s, making the movement of the families of Ghat into modern housing in the wadi more plausible than the enforced exodus from Ghadames.

We made our way along narrow passageways between sagging and fallen walls, gradually ascending to the highest point where the restored Ottoman-built Red Fort dominates the skyline. Legend has it that the eleventh-century Arab King of Seville, Mu'tamid Ibn Abbad, defeated and deposed by religious Berber warriors from Morocco in the Almoravid Revolt, was exiled in this fort. The imprisoned king, renowned for his creative talents, is said to have been a fine poet.

Before us was the wadi with the new settlement, and, leading from this, caravan trails headed north to Ghadames and east through the Fezzan to the Oasis of Augila, known for its excellent supplies of dates. Herodotus believes that Augila was the end of the salt-trade route since the people beyond this point could use salt from the flats of the Mediterranean Sea. To the west, he tells us, the salt trade took its reference point from the Pillar of the Sky in an approximately north–south line to the Niger River. Salt was loaded on camels in big blocks and exchanged at fixed rates between the weight of gold and the weight of salt.

My favourite story, told by fifteenth-century Venetian sea-captain and explorer merchant Alvise Ca' da Mosto, is one of the silent trading of salt for gold between the Tuareg of the Sahara and the more sedentary inhabitants of Sahel (Southern Sahara). The highly coveted salt, carried from the interior on the heads of black slaves of the Tuareg and Moors, was taken to a region near the Niger River. Once the slaves arrived at the region they formed the salt into little hillocks in a straight line and after marking them retreated out of sight. When the native people from Sahel arrived at the scene they placed next to each mound of salt a certain amount of gold. They too withdrew, leaving behind both the salt and gold. When those who left the salt returned, if they deemed the amount of gold to be sufficient they took it, leaving the salt; if not they took neither the gold nor the salt and left once more. When the local people returned they took the piles of salt with no gold next to them and placed more gold next to the others. And so they conducted their commerce, never seeing one another and never speaking.

This extraordinary silent commerce, said to be based on the African's fear of being taken as slaves, was being practised long before the fifteenth century. Herodotus too describes the procedure of silent trade used by Carthaginians to buy gold from a race of men beyond the Pillars of Herakles. Whether the salt and gold was carried by camels or slaves, Arab geographers report that the caravans that went from Ghat to the Niger followed guides who orientated themselves by the stars and that the smallest orientation error could be fatal. A fact confirmed by the Berbers who named the desert west of Ahaggar: Tazen Ruft – Land of Fear.

***

Before signing out of the hotel we were required to sign in – a task our late and unexpected arrival under cover of darkness had freed us from the previous evening. The forms required extensive details of our family histories, residence and travels in Libya. While we were preoccupied with the painstaking chore, a smooth-talking Libyan sidled up and spent his time looking over our shoulders and chivvying us with a range of inquisitive questions about our movements and intentions. His impeccable English and oily manner marked him out as yet another security agent. Even in distant Ghat we were under surveillance. It was a relief when Mustafa swept into reception with a guide in tow.

"This is Abu Bakr," Mustafa announced, introducing a short and wiry-looking Tuareg. "He knows the desert like the back of his hand and has some English."

Abu Bakr's coal-black eyes sparkled in a face the colour of polished mahogany. His nose was bent slightly to one side over a shaving-brush moustache. Dressed in a full-length collarless white shirt-like garment over dark trousers and with his *tagulmust* knotted jauntily about his head, he bore no resemblance to his solemn namesake in Ghadames.

"Abu Bakr very happy," he said, grinning widely. "Abu Bakr love desert. England plenty money. Abu Bakr show England desert."

Feeling like royalty, we left Ghat on the road north and then turned west to cross open desert, following intermittent tyre tracks into the wilderness. The surface of the desert was covered with small, black, hard stones of cindery appearance and surrounded by black isolated hills. When the tyre tracks disappeared Emad followed the deft hand signals of Abu Bakr. Although the only remaining landmarks were occasional rocks or alterations in the texture of the desert floor he showed no hesitation in indicating a change of direction.

An hour later the surface was covered in slabs of flaking beige rock. At times these were so smooth it was as if the entire place had been as painstakingly paved as the magnificent roads of Roman cities. At other times loose and broken slabs and pieces of rock, as hard as marble, crunched and snapped and jumped under our wheels or grated disconcertingly against the undercarriage, reminding me of the approach to Waw al Namus and of past volcanic activity in the Akakus region. Now huddles of rock were appearing in strange shapes that became the animals, birds or people of a nightmarish, petrified landscape. Tufts of green and the occasional spindly thorn tree showed that we were following the course of an ancient wadi between a labyrinth of sculptured turrets and rocky canyons, blasted and hollowed by sand-laden searing winds aeons ago.

As shadows lengthened we left the wadi and followed a track, winding between rocky outcrops through deeper sand, until finally Abu Bakr directed Emad to the entrance of a wide low-roofed cave. This, it transpired, was our camping place for the night. Relieved to flex our cramped limbs and eager to explore, we left Emad stretched out on his back to sleep on the stony floor and followed Abu Bakr through an avenue of pillars of sculptured rocks. The silence, the shadows and exquisite light of the dying metallic sun kept us immersed in our own thoughts as we trailed our leader through an archway of rock into the shadowed and cool interior of another huge cave.

Once we'd adjusted to the change of light we found we were standing in front of a wall of grey rock, face to face with rock carvings of a row of near life-size cattle. The outlines had been deeply incised in the surface in a style so naturalistic that the stance and gait of the creatures was suggestive of the melancholic yet contented demeanour of domestic cattle seen plodding in English countryside today. Some of the beasts, walking head down, had short, stubby horns while others strung between them, boasting long, curved horns, stared soulfully at us in the way that curious yet unafraid creatures do.

In an interconnecting cave, this time on pitted red-brown rock, two more strolling cattle images filled the wall. Again, and immediately behind the pair, the head of a forward-facing beast with long, upward-curving pointed horns stared straight at us. As flashlights from our cameras momentarily lit the surface, highlighting the images, I imagined a cave fire sending flickering light and shadows onto the artwork and a family gathered about the flames, enjoying the warmth and safety of their decorated rock home on a starlit, frosty desert night.

Lord of his domain, Abu Bakr's dark eyes shone as he escorted us to another set of caves to view further displays of the rock art of his ancestors. Interpretation and understanding was left to us – what we didn't know we compensated for by imagination and guesswork.

This time the caves were wider and deeper yet enough light filtered onto walls of pale sand-coloured rock to highlight an isolated example of each of two distinct styles of cattle on opposite walls.

"Wow!" enthused Henry, his face lighting up. "Just look at these pointed lines!" he continued, gesturing towards a creature with a pointed muzzle, long, curved pointed horns, and with both its legs and tail ending in pointed lines. "It's not a different art form or even time – it's the texture of the rock. On this wall the rock is smooth and hard – difficult to chisel rounded ends – the engravings taper off."

Further into the cave a juxtaposition of creatures and styles, facing in various directions, covered the pitted surface, including the elegant outline of an ostrich. One image in particular provided some lively debate. I was convinced that we were looking at the shorter more solid outline of a young rhinoceros and behind it the deeply incised and rounded form of an adult of the same breed.

"Impossible," Henry insisted. "These carvings are from the pastoral period. Rhinoceros were no longer around. Could be buffalo," he conceded.

"I think not," Simon challenged unexpectedly. "Not with sides rounded like these! I'm no expert but these inner caves have probably been in use for centuries. After all this is Africa – rhinos are still around to this day – even here they didn't die out overnight. What's more, I understand the people used the shape of the rock as part of the design." He was pointing to where the rock edge coincided with the outline of the larger creature.

"That may be true," Henry responded, a peevish note creeping into his voice, "but it doesn't prove anything."

Suspecting that Henry's insistence was as much a testing of antler strength as conviction, I remained silent.

"Come on, guys. Let's agree to disagree," Gerry suggested before deftly changing the subject. "What interests me are the cattle in the first cave – surely those with long, curved horns – the ones staring straight at us – aren't they the ones that were forced to graze backwards?"

His diplomacy was effective in ending, if not in resolving, the debate. Neither guy was prepared to back down. That the images of long-horned creatures carved into the cave walls could be the very ones described by Herodotus was less contentious:

'it is amongst them [the Garamantes] that cattle are found which walk backwards as they graze. The reason for this curious habit is provided by the formation of their horns, which bend forwards and downwards; this prevents them from moving forwards in the ordinary way, for, if they tried to do so, their horns would stick in the ground.'

Whatever we said, Abu Bakr smiled and nodded his head in agreement. Standing in the very footsteps of the people who had executed the artwork was deeply satisfying. The images were from the distant past and yet there was a feeling of continuity as if the spirits of the artists lived on through their artwork – a feeling that had been so absent in the ruins of the abandoned city of Garama.

The opening and closing of shutters broke the spell of silence that had fallen upon us. We followed Abu Bakr into the slanting shadows of the wadi where thousands of years ago his ancestors, the artistic tribesmen, watered their cattle and hunted. In evening light the weird and tortured shapes of spiralling pillars of rock, silent witnesses to the past, were silhouetted against the deepening lilac hues of the sky.

Our voices roused Emad from sleep. As soon as he was on his feet Abu Bakr directed him to an especially fertile oasis a few kilometres away to find wood from dead trees for a fire. It was a magical place where underground water and sudden rain showers give life to a variety of flowering plants: the bright yellow furry heads of chamomile, galaxies of tiny mauve stars like the heads of forget-me-not and delicate pink and white miniature foxgloves. Among the tufted grass, under the thorny trees with flat green heads, we found and armed ourselves with dead stumps of trees, handing them to Emad who tied them to the roof of his vehicle.

Back at camp we all set about helping to unload the wood and build the fire then Abu Bakr took control. Before long he had the fire blazing and was preoccupied making mint-flavoured tea over the charcoal edges. He inserted a generous sprig of mint into a metal teapot which he filled with water, added some green Libyan tea leaves and left it to boil. Meanwhile, he spooned several heaps of sugar into an enamel mug. When the water had boiled he emptied the mixture onto the sugar, then poured it all back into the pot to simmer while he set out the food. Finally, Gerry poured and handed round mugs of the hot, sweet, mint-flavoured tea and we helped ourselves to great rounds of Arabic bread, filling them with slices of tinned meat, cheese and tomatoes.

"Not quite what we had in mind," Simon said, raising his mug of syrupy tea to the stars and winking at me before toasting the success of our trip and tucking into his doorstep sandwich.

The meal over and cleared away, we wriggled into sleeping bags and arranged ourselves like the spokes of a wheel round the fire. Overhead the sky was tremulous with stars. Layer upon layer throbbed, sparkled and cobwebbed the sky with feverish light. I settled down to make the most of one of life's great awe-inspiring experiences: a night under an African sky, feeling the pulse of life as our early ancestors had done.

I thought back to the ancient curled skeleton in the museum, to the map of the world showing mankind spilling from the heart of Africa. Then from the stillness of a desert night something stirred. At first I heard a sound I had heard before like falling raindrops or the pattering of dozens of tiny feet; then a stinging sensation as a cold breeze lifted and whipped sand into the air. Fine grains bounced off exposed surfaces; as the attack thickened they accumulated round my eyes and nostrils, in my ears and even in the corners of my mouth. Clamping my lips together, I resisted an urge to moisten them with my tongue. Smoke from the stirred remains of the fire was the final straw.

This wasn't how I had imagined it would be. The stars were still there, filling the lake of sky with luminous light but, forced to keep my eyes closed, I couldn't see them. The wind was cold and the ground so hard I might just as well be lying on rock. I raised myself onto my elbows and surveyed the scene. To one side of me was Simon. Too long for his sleeping bag he'd wrapped his head in a towel and was lying face down resting his smothered head on his arms. On the other side Gerry was lying on his back with his eyes closed, his face protected by his mop of hair and beard; his heavy breathing threatened to become a snore. From a sitting position I saw that Henry had all but disappeared into the folds of his sleeping bag while the shrouded forms of Emad and Abu Bakr were as motionless as mummies.

Wriggling free, I left my companions cocooned round the glowing embers of the fire and, taking my sleeping bag, I crept into the cave. The floor was just as hard but now I could hear the wind and not feel it and beyond the black lip of the rock cave I could feast on the star-crazy sky.

***

The next morning, bones aching from a night on the ungiving cave floor, I woke early and surveyed the scene before me of sunlit pockets of sand in distant rock hollows and dunes rolling to infinity. Leaving the sand-swept bodies of my companions, resembling discarded bundles distributed round the remains of the fire, I set off to explore.

Last night's wind had smoothed the surface of the dunes,

creating a perfect canvas for the delicate hieroglyphs left by gazelles. Following their trail into a narrowing passage of deep, loose sand flanked by phallic rock formations, I left my own set of smudged prints in small hollows. From the summit I looked across great buttresses of rock and crenellated ridges that acted as a barrier to a line of wind-driven dunes. Soft sand had blown and trickled into crevices and hollows like mountain snow, cloaking the back of the rocks, while seductive lines of dunes stretched and curved, forming a range of hills that were inexorably changing shape and position as silently and mysteriously as water.

Intoxicated by the wild beauty of my surroundings, I followed the crest of the nearest dune, the sun on my face, a light wind rippling the sand and fingering my hair. One minute I was trudging along, the next I was on my knees as a terrible emptiness swept through me. Cold tears ran over my cheeks and dripped from my chin as quite literally joy spilled over into sadness. One of the benefits of previous overseas postings had been the facility to share the experience with family and friends through phone calls, letters and even visits. I had been in Libya for close on four months and out of contact for over six weeks. The moment of intense spiritual beauty had triggered not only a feeling of isolation but the breakdown of reserve built up to cope with weeks of pent-up frustration: the direct result of the game-playing and control exerted by security, denying residents the facility of making a single telephone call in the weeks before and throughout Ramadan.

Back at camp the others were getting ready for the start of a journey that would take us near the Algerian border, across the caravan route leading to Ghadames and through a huge wadi skirting the Akakus range. And so we continued our travels from oasis to oasis and from spring to spring, as the ancient travellers recorded by Herodotus had done. We crunched and bounced over the surface towards Jabal al Ginn: Mountain of the Genie. "Ghosts live in mountain," Abu Bakr called as we trundled past huge pillars of sculptured rock that dominated the skyline and fed the imagination. Then leaving the mountains behind us, we trundled across mile upon mile of burning sandstone. Small tornadoes whipped whirlpools of sand into the air and sent them spiralling into the distance where the rose-pink and ethereal outline of the Tanezzuft Dunes blended into the horizon.

Suddenly Abu Bakr pointed to a dark blob on the desolate surface. We headed towards it, watching the outline of a lone camel emerge. At a reasonable distance from our quarry we slowed down, cameras at the ready. As Emad brought the vehicle to a standstill, black eyes sparkling, Abu Bakr scrambled out. Cautiously approaching the camel, he was attempting to persuade him to come our way. Then it was all action: photographers at the ready and even Emad, in an unusual display of animation, hopped down to assist Abu Bakr. The camel argued for a while, hackles raised and tail erect, providing some lively postures for the photographers. His hobbled front legs kept him from escaping, allowing us to obtain a range of shots. An hour or so later, surrounded by sand in every direction, we crossed paths with another four-wheel drive. The owner circled back to ask if we'd come across a stray camel. He disappeared across the desolate sandscape in the direction of Abu Bakr's outstretched arm.

Close up the soft curves of the dunes transformed the landscape from bleak exposure to sensuous beauty. In front of us a mirage of a lake, as flat and glazed as a mirror, slipped over the skyline. The occasional arthritic thorn tree, twisted and gnarled with a head of green flattened against the sky, traced our route. Coming upon a grove of trees with thick spongy leaves and mauve heads of blossom-like desert lilac, we asked Emad to stop and tumbled out to explore the magical scene. At the foot of a thorn tree we found seedpods, brittle as eggshells and the size of billiard balls, that rattled like castanets, and strange white and yellow dried flower heads. Beautiful scented bushes filled the air with a heady fragrance. Shrubs with dagger-like thorns spiked the air. It was a place full of oxymoronic images, worthy of a setting for Keats' 'La Belle Dame sans Merci'.

Out of the wadi we were in hostile desert again. Then as the landscape softened into sandhills we headed for a line of trees on a ridge that marked the setting of a village.

"Here buy sheep," Abu Bakr announced.

He was pointing to a dozen or so rush-built huts, each supported on a framework of sticks, in a scene that was quite literally straight from the heart of Africa. "Buy sheep. Cut throat for dinner," Abu Bakr enthused while demonstrating cutting his own throat with the side of his hand. Simon responded with his thumbs-up sign of approval. As we drew near some of the villagers emerged and were viewing us with wide curious eyes. The women, dressed in bright swathes of silk shot with silver and gold, and the men in embroidered robes were preparing to celebrate the end of a month of fasting. We had come too late. No sheep was available. Secretly, I was pleased. I had no wish to be party to another throat-slitting ceremony and the ensuing smell of blood and intestines to precede dinner.

Some twenty minutes later we stopped at a second village. Again it was a settlement of several casually built rush huts set amongst trees against a backdrop of red dunes.

"Village of my uncle," Abu Bakr announced, hopping from the vehicle to greet a group of smiling children and then some adult males. "Come!" he invited. "Come. Take tea with my uncle!"

We followed him into one of the rush huts. Apart from a carpet spread on the sandy floor there were no furnishings. In spite of the heat, the inside was kept remarkably cool by the thatched conical roof and the passage of air through gaps in the rush walls. Its absolute simplicity was an amazing throwback to the long-past days when the characteristic dwelling for native Libyans was *mapalium* – a flimsy hut made of wattled grass or asphodel on a framework of sticks.

Within minutes Abu Bakr's uncle, looking young enough to be his cousin, as well as several male relatives, had joined us, bringing with them a silver teapot, a jug of water and a selection of small glasses. Dressed in a loose white overgarment, gathered and embroidered across the chest – not unlike that worn by Emad, our host motioned for us to be seated. Cross-legged in a circle, we practised Arabic as we sipped *mayya* (water) and *shay* (tea), passing a single *tassa* (glass) of each from person to person. The glasses were refilled and passed again until the teapot and jug were empty. Emad, his face relaxing into a smile as he conversed with our host, looked more at ease than at any time on our journey.

It seemed that I was the only one who wasn't totally relaxed. The occasion and the company were more than I could have hoped for, but I was apprehensive about sharing alien germs. To refuse would be impossible without causing offence. The situation reminded me of the story told of Joan MacArthur, an English traveller in Libya in 1949. When offered tea by a Bedouin at the roadside she 'pours hers into the sand undetected, because, in Barbary, it does not do to take unnecessary risks'. I too was of the mind that 'it does not do to take unnecessary risks'. But we were guests, seated in a circle, sharing one glass – every movement and gesture was followed by a ring of eyes.

It was as much an act of friendship as trust, as was the rather more intimate custom of the men of the Nasamones tribe. When making a solemn oath 'each party gave the other water to drink out of his own hand, or, if no water was available, earth to lick'. Fortunately, we had water and tea to drink and continued to pledge our faith by sitting in a circle, hosts and guests, sipping and smiling until the teapot and water jug were empty and the last glass drained in yet another out-of-time and out-of-place experience.

Outside in bright sunshine we were surrounded by inquisitive smiling children, their skin colour and features ranging from near black with short frizzy hair to pale brown with aquiline features and brown straight hair: a *pot pourri* of nationalities. One plausible explanation was that some of the group were the descendants of slaves taken by the Tuareg in former days. Today, they appeared to be happily integrated into the Tuareg families. I shall remember the visit to their village for the simplicity of their lives as well as for the warmth of the hospitality we received.

***

'Thus far', Herodotus says, he is able to give the names of tribes that inhabit the sand belt, but beyond that point his knowledge fails. Herodotus was referring to the region beyond the Pillar of the Sky where the land is 'waterless and devoid of living creatures or trees and where there is no moisture at all'.

After just three days of travelling it was not difficult to imagine such a place. Fortunately, with Abu Bakr and his precise knowledge of the region and Emad and his reliable four-wheel drive we were in no danger of getting lost although the possibility of breakdown could not be dismissed. I thought again of the remarkable story about Barth – his desperation in resorting to sucking his own blood in an attempt to stay alive – and of Simon's mischievous response, offering a practical alternative. Now, it was winter yet daytime temperatures were sufficiently high to have a debilitating effect. Travel in the desert in summer is best left to the Tuareg, of that there is no doubt.

Followed by the bald head of the metallic sun we began the last stage of our journey along a desert plain at the foot of the Akakus Mountains. We were heading towards Ghat through a wadi blessed with underground supplies of water providing pasture for the many hobbled camels grazing and resting in lengthening shadows. Flat-headed acacia and the occasional bed of shrubs and reeds marked the course of an underground stream.

Then Abu Bakr was directing Emad across a stony plain towards a distant group of trees. As we drew near we could see that they were bunched alongside a square concrete building. Once the engine had died, before we were out of the vehicle, we heard the sound of rushing water. A doorway led into two square brick-built bathhouses, open to the sky and fed from hot water gushing from a metal pipe: an amazing open-air bathhouse literally in the middle of nowhere. Within minutes we were sitting in a row along the edge of a containing wall, feet dangling in the warm, clear water and leaning forward to bathe our hands and faces. The temptation to slide in, even fully clothed, was strong.

"I will if you will!" Simon muttered as if reading my thoughts.

"Get in?"

"Strip and dip!"

"And risk arrest?"

"It's a bathhouse!"

"It's Libya, and I'm a woman."

"We're alone."

At that moment an elongated shadow fell across the wall opposite. Turning, I exchanged glances with Emad, standing in the doorway behind us. The look on his face was warning enough of the penalties we could face for such outrageous frivolity.

"Not any longer!" I warned.

"Another time. Another place!" Simon concluded wistfully.

We contented ourselves with some competitive and reciprocal splashing until a wrestling session between Henry and Gerry threatened to end in total immersion. Finally, wet and bedraggled but contented, we prepared to face the last lap of the journey to Ghat.

By now the sun had slipped behind a row of dunes, leaving a glowing trail of red on the horizon. Opposite, over the dark silhouettes of rock mountains, the first stars pricked the sky in diamonds of light.

Mustapha was waiting to greet us on our return. Although dressed in a richly embroidered white garment over white narrow ruffled trousers, the untidy *tagulmust* had been wound about his head with an end left pointing into space like a radio antenna and his overall appearance was shambolic. Suddenly, I was struck by the ironic similarity between his overgarment and the chasuble worn by a priest when celebrating mass – resurrecting once again the question of the Tuareg's Christian past. Not only was the garment similar in style to a chasuble – loose, sleeveless and with an opening to slip the garment over the head – but at least two symbols of the cross were visible in the blue embroidered design: one on the centre front and one on the right shoulder. Meanwhile, Mustapha's fulsome and charming greetings included an invitation to his home that evening for a traditional celebratory meal.

We were especially thankful for his invitation when we discovered the sandstone hotel open but, once again, devoid of staff. We waited in the reception area until it was almost too dark to see anything then decided to risk moving into our original rooms and taking showers. While unloading, collecting and carrying luggage into the hotel our smooth 'friend' from security turned up and followed on our heels, asking irritating questions about our comings and goings and generally getting in the way. As we set off for Mustafa's house he called after us, promising to tell staff from the hotel that we had moved in.

Our host for the evening lived in a large modern villa – a symbol of the success of his business techniques. Given the complete absence of organised tourism, that he had any business was remarkable. The lone female traveller, I was taken to the kitchen and introduced to his wife, daughters and sisters who, in the customary Arab practice, were preparing our food but excluded from joining the mixed company to eat. With few words of each other's language between us communication was through smiles and pointing to items of food and repeating the words: bread – *bazin*; lamb – *alloush*; dates – *tamaar*. Then leaving the women to complete the preparations for serving the food, I was escorted into a room furnished with carpets and large floor cushions reserved for the men of the household for entertaining guests. A mammoth TV, broadcasting light Arabic entertainment, suspended from the ceiling, was on full blast.

Fellow visitors included our host's brother and two travellers from Switzerland. Like desert foxes the Swiss appeared in remote and distant places and were, in fact, the only travellers we had come across on our expeditions into the desert. I watched Mustapha moving between the visitors with easy charm, advertising his tours, taking and giving contact numbers and addresses. For him the evening was an opportunity to entertain the trickle of visitors and make contacts for further business.

We were sitting in two groups; each forming a circle in readiness for the food to be placed in bowls on the floor between us. After the traditional hand-washing ceremony we were offered glasses of camels' milk and bowls of fresh dates. Nutritious and filling enough to live on in the desert, this repast is also offered to break the fast during Ramadan and to prepare the stomach for the full meal which follows the muezzin's call to prayer. Today it served as a filling starter. "Eat!" invited our generous host, gesturing to us to help ourselves from the dishes being served containing bazin – a bland flour-based doughy bread – boiled mutton and salad. The meal was to be a 'hands-on' experience, dispensing with cutlery. As local etiquette demanded, I was ready to use my right hand to tear pieces off the large pancake-shaped bread in readiness to scoop and wrap dollops of mutton and salad placed before us in separate bowls. Finally, with a dessert of coffee and doughnuts my stomach felt bloated and leaden.

We arrived at the hotel to be confronted by a tall, thin, unshaven Libyan, wrapped against the cold in a dark *baracan*. In spite of having our details on record from our recent visit he insisted that we begin the tedious form-filling procedure all over again. By candle and torchlight it took twice as long. Finally, we were handed buckets for flushing the loos and the added bonus of blankets for our austere beds.

Sleep fell like an executioner's axe. Just as swiftly I was awake and feeling desperately ill. I knew with a horrible certainty that I was going to be sick! It was the start of a night I was unlikely to forget. Not only was I throwing up at frequent intervals and with such force that I feared losing all my internal organs, but on each occasion I had to find my way to the toilet, through the thick darkness of a windowless corridor, by candlelight. Flimsy matchsticks, supplied to light the diminishing candle, splintered in my unsteady hands or lost their heads. All the while I was exerting desperate willpower to hang on to the churning contents of my stomach. The aftermath of temporary relief was short-lived and undermined by the practical efforts of filling a bucket with water to flush the detritus away.

Weak with exhaustion, I thought it couldn't get worse. It had to end soon. Then on the way back to my room after a particularly violent attack I trod on something with my bare foot. From the shape and shell-hard texture I knew what it was and jumped involuntarily, dropping the candle. Now I was in absolute darkness with my worst nightmare: a huge walnut-brown cockroach with an armour-plated shiny shell, hairy legs and restless probing antennae. I could see it in my mind's eye.

Spiders or lizards or even snakes I'm less scared of. They go away if you leave them alone. Even in daylight dead-skin-eating cockroaches come straight at you.

Completely disorientated in the deep darkness of the windowless corridor, I was not only unsure of the whereabouts of the cockroach but equally unsure about which way to go. Finally, in spite of the possibility of a second encounter I dropped to my knees, exploring the sandy floor with tentative fingers until I found the candle. With a candle and no matches I resorted to feeling my way along the rough surface of the sandstone wall across two closed doors then at last an open doorway. Through it I could make out the shape of a bed under a star-freckled window. Feverishly checking there was no occupant, I clambered onto the bed and fell into uneasy sleep until stomach cramps woke me again

The Ottoman built Red Fort stands guard over the settlement

Remains of the walled city of Ghat cover the hillside

Pillars of rock take on the shapes of petrified creatures in Wadi Tanezzuft

Life-size outlines of cattle dominate Tuareg rock art in Tanezzuft caves

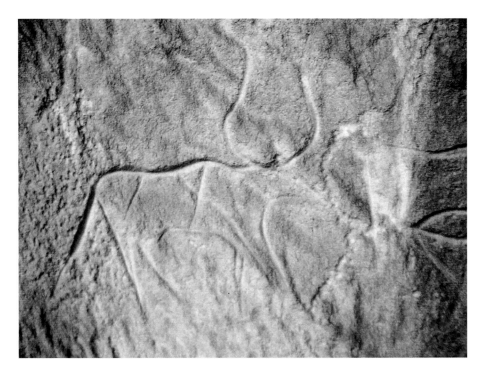

Stylised rock carving of long-horned cattle

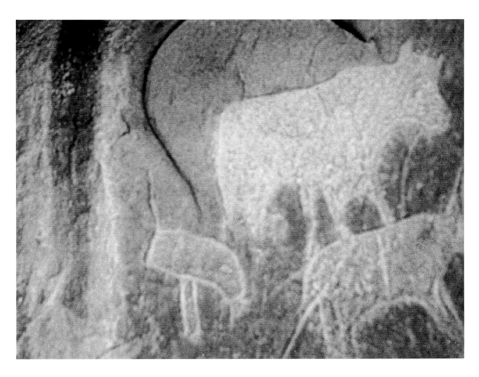

Rock carvings that prompted a lively debate

Life-saving oases make travel in the desert possible

Emad loading wood for our camp fire

Emad in action: an unexpected encounter with a lively camel

Abu Bakr's uncle between Emad and Abu Bakr

Tanezzuft dunes line the wadi en route to Ghat

Mustapha welcoming traveller and guide on our return to Ghat

Back to Reality

By the time daylight was filtering through my square of window I was unfit for travel. The thought of being left behind and ill in the no-services hotel in Ghat was making me panic. I tracked down Gerry. As I suspected and hoped he had a supply of pills. "From a Polish doctor!" he assured me. An hour later with the combined help of the pills, willpower and muscle-clenching techniques I believed I could risk the journey. I took a shower, put on my last set of clean clothes and determined to exercise mind over matter. As desperate as I was for drinking water, I was reluctant to drink the warm spring water from the taps. It may have started out as pure, but after its journey through corroded pipes and open tanks visited by rats and bathed in by local people it was likely to be contaminated and in my present state not worth the risk.

We toured the local shops for bottled water without success. As a last resort Gerry stocked up on a supply of Mirinda – oversweetened canned orange – to sustain us throughout the journey. I warded off dehydration by sipping the syrupy orange between falling into bouts of feverish sleep. From time to time I woke with intense cramping pains, overdosed on Gerry's pills and waited for sleep to take over again.

Our plan had been to end the trip with a visit to a set of lakes that lie between the fingers of a group of sand dunes north of Ubari, about fifty kilometres from Sabha. The mysterious presence of the lakes amidst towering shifting dunes is said to be the result of geological faults and earth movements that have allowed underground water to rise to the surface. During the summer months all but one of the lakes are said to disappear. This strange and isolated region has been the home of the Dawada tribe for centuries, hiding them from other desert people. Their diet of tiny shrimps, gathered from the lakes, has earned them the name of 'Worm Eaters'. At this time it was said that the few remaining Dawada people still lived by the lakes in their palm-frond dwellings; we had hoped to end our exploration of ancient desert tribes by meeting with them in their unique setting before they disappeared without a trace into the wastes of the Sahara as the Garamantes had done.

Once again we had no maps or precise directions and without Abu Bakr, his enthusiasm and intimate knowledge of the desert, we had to rely on Emad. Predictably, he professed to have no knowledge of the route to the lakes or of the tribe. I was not convinced. I knew that in his heart he was not interested in exploring and now he was bent on getting home. However, in an act of appeasement he offered to take us across the dunes north of Ubari to visit a well in Wadi Shatti – the most isolated and northern of the three great wadis that cross the Fezzan from east to west and used by camel trains en route to Brak. I clung on to the belief that there was a chance that from the crest of the dunes we might be able to sight the lakes that like dunes are said to change colour in changing light.

Finally, a few kilometres west of Germa we reached a Moorish café tucked down a side street in Ubari. With its bright exotic posters, wooden outside tables and guitar music it was a small haven in a drab and dusty Arab village and an unexpected treat. I began to feel vaguely human. A cup of milky cappuccino completed the part-rehabilitation. It was just as well, for the next stage of the journey was across a gravel plain of the teeth-rattling, conversation-stopping variety.

In fact, anything and everything on board that wasn't firmly anchored or tied down vibrated and jerked and shook. You discovered parts of your body that you didn't know existed and couldn't control. Then an unpleasant grinding noise and we lurched to a halt. One of the tyres had split. While Gerry helped Emad change the tyre Simon and Henry set off across the baked featureless plain in opposite directions – in Henry's words, "To give life to a tree." I focused my zoom lens on tracks in the sand

and then, still feeling fragile from my night of illness, took up residence on the damaged tyre until the spare was in place.

About halfway into the next stage of our journey, against a background of golden sands and intensely blue sky, what appeared to be a mirage of camel silhouettes stretched along the skyline. As soon as we lost height it became clear that it was no mirage but a train of twenty camels heading north towards Brak, the main oasis in Wadi Shatti. The timing was perfect and the scene like a perfectly executed painting showed the lead camel, wearing an emerald green cover on its saddle, walking ahead of the main body while the Tuareg herdsman, wearing a matching emerald green jacket over his white robe, walked at the rear.

As the herdsman strolled over to chat to Emad the orderly train broke into confusion: some were turning to look at us, others were bunching together and turning back the way they'd come, while the more adventurous were making for a clump of greenery sprouting from a distant mound. As soon as the herdsmen rejoined them they reassembled and continued strolling in an orderly procession again. The goal was to reach Brak by midnight.

A sensation of driving through water indicated a change from corrugated gravel plains to deceptively smooth soft sand. As the sand got deeper and the slope steeper Emad maintained a steady speed and navigated the loose sand by executing long sweeping curves as expertly as a sidewinder. Finally, he crested the dune and stopped to a round of applause. His usually solemn expression relaxed into a smile. He was nearing his territory and the pleasure showed.

Perched on the ridge of the dune, we were surrounded by an ocean of bronze waves stretching to the far-reaching curve of the horizon. Knowing it was our last chance of locating the lakes and the Dawada people, I searched among the kaleidoscope of changing colours streaming across the dunes but in evening light among the browns and greens and rust-golds not even a mirage was visible. For us the last of the Dawada people and the magical lakes were to remain an enigma. Before us the dip slope of the dune fell to a wadi. We lurched forward a few inches and stopped nose down, the back wheels spinning – the chassis wedged in deep sand. "All out!" Gerry directed. On our knees we scooped and removed armfuls of loose sand like burrowing turtles. Next we hunted for objects to slot under the wheels: a rope, shoes, a notebook, garments – anything for the wheels to grip on to – then into pushing mode. Emad rolled the vehicle back then forwards before taking flight across the steep slope at a sharp angle, sending a great wall of sand cartwheeling over the vehicle as high and perfectly curved as the wave of a surf riders' dream. We collected our scattered 'wheel grips' and followed, feet and legs disappearing into sand as soft and deep as snow as we staggered laughing to the wadi below.

Ahead of us the sky was a furnace. We were following tracks through a wadi marked by the occasional thorny flat-headed tree, heading straight towards the sky's fiery centre. Suddenly, Emad slowed and pointing to a red plastic bucket, attached to a piece of rope lying in the sand, drew alongside it. It wasn't until he directed us that we saw it had been left next to a round wooden lid. He removed the cover and we peered into a black hole; just a few metres below the surface dark underground water reflected the sky. While Emad let down the bucket we delved into our baggage for drinking receptacles. I savoured the first mouthful then swallowed. A trickle of pure, cold water traced every intricate twist and curve of my intestines on its way to my stomach. It was the sweetest moment of the last twenty-four hours. This, without any doubt, was the elixir of life.

The place reminded me of a story told over 100 years ago by the intrepid traveller Cowper. He and his guide had been travelling in intense heat through the desert for many hours and came upon a well. They were in need of water for themselves and for their camels:

We found there about a dozen Arabs with horses to water, and although there was neither bucket nor rope at the well, nobody thought of going for one, but simply sat down to wait until someone more business-like bethought himself to bring one with him. In vain I stormed and implored and offered '*bu-*

tisains'. They only smiled at the absurd impatience of the Frank and remarked that there was no house (tent) near, where anyone possessed either rope or bucket, but *'Insh'a allah'* one would come by and by. At last, after an hour and a half, a man said he would go and hunt for one, and returned with it in ten minutes.

The *Insh'a allah* syndrome has a long history!

***

Back in Sabha, Emad took us to his family home – a square concrete farmhouse – to meet his sister, his brothers and their wives, a host of children under the age of six years and a tremulous captive gazelle. The women, preparing to attend a female pre-wedding celebration, were dressed in bright robes shot with silver and gold thread and wearing traditional heavy pendant necklaces from which a series of gold suns, stars or disks link to cover the chest and reach the waist. Their feet and hands were covered with henna designs: the central motif, an open flower on the palm of the hand. The heavy all-encompassing jewellery and henna decorations are a time-long custom of tribes from the Arabian peninsular. The nineteenth-century traveller James Hamilton, after attending a wedding feast in Aguila Oasis in the eastern Sahara, expresses surprise over the size and weight of the jewellery, especially the earrings which were so elaborate and heavy that he was curious: 'to see the cartilage capable of supporting such a weight'.

That tradition and change move hand in hand is evident. Abu Bakr's comment that women in Tripoli and Benghazi no longer want gold for a dowry but demand a villa and a Mercedes was confirmation of that and of the time-lag between those living on the westernised coastal strip and those still living in rush huts in remote oases of the interior. Wedding preparations aside, we were treated with warm hospitality and expected to share a meal with the family.

The invitation to participate in another 'hands in the same dish' meal so soon after my recent attack made me uneasy. I did not want to offend my hosts yet I dared not risk further illness.

Fortunately, the number of people and the arrival of more guests provided a shield so that, on this occasion, I was able to use discretion. I nibbled on Arabic bread without drawing attention to my otherwise empty hands. News of our arrival had spread. Among the curious visitors was an uncle in the police force; another uncle who was a colonel in the army; and a nephew of Colonel Gaddafi! With such powerful relations I was beginning to feel uneasy and to wonder if Emad was more than a farmer with a four-wheel drive!

Expectations of a comfortable reception at the modern Al Fateha Hotel in Sabha were not realised. In common with its ageing counterparts in Ghadames and Ghat it seemed that services over the holiday period ground to a halt. There was no visible member of staff. A crowd of local males celebrating the last day of the Eid remained glued to the television set in the hotel lounge. It took some insistent demands to get one of them to find a receptionist and give us rooms. Next we discovered that the sheets and towels had not been changed. Finally, after more demands a young man appeared at my door, armed with clean linen sheets and complaining bitterly that he was a technician and had been forced to bring clean laundry. Once our rooms had been organised, Gerry tracked down someone to bring us a tray of coffee and biscuits. We were all ready for an early night.

Apart from the oily character hovering round us at the hotel in Ghat, the trip itself had appeared to be gloriously free from any sense of being watched by security. Our treatment at Sabha airport was a sharp reminder that we had not been forgotten and confirmation that, in all probability, Emad had indeed been engaged for the specific purpose of keeping an eye on us. He had been courteous and a reliable driver throughout the trip, but he had never relaxed or become part of the camaraderie that we had shared with the friendly and humorous Abu Bakr. He had never shown, or else he had declined to show, any knowledge of the places we visited; he professed to have no knowledge of the rock carvings, the Garamantes or Dawada people and had no interest in exploring. Although none of us believed he had evil intentions towards us, we were now convinced that he had been directed by security to drive us to Ghat and back and to keep a watchful eye.

As soon as we arrived at Sabha airport a Libyan official dressed in the customary security uniform beckoned us to the front of a long queue. We were taken one by one into separate male and female cubicles for a 'hands on' search. Next our luggage was opened and scrutinised and finally a security officer casually dressed in jeans and an open-necked shirt escorted us to a row of seats on the aircraft and took up a central position between us on the return flight from Sabha to Tripoli. This low-key end to our adventure kept us silent and immersed in our own thoughts throughout the flight.

Just days after our return, convoys of armed military vehicles, police cars with blue flashing lights and blaring sirens and a proliferation of roadblocks kept the main Tripoli road at a virtual standstill for days. Gradually, news filtered through. Preparations for a suspected coup had been discovered and dealt with in Tarhuna – a settlement on the eastern curve of an escarpment separating the coastal plain from the Saharan Plateau. It was said that Syrian fighter planes had been employed to wipe out a column of assembled tanks and raze Tarhuna to the ground.

The buzzwords were 'military' and 'Berber'. A column of assembled tanks spoke for itself, and Tarhuna was situated at a meeting place of roads to Tripoli, Khums, Bani Walid and the Berber stronghold of Gharyan, located in the Jabal Nafusa. Berber hopes of having their own autonomy had gone underground since Libyan independence. Driven into the Jabal Nafusa by Arab invaders in the eighth century, they built and settled into troglodyte citadels, running highly successful farms. The result has been the survival of their language, close ties of kinship plus distinct housing and culture differences from the coastal Arabs.

In modern times the Berber people had looked for a semi-autonomous province under the Italians, moved into modern villas in the open land around their old settlements and hoped for cultural separateness with their language being given equal status with Arabic. The rise of Arab nationalism has forestalled this and Gaddafi's series of failed ideologies has done nothing to win Berber support. Now, political tension had erupted around us once more and, if the rumours were true, Tarhuna no longer existed.

Untimely puncture en route to Wadi Shatti

Camel train hoping to reach Brak by midnight: Wadi Shatti

Tracks disappear into the great sea of sand

Jabal Akhdar

We Never Walk Alone!

The Jabal Akhdar, or Green Mountains, are the greenest place in Libya, but the fact that they are skirting the biggest desert in the world is evident. Tree-covered hills have little or no undergrowth and desert sands advance inexorably. Should the annual rainfall – the most generous in Libya – of up to 300 mm per annum fail, farming and trees will no longer be sustained and desert conditions will take over. One thing is certain, life forms in the hills are nowhere near as colourful or exciting as they were in Herodotus' days: 'It is here that huge snakes are found – and lions, elephants, bears, asps, and horned asses, not to mention dog-headed men, headless men with eyes in their breasts (I merely repeat what the Libyans say), wild men and wild women, and a great many other creatures by no means of a fabulous kind'.

It is possible that the inhabitants of the ancient Greek city of Berenice that once formed part of the Pentapolis, or 'land of five cities', may have witnessed some of the creatures cited by Herodotus. As for the weird and wonderful dog-headed men, an explanation may be found in the prehistoric dog-man carvings in the canyons of the Messak Settafet (Black Plateau) south of the Fezzan. Although speculation about the meaning and symbolism of the carvings of these mythical animal-headed beings continues, their predatory appearance has been associated with the Cape hunting dog. A formidable hunter, it would have made an appropriate emblem for the early inhabitants and hunters of the Messak. On the other hand, 'headless men with eyes in their breasts' are less easy to account for!

Inhabitants of modern Benghazi are far more likely to witness the growing urban developments of Libya's second largest city.

Located 1,050 kilometres to the east of Tripoli, it is the starting point for a visit to the Graeco-Roman sites fringing the coastline on the edge of the Green Mountains. Simon, Gerry and I were planning a tour of Tolmeita, Cyrene and Apollonia, and to do this we had to arrange a flight to Benghazi to coincide with the public holiday to celebrate the Eid al Adha, marking the pilgrimage to Mecca. Although we knew that horror stories about oversubscribed flights to Benghazi were not unfounded and that the dangers of flying were increasing, we couldn't afford to spend two days of the holiday travelling by road to and from Tripoli.

It was in the departure lounge at Tripoli Airport that I learnt the literal meaning of jam-packed. I could no longer tell where my body ended or where an adjacent passenger's began. I was attempting to snake-ease out of my backpack to use it to protect my front when my attention was drawn to Simon who, head and shoulders above the crowd, was responding to a security agent's urgent beckoning. It was the usual scenario: we were not Libyan; we were travelling and therefore we must be up to something; we needed watching! Signalling to us to follow, Simon was attempting to forge a passage to the front. I wedged myself behind Gerry, relying on his tunnelling techniques to get us through. "Priority treatment," he muttered as he led me forward.

At times like this, the tag of 'security risk' in Libya had its advantages. Then, once we'd been vetted, I was directed to join a handful of Libyan women travellers to board the aircraft first. 'Vantage number two!' Not only was I certain of a seat but also I could save seats for Gerry and Simon. When Simon arrived to join me he was alone and muttering that one minute they were walking along together and the next Gerry wasn't there. It's easy to disappear from the face of the earth in Libya with no questions asked, so minutes later we were relieved to see Gerry, his crimson face warning us that security were on our heels. He'd been escorted to identify our luggage, which had been separated and searched, before he was allowed to board. Along this highly populated stretch of coastline we would be considered a high security risk. We resigned ourselves to a shadowed trip.

Emerging from Benghazi Airport, I found myself propelled to a waiting taxi by my two escorts. Two weeks previously Simon had made an exploratory visit and, on his recommendation, we had agreed to try the Hotel Omar Khiam. There were, in fact, two luxury hotels by Libyan standards but Simon thought we would lose 'the flavour of the place' if we went too modern.

Grand and dark with strong colonial overtones, the Omar Khiam sported high ceilings, lofty columns and a wide sweeping marble staircase just waiting for Scarlet O'Hara to make an entrance. It felt empty. In fact, it was so yawningly empty that it echoed, yet we had been given rooms on the ninth floor! We had rooms on the ninth floor in Sabha. Was there some significance, I wondered? Dante came to mind. The ninth circle of hell rather than the ninth sphere of heaven. On a more practical level, why were we nine floors up when porters didn't exist and we had baggage?

"This way," Gerry was calling. "I've found a lift. Genuine antique cage variety," he boasted.

Complete with straining cables that creaked and swayed, the antique cage finally jolted to a halt inches below the floor level. From death-defying adjoining balconies – wrought iron railings had come away from the walls and parts of the concrete floor were missing – views of a range of naval vessels in the outer harbour, including ships with radar equipment and a battered submarine, begged the question. Was Benghazi preparing for war? From below, a slow grinding war of vehicles fought for position on the harbour road. With the door to the balcony closed, the room was stuffy. The rust-eaten cage of a defunct air conditioner hung from the wall. There was a choice: the grind of traffic or a private sauna.

The deserted dining room was the perfect post-war setting for a forties' film. Forget Scarlet O'Hara! This was the backdrop for Celia Johnson, her face shielded by a felt hat, waiting for a close encounter with Trevor Howard. Yellow ceiling lights hung like drooping flowers from the brown dome of the ceiling and white linen tablecloths were starched to match the waiter's shirt collar topping his shining evening suit. There was a film set but no film crew and no celebrities – just three CIA suspects disguised as tourists making the best of the ubiquitous menu of a nondescript-flavoured, watery soup followed by chicken, cold chips and salad.

Necessity had made us resourceful. I had a flask for hot water and a small jar of instant coffee tucked in my bag for our after-dinner rush of caffeine and Simon had a supply of Glenfiddich in a container in the shape of a book. Although dark bronze in colour the hint of green was sufficient to merit it being christened the Green Book! Once dinner was over, leaving Simon to organise the hot water, Gerry and I headed upstairs to take advantage of the long-awaited opportunity of making a prearranged international call. I opened the door to my room, and we both stopped on the threshold. Noises, like someone playing with a loud-speaker system, were coming from the wall behind the bed.

"Microphone," mouthed Gerry. He was pointing at the red velour-covered headboard. "They're listening in."

He was moving stealthily forward to inspect the headboard when the phone rang. I jumped involuntarily then lifted the handset to hear three beeps and an achingly distant but familiar voice: "We're not in, please leave a message." A click was followed by a dull tone. I had been cut off without the opportunity to respond. Frustration, self-pity, anger were interrupted by the phone ringing again. This time it was the operator telling me that since I hadn't made contact there would be no charge. We commiserated in muttered undertones until Simon joined us with the flask and sotto voce we passed on the news about the failed telephone call and the bugged room.

"That's why we're in these rooms," he muttered. "I remember now. I was here – in this very room – on my last visit."

Meanwhile, Gerry had found some clumsy wiring on the balcony. "Here," he was pointing at a region of the outside wall on a level with the headboard. He made a brief inspection, tracing the wires beneath the balcony until they were out of sight. Signalling to us to that there were ears in the walls, he led us inside and, picking up his guidebook, began pointedly discussing our route for the following day. The smell of Simon's Irish coffee was almost as good as the taste. Even the plastic cups could not detract from the sybaritic effects. We toasted our new adventure in silent mode and agreed that although Cyrene was the main focus of our visit we'd begin at the beginning with Tolmeita and then, as time and circumstances allowed, work east to Cyrene and Apollonia.

By the time Gerry and Simon had departed I was ready for sleep but even from nine floors up night was plagued by noise: heavy traffic till the small hours accompanied by the incessant howling of dogs prevented all but fitful dozing.

***

Awake at first light, I amused myself by browsing through Herodotus' descriptions of coastal tribes and was especially taken by the discovery that Libyan women, from the Zaucces tribe, were drivers of war chariots and much envied by the Greeks. In fact, charioteering Libyan women were not only on a par with Boadicea and her army of female warriors in Ancient Britain but also confirmed the presence of a women's army in Libya that could outshine the one set up by Gaddafi. As for Herodotus' comment that 'Everybody here paints himself red and eats monkeys' – travel in high temperatures ensured red complexions and we were delighted to be served a run-of-the-mill English breakfast of hard-boiled eggs, toast and honey, and coffee.

Our first planned stop, the Greek coastal settlement of Tolmeita, was originally the harbour for the inland city of Al Marj. Well armed with material on the Graeco-Roman sites, Gerry briefed us with a potted history over breakfast:

Named Ptolemais after the Hellenistic King of Egypt Tolmeita grew in importance under his rule becoming an important city in its own right. The city continued to flourish under the Romans. Decline began with attacks by the Vandals in the 5th century and continued under the Arabs who used the remaining buildings to provide materials for a new settlement. Said to have once been larger than Cyrene the site wasn't discovered by the Italians until 1935 when excavation work revealed scattered remnants of the remains of an extensive city spread across the wide coastal plain.

All that remained was to find transport for the first leg of our journey to Al Marj. With help from the hotel staff we located a taxi, and within minutes the suburbs of Benghazi were behind us and we were crossing a plain of semi-desert that increased in height until we were travelling east across the once intensely fertile Al Marj Plateau. The region's history of highly productive intensive farming, made possible by an underground water supply, earned it the title of the 'Breadbasket of Rome'. Some Roman emperors, notably Hadrian, offered inducements to Libyan tribesmen to farm neglected or uncultivated ground. Those who did were granted security of tenure and paid no taxes on their olives and vines until they were fully grown.

Although today's declining water-table levels are causing some problems, it is evident that the area is still productive: blond cut fields littered with parcels of dried hay, vines – cultivated now purely for the fruit – and olive groves clothed the higher slopes. The appearance at regular intervals of identical one-storey farmhouses was a legacy of the 1930s' Italian land resettlement programme; each house, painted pink and featuring a small contained garden filled with flowering shrubs, was framed by two archways: one over the entrance to the house and the other leading to a covered terrace.

The first indication that we were approaching Al Marj was the sight of twin minarets that stand guard either side of the gigantic new mosque built to replace the original destroyed with the city by an earthquake in 1963; it was also the landmark for finding the bus-cum-taxi station. Here we made a deal with another taxi driver to take us to Tolmeita, wait while we explored, then take us east to Al Bayda for our next overnight stop.

As we neared the coastline, mountain spurs became more

defined and hairpin bends grew sharper. Between them we caught occasional glimpses of sea. Finally, the road straightened out across a low plain and we were heading for the beach. Simon had previously explored the site and intent on finding sunken treasure in the harbour had come armed with snorkelling gear. Our warnings that, given security's accusations that we were searching for the whereabouts of Libyan submarines, his underwater activities could put him in danger, fell on deaf ears. Pointing us in the direction of a distant line of columns, he waved and retreated in the direction of the sea.

Leaving him to his solitary marine explorations, we skirted a grove of tamarisk trees and followed a track for about 200 metres across coarse grassland to find that the entire site was cordoned off. To gain access there was no alternative except over and, in my case, assisted by Gerry through tangles of barbed wire. We stood for a moment, examining Gerry's plan of the site and surveying the hugely overgrown complex before us. The only way of identifying key monuments or buildings was by columns reassembled in lines, squares or rectangles. Believing we had spotted the outline of our goal, the appropriately named Palace of Columns, we made our way along an east–west route, marked by a row of eucalyptus trees, to an overgrown crossroads then headed south.

We'd gone no more than a few metres before Gerry was distracted by two sections of ten-foot-high brick-built tunnels running parallel to our route. Believing they were connected to a series of vaulted chambers built under the former gymnasium, he set off to explore. Preferring to keep in the shade of eucalyptus trees obligingly fringing the route, I carried on, finally taking up residence on a trunk of a conveniently fallen tree. It turned out to be a well-shaded spot in a clearing, just opposite a flight of stone steps leading to the upper floor of the palace; in fact, it was ideal as a retreat from the sun as well as a convenient spot for checking on other places of interest on the site.

Aided by Gerry's guidebook, I set about attempting to identify buildings that had retained or regained some semblance of their former glory and were not too distant. Apart from a tower-like mausoleum, said to mark the burial places of Ptolemaic rulers of Cyrenaica, and a small Greek-cut theatre few Hellenistic buildings have survived. From the Roman era partially restored buildings included luxurious private villas and palaces; a theatre and amphitheatre; a gymnasium built over a complex of water cisterns that Gerry was currently investigating as well as a Byzantine gate and basilica. It all sounded very grand but in reality Tolmeita was hugely incomplete and overgrown. Vandalised by the Vandals and with building materials heavily looted by the Arabs for their own settlement, the Italians' task of attempting to rebuild must have been a real test of determination, dedication and devotion.

I heard before I saw Gerry when he tripped over a tree root and stumbled into the clearing, his red face signalling more than climbing temperatures.

"What is it? What's happened?" I asked. Recovering his composure, he took me by the arm and guided me up the palace stairway.

"Two men," he said by way of explanation. "Tailing us. They caught up with me. The usual mindless questions!"

"And now? Where are they now?"

"Lord knows. They headed that way," he said, gesturing in the general direction of the beach. He stood for a while, dabbing at his sweaty brow and wiping his glasses with a handkerchief.

Suddenly aware of how remote and desolate the place was and unnerved as much by Gerry's agitation as by the men's presence, I suggested we keep the visit short. Even the palace, with its rows of incomplete columns – some no more than stumps – and sand-strewn floors, was failing to suggest its former splendour.

"You have to be something of a ruin freak on a good day to enjoy Tolmeita," I concluded disconsolately.

Gerry nodded in agreement. For memories' sake we each set about taking a series of shots before leaving. Beneath layers of gritty sand, marble and mosaic floors of two adjoining courtyards occupied most of the upper floor. I succeeded in clearing one area, revealing a large flower mosaic, then gave up and focused on an ornamental fountain – all that remained of a rectangular pool that was once the central feature of the main courtyard. Once again it was the sea views that fed the imagination.

"God damn it! I don't believe it!" Gerry hissed in an out-of-character outburst. Following his directions, I made out the shape of one of the vigilante's jutting limbs and part of a torso protruding from behind a column between us and the sea. While focusing his camera to take some seaward shots he had spotted the men through his view finder. As we watched a head appeared and, almost immediately, disappeared, then both men remained partially hidden, slouching and smoking until the next action replay. Although the familiar Inspector Clouseau-style pursuit was more of an irritation than a threat we were not in the mood to be amused.

"Come on!" Gerry suggested. "Let's go for a mosey. Let's take them for a walk. Over there!" he said, pointing to the distant outline of the small Greek theatre cut into a spur of the north-facing hillside. "It's too far and too hot," he added, "but I want them to suffer."

Almost as soon as we set off we saw first one then the other vigilante retreating towards the sea. They had no intention of suffering! On the other hand we were: the sun burned white hot in the azure sky and we were under attack from a plague of flies. What is more we were still some distance from the theatre and becoming increasingly concerned that the men were now heading for the beach where we'd left Simon alone. Deciding that our priority was to check that Simon was okay and to make sure our taxi was still waiting, we abandoned our trek. Waves of heat washed over us as we trudged back towards the beach. Finally, the first semblance of a cool breeze, lifting damp strands of hair from our foreheads, and the sight of Simon's prostrate form in the shadow of our waiting taxi, brought relief.

***

At 880 metres, the highest point in the Green Mountains, Al Bayda is conveniently situated for visits to Cyrene and Apollonia; renowned for a plethora of sanctuaries and temples of Athenian and Eastern influence, both cities were dedicated to the deities of ancient Greece. A large number of the Libyan tribes – not less than thirteen described by Herodotus – that lived along the coastal strip not only had colourful individual traits but also show evidence of cultural interchange with Egyptian and Greek settlers. One of the most remarkable was an ancient rite performed at the festival in honour of Athene when girls from two opposing tribes – the Machlyes and the Auses – fought each other with stones and sticks. While paying honour to Athene undoubtedly has its origins in Greece, the outcome of the 'rite' – any girl who was fatally injured was considered no maiden – is reminiscent of forms of justice practised throughout Medieval Europe. Just as fascinating is the knowledge that the ancient sport of stick-fighting continues to this day among some African tribes – albeit with a gender leap. Men from some tribes, including the Mursi and Surma from Ethiopia, still engage in barbaric stick fights which can result in severe maiming if not death – a test of manhood rather than maidenhood!

As we approached Al Bayda the mountains grew taller and more rugged until we were following a narrow valley between vertical rock slopes in an area steeped in more recent history. We were approaching the bridge that spans Wadi al Khuf, a dramatic and historic 500-metre-deep gorge that cuts across the west–east route. Riddled with caves and weird rock formations, the gorge was the territory and hiding place of the legendary Libyan hero, Umar al Mukhtar. It was in the caves of this gorge that Umar al Mukhtar – played by Oliver Reed in the film *Lion of the Desert* – and the Sanusi tribesmen hid and planned their relentless war against Italian fascism. This ended in 1931 when Umar al Mukhtar was captured and hanged by the Italians at Soluk, a village to the west of Benghazi, turning the seventy-year-old guerrilla leader into a hero and martyr for Libya overnight.

The sense that Al Bayda was different was apparent from the moment we stepped out of the taxi. In part, this may have been its hilltop location; the air was clear and, on this day, distinctly chilly. But there was more than a chill in the air. Hostility of the 'if looks could kill' variety was apparent. Al Bayda's long-standing reputation for resistance to colonial powers and its history are impressive. In 1843 it was the seat of radical Islamic movements, led by Mohammed al Sanusi, which spread throughout Cyrenaica. The Al Sanusi hold on the population kept the Turks at bay in the nineteenth century, led a rebellion against the Italians and finally led the Sanusi leader Sayyid Idris to the throne and Libyan independence in 1951.

Today, Al Bayda is the site of an important Islamic university and is believed to be a stronghold of opposition to the current regime. Compared to the desert oasis settlement of Sabha – Gaddafi's 'Cradle of the Revolution' – with its huddles of scruffy armed locals, Al Bayda had a tangible sense of purpose and order and of 'something in the air'. You could feel it in your bones.

It was soon apparent that the Al Bayda Palace Hotel was no palace. Nevertheless, it was a convenient stopover to explore Apollonia and Cyrene. Of similar colonial design to the Omar Khiam, the building sported high ceilings, marble floors, lofty pillars and wheezing lifts that creaked threateningly and stopped with such frequency that for me one journey was enough. From then on I decided to use the stairs more for safety than fitness. By now it was late afternoon and, Gerry reminded us, the shops would be closing. Unsure of the hotel's services once the Eid started we decided to make a quick tour of the high street for emergency provisions. The less than friendly stares of local people confirmed our initial feeling of antagonism in the air and the rumour that east of Benghazi the entire Jabal Akhdar region remains notorious for its anti-colonial stance.

Austere and empty, the dining room with its brown walls and colour co-ordinated ceiling held no surprises. There were no other visitors and there were no prizes for guessing the menu. Simon muttered throughout the meal something about developing a squawk and then disappeared into the region of the kitchen not, as Gerry feared, to dismember the cook but to get boiling water for the flask. Upstairs Gerry did a quick bugging check then gave the thumbs up and all clear sign before we retired to his room. We supplemented our customary nightcap of black coffee laced with a dash of Glenfiddich from Simon's Green Book with a bag of pastries, bought on our earlier shopping expedition.

The action replay of noise from heavy traffic in the street below and stuffy rooms with ancient air conditioners that didn't work guaranteed another disturbed night. Then at first light an overenthusiastic and distinctly adenoidal muezzin, heralding the arrival of the Eid, provided an unwanted wake-up call. Finally, I fell into a deep sleep to be woken by Simon, banging on my door and summoning me to breakfast.

By the time I was on my feet, in full view of my window throats were being slit. Sheep were being quietly and, therefore, I liked to believe, expertly slaughtered on balconies, rooftops and pavements to celebrate the Haj: the arrival of the pilgrims at Mecca. The air was heavy with the smell of blood. Attempting to put the blood-soaked scenes behind me, I made for the starched dining room where a breakfast of hard-boiled eggs, bread, jam and a jug of coffee was a pleasant surprise and fortified us for another day among the ruins.

View to the sea from the Hellenistic Palace of Columns: Tolmeita

Eucalyptus trees line the way to the palace

Colonnaded courtyard on the upper floor of the palace: Tolmeita

A Hole in the Sky

The history of Cyrene is a wonderful mix of myth, legend and real-life drama. Battles and negotiations, arrivals and departures of settlers and invaders include Greek, Persian, Egyptian, Roman, Barbarian, Byzantine and Arab. Herodotus tells us that the first Greek settlers were directed by the Delphic oracle to found a settlement in Cyrene. An expedition was organised under the leadership of Battus who, with a party of men, sailed for Libya in two 50-oared galleys, establishing themselves on an island and then on the coast at a lovely spot called Aziris where they lived for six years until the Libyans agreed to show them a better place:

After getting them to consent to the move, the Libyans took them further west, and so timed the journey as to pass through the finest bit of country – called Irasa – in the dark, in order to prevent them from seeing it. Finally, they reached the spring called Apollo's Fountain and the Libyan guides said to the Greeks: 'This is the place for you to settle in, for here there is a hole in the sky'.

A poetic way of telling the Greeks there was no shortage of rain, perhaps. In fact, there are two versions of this story. In the first, guided in his choice of site by the Delphic Oracle, King Battus established the first Greek settlement in Cyrene in 631 BC. Here he ruled over his tiny immigrant community for forty years. I prefer the version that tells us that Battus consulted the Oracle in order to seek a cure for his stammer. The Oracle reminded Battus that he'd been sent by the Lord Apollo to found a city in Libya and not to find a cure for his voice. Nevertheless, the story continues: when Battus arrived in Libya he encountered a lion and was so frightened that he never had trouble with his stammer again.

Our plan was a round trip to Cyrene and Apollonia and at Simon's request we would then proceed east to the port of Derna. Though neither Gerry nor I were keen on travelling further east, tempted by Simon's insistence that Derna was a favoured holiday resort in the Italian era and that we would be able to spend a relaxing night there, we finally agreed to accompany him.

The approach to Cyrene along a winding road took us downhill through a valley to an avenue of eucalyptus trees marking the entrance to the site. From the north-eastern hill we found that we were looking down on the Sanctuary and Temple of Apollo. On a wide terrace, to the south and above the Sanctuary, was the site of the Agora-Forum and Acropolis while to the north the land dropped away in a steep slope to an extensive plain beyond which the sea was visible. Cyrene's elevated and staggered position overlooking the Mediterranean Sea is without doubt the most spectacular setting of the Graeco-Roman sites in Libya.

We arrived at the North Gate to find it shut. Like kids at a zoo we pressed our noses between the iron railings and stared in wonder across the plethora of pillars and archways and temples, littering the stepped hillside and staggering towards excessively blue sea. Slowly, a trickle of expatriate visitors began arriving – more than we had seen on our travels so far. One couple had driven for fifteen hours, from west of Tripoli. Speculation and rumour about when or if the gates would be opened was given a lift when a small café near the gate started selling drinks.

An hour later there was still no sign of the gate opening. Then four young men, who had driven from Benghazi that morning, decided to explore the perimeter to see if there was an alternative way to get in. Just as we were thinking it was time to cut our losses and move on to Apollonia they returned. They had discovered a hole in the fence near the East Gate. By now a grand total of fifteen people was waiting and everyone was intent on entry, illegal if necessary. We decided to join them. No one was prepared to miss such an opportunity. Banking on leniency for an en masse break-in, we followed our leader along the Sacred Way to the Forum and Agora complex and one by one squeezed through the hole in the fence.

A magnificent Roman propylon (monumental entrance gate), excavated and reassembled by the Italians in the 1930s, guards the eastern entrance to the Forum. Overawed by the size and grandeur of colonnaded porticoes towering over us and framing the great rectangle of the Forum, we paused inside the gate, absorbing the place and the silence; it was a powerful reminder of our ant-like insignificance in the scheme of things. Then Gerry drew our attention to a flight of steps leading to a raised base in the near centre of the otherwise empty enclosure. This, he informed us, was once the site of a temple to Battus. Guiding us to a plaque at the base of the steps dedicated to Battus, he explained that the now empty platform once held a colossal statue of the founding father.

In spite of invasions and counter invasions, a Jewish revolt and a massive earthquake in AD 365, a number of the restored buildings erected under the rule of Battus are said to be among the most memorable on the site. In fact, the founding father's importance was such that when he died his tomb was venerated and the Agora, a public place of assembly, grew up round it.

We had a limited period before returning to our taxi and we each had different plans so we agreed on a time and place to meet and went our separate ways. I wanted to explore the section opposite the forum, including a private villa and an area containing the remains of various shrines and temples, and then take a leisurely route via a Hellenistic theatre and a fifth-century Byzantine house towards the steep edge of the plateau. From there I hoped for panoramic views across the lower plateau.

Leaving the Forum by the equally imposing propylon marking the South Gate, I entered the Street of King Battus. With Goodchild's *Historic Guide* in hand I made my way past the remains of a small Roman theatre to an area littered with fallen and partially reassembled temples and altars. I had set my sights on one particular shrine once dedicated to the worship of the Goddess Venus. Remarkably, it was the discovery of the famous statue, dubbed 'Venus of Cyrene', that gave rise to the start of Italian excavations in Cyrene. In the form of the Goddess Aphrodite rising from a sea of foam the statue was miraculously brought to light by a torrential rainstorm in 1913.

Fortunately, the shrine to Venus is as outstanding for its size as its composition so that even from a distance it was not difficult to identify. Standing before it I could make out three separate stone sections; reassembled one on top of the other, they reached to about twelve feet in height. From ground level the base, made up from loosely assembled stone blocks in the form of an altar, supported a huge open-fronted stone tabernacle. The monument was crowned by an enormous pair of open, uplifted and headless wings. Lacking the elegance of the Greek world and appearing neither wholly pagan nor wholly Christian, it was an impressive if strange ensemble! Standing as it did among a collection of randomly reassembled columns at the near centre of the former Temple of Venus, it was thought-provoking and, I decided, worth committing to film for further contemplation and enlightenment!

Clues to the identity of crumbling monuments and buildings, I discovered, are very often found inscribed in mosaic floors and the nearby and once splendid House of Jason Magnus was no exception. A mosaic-paved corridor bordering the central courtyard of the west wing of a former palace contained a plaque with inscriptions of his family name. The floors of rooms feeding off the courtyard were awash with coloured marble inlays and mosaic surrounds.

Rejoining the Street of King Battus, I came face to face with the remains of a great wall, lined with alternating busts of the two deities facing onto the street: the Stoa of Hermes and Hercules. Formerly a roofed gallery with a central row of columns it once extended for 130 metres, providing covered access between the Forum and the Agora. Sadly, all but one of the busts was headless or incomplete but since much excavation and restoration remains to be carried out it is highly possible that remaining heads are lying among the tumble of stones and rubble at the base of the wall. The lone survivor, resembling the worn figurehead on a ship, gazed over the open gallery as she had done for hundreds of years.

The importance of drama in ancient Greece is evident from the number of theatres. There are two pocket theatres on the upper plateau. The small Hellenistic theatre alongside the west wall of the Forum, easily accessible from the Street of King Battus, was my next port of call. Taking a seat in the near centre of the curved auditorium, I surveyed the scene before me; marble columns that once formed an elegant backdrop to the stage were lying strewn about the orchestra area – others have been taken. To my right one of five vaulted corridors provided access to the auditorium from an outer semicircular corridor. In spite of damage – reputedly by fourth-century military occupants – it had a certain ambience evocative of 'All the world's a stage' of 'exits and entrances' not only to the theatre but to the abandoned site itself. On a more practical level it was also a convenient resting place to check up on historical and mythical details as well as the route to my last stop: the House of Hesychius.

In common with so many partially excavated buildings on the sites, the starting point and sometimes the ending point was the entrance to a building – two pillars supporting a lintel. Evidence once again of the marathon task and interrupted excavation work of the Italians. A set of stone steps, flanked by headless sculptured figures, led through the doorway into a central courtyard around which rooms were once symmetrically arranged. Like Jason Magnus, Hesychius had taken the trouble to record his family name in a series of inscribed mosaics in the paving surrounding the courtyard. It was not on the same scale as the House of Jason Magnus. Nevertheless, in spite of his modest home, Hesychius was said to have been a prominent citizen of Cyrene – a president of the local council of Cyrenaica. Inscriptions referring to Almighty God and to Christ leave us in no doubt of his religious beliefs.

Leaving the site, I picked my way across open ground inhabited by butterflies and lizards, waves of heat shimmering and dancing hypnotically in front of me. The song of a skylark rose and magnified in the clear air. From the edge of the plateau there were excellent views to the lower terrace. I could make out the blue rectangle of the baths, rows of columns and great swathes of unexcavated land dotted with the litter of partially exposed walls. For the most part it resembled an extensive building site. Beyond the terrace a slope of green trees fell to a wide parched plain, dotted with more ruins. In the distance sea merged with sky.

At the agreed time Gerry and I met at the small café near the North Gate just in time to see Simon's lanky form striding towards us. Gerry's explorations had included a visit to the tomb of Battus in the Agora complex. Simon had been more adventurous. He arrived looking red in the face but sporting a self-satisfied grin. He had more than made up for my leisurely morning by completing a marathon walk round the perimeter of the entire site. After following the Byzantine defence wall along the top of the plateau and skirting the largely unexcavated Acropolis, his route took him downhill to the Greek Theatre and to the entrance of the Sanctuary of Apollo.

"Drinks are on me," Gerry insisted. "Let me see," he added, casting his eye over the remaining supplies on the near-empty shelves. "You have a choice. Mirinda or Mirinda?"

The twenty-kilometre journey north to Apollonia, Cyrene's port for over a thousand years, followed the course of the ancient highway linking the city to the port, descending and winding through the Northern Necropolis to the lower plateau. Renowned as one of the most extensive cemeteries in the ancient world, the Greek Necropolis covers many square miles. A vast and little-visited 'city of the dead' it is said to contain three main groups of elaborate tombs: built-up rectangular and circular tombs; rock-cut built-up tombs and rock-cut graves. Apparently, damage has been extensive. Many tombs have been vandalised and robbed while the huge rock-cut tombs, arranged in tiers descending the side of the mountain, are reputed to have suffered considerable damage from local people who have occupied them from as far back as the early nineteenth century.

Occasional glimpses of the elaborate portals marking the

entrances to tombs that once stood close to the road were all we had time for on our journey. They served as a reminder of the importance of the cult of the dead and the extraordinary lengths that the Greeks went to to provide extravagant burial chambers. We learn from Herodotus that although, in general, nomad Libyans buried their dead in the same way there was one exception – the colourful Nasamones, whose home territory extended to Cyrenaica: the Nasamones' belief that the dead were a power for good was such that when anyone was dying they took care 'to make him sit up, and not let him lie flat on his back'.

In this way it was believed family members could come to the deceased for advice. In the matter of oaths the Nasamones would lay a hand on the tomb of some person noted for justice and goodness and swear by his name; and a member of the tribe in doubt about the future would visit the tomb of an ancestor and, after praying, lie down on it, accepting as prophetic whatever dream might come to him. On the other hand, the practice of crying at religious ceremonies, admired by Herodotus, is more like pure Greek drama: 'I think too that the crying of women at religious ceremonies also originated in Libya – for the Libyan women are much addicted to this practice, and they do it very beautifully'.

We cruised past the last of the Greek tombs and towards the remains of Apollonia spread across the coastal plain. Most of the surviving ruins are from the Byzantine era when its prominence and importance increased to such an extent that it became the principal city of the province. Over the centuries devastation has been wrought by earthquakes, vandals, marauding tribes and, finally, by the sea, invading and swallowing those sections built near the coastline. It is a miracle that anything has survived. It has and it's worth seeing. It has some of the most impressive remains of Byzantine churches in Libya and what is more they are easily accessible.

Of the three remaining churches the Eastern Church is the most complete. A porch from the street provides access to the nave and aisles, separated by lines of reassembled monolithic marble columns, each marked on its inner surface with the raised form of a cross. Just standing before these simple yet potent symbols reinforced the powerful message of the dramatic changes that took place under the Byzantines. Further discoveries of Christianity we made were a fine mosaic in the apse and a marble-faced baptismal tank. There was a tangible feeling of the past. Not unexpectedly, the museum was closed so we were unable to see many of the treasures rescued from the site, including the sixth-century panelled mosaic depicting scenes of wild beasts and one of Noah releasing the dove from the Ark.

As we left the church and started to climb the hill, heading for the remains of a Byzantine palace, my head was buzzing, not so much with the effects of the dramatic arrival of Christianity during the Byzantine era, but with one particular person: Simon of Cyrene. Although I have been familiar with the name and the role Simon played in helping Christ carry his cross since my early school days, it wasn't until I was standing on the very soil he would have trodden that it came home to me that his roots were here in Libya. Like Joseph of Arimathea, the name has a memorable ring but I had never questioned the origin.

As if a light had been switched on, Simon of Cyrene – the very first African Christian – became real for me. Believed to have been an African Jew who had returned to Jerusalem for the Passover festival, he was among the crowd of onlookers at the time of the crucifixion of Christ and was pressed by Roman guards to help Jesus carry his cross. Tradition states that he not only became a convert to Christianity but his two sons, Rufus and Alexander, became missionaries of sufficient note to be included in Mark's gospel.

Leaving the churches, we made our way uphill to the palace. A paved corridor separated the building into two distinct sections – the east and west wings. From the west wing fine stone-built portals provided access to a series of interconnecting rooms arranged round a central courtyard. From its hillside setting there were excellent views of the Byzantine churches and down to the sea, stirring my imagination once again. Was it from this harbour, Cyrene's port, that Simon of Cyrene left for Jerusalem as an African Jew? And did he return to this same place a changed man?

One minute I was standing alongside my companions, albeit lost in contemplation, the next I was alone. Quickly surveying the area, I was just in time to see the top of Simon's head and then, tailing him, Gerry's head and shoulders disappearing over a ridge. Our plan was to follow the Hellenistic city wall east to the Greek theatre. I set off in the direction they'd taken and caught up with them just as they reached the outer perimeter. Negotiating our way up a stairway, we took seats in the near centre of the auditorium.

It was impressive – both the theatre and its splendid location. Although the original building has suffered extensively from successive invaders, including the Byzantines who had no qualms about dismantling sections to provide building materials for their own uses, nevertheless, twenty-eight tiers of rock-cut seats remain intact. I counted them! That it was in sight of the sea but not built on the original coastline was fortuitous. It had a romantic setting but was safe from the fate of great sections of the city which have suffered from gradual yet dramatic coastal submergence. Much of the port and early periods of its history have been claimed by the sea.

Then, in an out-of-no-where fashion we were becoming accustomed to, a figure appeared. Not an actor and not security in Roman garb but an old man with rheumy eyes and looking pitifully thin. Shabbily dressed in a garment that was neither fully Roman nor Arabic, he shuffled towards us and with shaking hands unwrapped a grubby cloth to show us a handful of Roman coins marked with images of wild animals. He was offering them at 10 dinars each – more than £20 each at the current official rate. Simon was interested and started to bargain with him. Gerry pulled him aside.

"Better not," he warned. "We could be being watched. Could be security in drag or a plant! Don't give them a reason to pick us up."

Reluctantly Simon gave in and slipped the old man a few coins for a meal.

The Eastern propylon: an imposing entrance to Cyrene's Forum

View of part of the splendid colonnaded Forum: Cyrene

Headless statues guard the entrance to House of Hesychius: Cyrene

The Hesychius family name in a floor mosaic: Cyrene

Ceremonial gateway into the Street of King Battus

Stoa of Hermes & Hercules: Cyrene

Escape from Derna

Leaving Apollonia, our taxi headed east along the twisting coast road that traces the lower spurs of the Green Mountains en route to the east and Derna. A series of dramatic bends provided glimpses of sandy bays between rocky headlands though for the most part, like much of the Libyan coastline, it was stony and barren. Simon assured us that during the Italian era and until the 1960s Derna was reputed to be a popular holiday resort, offering an up-market hotel and promenade as well as a selection of excellent beaches; the final lure was the promise of opportunities to view cliff-side caves used by Christians escaping persecution; a gorge with a spectacular waterfall; and an old but inhabited souk.

Finally, the road straightened and dropped until we were following a stretch of stony beach. It was Gerry who first saw the unmistakeable '*funduq*' (hotel) sign, pointing towards a seven-storey dilapidated concrete building facing the sea on the far side of the road, and asked the driver to pull over. Was this, I wondered, the remains of the 'fashionable' hotel used by Simon to persuade us to make the trip? The frontage, in a major state of collapse, clung to the remains of windows – some broken and some boarded up – while the forecourt and car park had been used as a tip for rubble. The driver shrugged his shoulders when we repeated, "*Funduq?*"

"Wow! So this is Derna's fashionable resort?" I teased.

"Good enough for Mussolini in its day!" Simon cheerfully responded. "Let's try the town centre. Hotel Jabal al Akhdar!" he directed the driver. "Town Square."

From the outside, it seemed possible that the Jabal al Akhdar Hotel could live up to the guidebook descriptions of 'very good' and 'central'. We dismissed the taxi driver before checking on 'clean and quite cheap'. That was our first mistake. In spite of the grandeur of a mosaic floor and a huge central domed entrance, an air of gloom pervaded the dimly lit reception.

We handed our employment cards to a heavily jowled, unshaven character. That was our second mistake. With sluggish movements, suggesting that he was either half-witted or heavily drugged, he locked our cards into a drawer, handed us room keys and gestured towards a dank, windowless corridor. On either side, lavatories and washrooms with missing and smashed tiles and leaking walls from which hung heavy broken chains looked as if they'd been used as torture chambers. My head didn't want to believe what my eyes had seen. The suffocating smell of stale urine followed us as we silently trailed along the dark passageway.

I turned the key, pushed open the door to my room and stared with disbelief at the scene before me. Pale sunlight filtered through torn rags covering a high, filthy window onto three single beds. Opposite, a lopsided wardrobe straddled a thin grey and heavily stained carpet. One of the beds held the shape of the last occupant's retreating body like a discarded animal skin. The other two were covered with dark wool blankets and thick heavily patterned sheets. I lifted a corner of the blanket on the nearest bed. Several huge walnut-coloured cockroaches ran out. Gerry had followed me and lifted the mattress of the second bed. Cockroaches scattered across the wooden mattress support and disappeared, others were climbing the walls. The bedding felt sticky with years of accumulated dirt.

"There's no way I'm staying here!" I protested as Simon joined us. "It's alive with cockroaches and this is daylight. Heaven alone knows what will crawl out in darkness!"

I pulled aside the blanket on the unmade bed. Two cockroaches obligingly ran for cover. Simon was not impressed. "My room's fine," he insisted. "We can swap. Whatever. I'm staying put!"

"Believe me. Your room will be no different. Look, I'm not out to prove anything. It's not just the squalor and sharing my bed with the local wild-life – it's the place – didn't you see the washrooms?"

"Come on, guys," Gerry intercepted. "Why don't we go outside? There's a terrace. We can have a drink. Let's talk – then decide."

As we filed along the corridor I looked again at the broken and rusted chains hanging from the walls, the cracked tiles. Unanswered questions raged in my head. I knew that the people of Derna had resisted the Italians. Was it possible that the rooms had been used as torture chambers in the Italian era? Had the Libyans kept the washrooms that way as a memorial to the suffering of local people? Or, once again, was it merely symptomatic of the lack of interest and ability to clear up, maintain and modernise?

At the front of the hotel a flight of stone steps led to a terrace filled with tables and chairs. In bright sunlight, in the shade of great ficus trees, I allowed myself to be persuaded to take a walk before a final decision was made. Having come this far, Simon wanted to explore. He was digging his heels in. I wanted to leave but wasn't confident about travelling alone. Gerry, in his customary role as mediator, was reluctant to take sides. One non-alcoholic beer later I found myself trailing my escorts towards the covered souk and medina which Simon insisted was known for its charming narrow streets and tiny ancient courtyards.

A modern, covered row of shops, built in front of the old souk, was closed. The ground was infested with litter, rotting vegetable matter and globules of spit. Small gatherings of men, dressed in a mismatch of crumpled and unusually grubby robes, their heads heaped and bandaged with scarves, were eyeing us suspiciously. We could see narrow lanes leading into the older part of the original settlement and followed one to a square where a group of old men were sitting round a rusted tap that capped the remains of a fountain. Above and behind them a magnificent magenta bougainvillaea created a bower, embracing the walls with long flowering fingers.

Our approach was viewed with such intense hostility that even Simon noticed and we retreated to make our way through a modern street of drab concrete buildings towards the harbour. As we walked litter, rotting vegetable matter, foul smells from leaking sewage and heat increased. My mood was becoming increasingly black. Then I tripped over a pile of severed sheep's legs and started to question my sanity. "That's it!" I announced. "I'm getting a taxi to Al Bayda. I'll wait for you there."

My outburst was received in silence but by the time we'd waded through more rubbish to reach the seafront Gerry had decided to leave with me, and before we were back at the hotel Simon's resolve had weakened. We faced one problem. We had to recover our employment cards. Without them we weren't going anywhere.

The receptionist shuffled towards us from the darkness of an inner room, reluctant to understand our requests for our cards or determined not to. Finally, attracted by the commotion, a small dapper guy wearing European-style trousers and jacket and an open-necked shirt arrived on the scene. He appeared to understand and speak English as well or as badly as he wanted to. Meanwhile, Gerry, who had been struggling to learn classical Arabic for a year, was doing his best to insist that we were leaving and demanded our employment cards whereupon the receptionist produced a bill charging us for the rooms. A heated argument followed and was finally resolved. In order to get our cards and escape we agreed to pay half the room rates. It was robbery, but we would have our cards and freedom. Minutes later we boarded a taxi and were speeding through the Green Mountains towards Al Bayda.

Now that we'd escaped, our experience was already turning into a hilarious after-dinner story. Then we became more serious and attempted to rationalise what had taken place. Although nothing could justify the state of the hotel, we realised that we should have done more research on the place and especially on the politics, but at the present time the problem was one of getting hold of up-to-date information. The guide-books we had between us were hopelessly out of date and didn't touch on such issues. Most certainly we had been unprepared for such open hostility.

Gerry reminded us that the people of Derna had fiercely resisted Italian colonialism and as a result suffered the horrors of fascist concentration camps and daily hangings, and reasoned that many of the older people had living memories of these atrocities as well as of the Second World War raging on their doorstep. Meanwhile, he was thumbing through the pages of a wad of dog-eared photocopied pages he'd rescued from his backpack.

"Listen to this!" he urged: "The only outside witness to the Italian atrocities in Derna was Knud Holmboe, a Muslim Danish traveller in the 1930s. Suspicious of his pro-Arab sympathies Holmboe was arrested by the Italians and imprisoned in Derna gaol. More fortunate than the four sheiks in the next door cell he survived to tell his tale ..."

It was little wonder that I'd detected raised eyebrows when that morning I told the staff of the hotel in Al Bayda that we planned to stay overnight in Derna. Neither did they seem surprised at our return. We were given the same rooms and the same sheets! Were they expecting us or saving on laundry?

We headed for the dining room. Simon was threatening to top himself if we had chicken again. The gods were with him. Boiled mutton was on the menu. Gerry urged him not to get too excited as it would be the leftovers from the Eid. He wasn't wrong. It was grey, it was rubbery and it defied any attempts to reduce it into a form that could be swallowed with any degree of comfort, never mind digested. I gulped several mouthfuls of water, forcing myself to swallow the first mouthful, then, fearing the worst if I persisted, gave up. Simon insisted that his was fine. Gerry was masticating manfully. He never complained. I wasn't complaining either. After the Derna experience the hotel could do no wrong. I'd changed my mind. The Al Bayda Palace Hotel was a palace indeed.

Postscript

It wasn't until some years after my time in Libya that I came upon the following plausible explanation of the intense hostility we experienced on our visit to Derna.

In the 1990s Derna was a hotbed of Islamic revivalism. A fundamentalist uprising in the Derna region was put down with considerable bloodshed in the late 1990s. Rebels took refuge in the Jabal Akhdar and were hunted down by the regular army. The escarpment where they took refuge was torched. Certain historic sites are said to have been damaged in the process. Few details filtered out to the outside world, *Libya Handbook*.

Temple of Love

Kyrene, a Thessalian princess, was a great huntress who guarded her father's herds in a region of Mount Pelion, destroying wild beasts with her bare hands. One day, while she was wrestling a lion, the god Apollo spied on her and became inflamed with love. Seizing her, he carried her off to the Hill of Myrtles in Libya where the Greeks would later found a colony named Kyrene (Cyrene) in her honour. Such was my early morning reading in preparation for our return visit to Cyrene, this time to the lower terrace used almost exclusively by the Greeks for the worship of their most revered deities.

Gerry and I were determined to explore the Sanctuary and Fountain of Apollo on the lower terrace. This, after all, was the starting point for the settlement as fascinating in fact as it is in mystery and legend. Doggedly intent on finding sunken treasure in the harbour, Simon planned a return trip to Apollonia. After dropping Simon at the beach our taxi driver delivered Gerry and me to the North Gate entry of the site. Since it was a public holiday, not only were the gates open but some local families as well as a straggle of expats had arrived ahead of us. In our usual strikes for independence we arranged to go our separate ways and to meet on the path leading from the Sanctuary to the theatre at an agreed time.

Backed by an easily defensible hill, the terraced hillside was supplied with a torrent of natural spring water, reliable rainfall from the 'hole in the sky', and a great plain for agriculture stretching north to the outstanding backdrop of the Mediterranean Sea! It is not difficult to see why the Sanctuary was an excellent place for the original Greek settlement. Four lofty Doric columns guard the entrance to the lower terrace where the ruins of numerous shrines and temples – some remain to be identified – cover the greater part of the terrain. In their midst stand the remains of the most important and conspicuous monument on the site, the great Temple of Apollo.

Easily identified by painstakingly re-erected Doric columns marking the perimeter and a flight of steps leading to the present-day floor level, the temple is memorable for what it was and what it stood for. Revered by the Greeks as the God of Light whose golden chariot pulled the sun across the sky each day, Apollo and his temple took centre stage. It was here that the great, sensuous statue of Apollo playing a lyre was discovered in 1861. Was it divine providence that the statue survived earthquakes, the Jewish Revolt and Byzantine Christian efforts to reduce pagan marble statuary to lime? Taken into safe keeping, the rescued statue was no longer present, but someone with a mischievous sense of humour had propped a grinning Gorgon's head relief, dating from the fifth century BC, on an outer wall – a silent witness to the tumultuous past. For memory's sake I decided to take some photos.

"Madam, I show you. I guide."

I spun round. A middle-aged Libyan was standing nearby.

"I guide," he repeated. "You want see temple. I show you."

"I have a map. I don't need a guide," I insisted.

"This love temple," he continued. "Many time fall down. Many time climb up."

Dismissing the innuendos as unintended and deciding that he was more of a nuisance than a danger, I planned to ignore him and again prepared to take a shot. Then out of the corner of one eye I saw a group of visitors a short distance away. Believing the principle of safety in numbers, I started walking along a paved terrace towards the group, so intent on losing my would-be guide that it wasn't until I had distanced myself from him that I realised that I was heading for a gathering of young Libyan males. I had shaken off a lone pursuer and plunged headlong into a gang. Armed with cameras and transistor radios and wearing a uniform of skin-tight jeans and open-necked shirts, they had arrived for a day out among the ruins. Their interest did not appear to be historic. They were on the lookout for diversions. There were few of these around and I had the misfortune of becoming the unwelcome centre of their attention.

I reacted to invitations to join them with a succession of explicit international versions of 'Go away!' These proved ineffectual. Now at some distance from the Sanctuary and other visitors I was feeling increasingly nervous.

"Hey, Germany!" one of the youths called. "I take you to theatre. I take you under the ground!" I backed away. I had neither the shoulders nor stature to merit the title or defend myself, and the idea of descending into the lions' pit with one, or indeed all, of these guys was not my idea of fun.

I'd arranged to meet Gerry on the pathway leading to the theatre. To do this I had to go past them on a path that was not only narrow but precariously near the eroded hillside. It was my only option. Then, miraculously, I spotted a mop of auburn hair. In his recognisable head-in-guidebook posture Gerry was standing fifty or so metres away on the cliff edge. "My husband," I informed the group, pointing to him. The effect was magic. "Thank you, James!" I murmured to myself, gratified that his state-of-marriage advice worked. A wave of nostalgia for James, his friendship and sense of humour washed through me as I walked purposefully towards the group. They parted like water, watching as I strode towards my spurious spouse.

Such was my relief at being reunited with Gerry that even his irritating habit of reading aloud great chunks from his guidebook about the 'Bizz'ntins' was forgiven. He offered to accompany me to Apollo's Fountain and then to see a huge sculpture relief depicting battle scenes that he'd sighted from Valley Street, or the Hellenistic 'Sacred Way'– the main access route from the Sanctuary to the Agora and Forum.

Guiding me further along the path from where we could look down on the theatre, he pointed out the wall built to replace the row of seats closest to the arena when the Hellenistic theatre was converted to an amphitheatre by the Romans. Herodotus records the terrible revenge taken on any person who opposed them, including captured members of the Garamantes tribe, who were dragged on stage by their hair to face death in the jaws of wild animals. Such was the entertainment of the Romans!

Leaving the amphitheatre and memories of the savagery of Rome behind us, we climbed the steps up the vertical cliff face to the more spiritual realms of the Greek world on an upper terrace. The centre piece is the Fountain of Apollo where two lions standing either side of an obelisk guard the place where fresh spring water, originating 300 metres inside the mountain, once gushed from a cavern; it is said that pilgrims came from all over Roman Africa to participate in the sacred rituals performed here.

That lions were a force to be dealt with at this time is reinforced by the number of images showing the nymph Kyrene strangling a lion with her bare hands; thus engaged, Kyrene can be seen as the guardian of the fountain as well as of the settlement against the savage forces of Africa. A bas relief from the Roman period showing the nymph being crowned by the goddess Libya while performing this feat of strength, more suited to the god Hercules, is on display at the British Museum. The only sign that the boyish-looking nymph has been engaged in a struggle is her displaced robe revealing her navel. On the other hand, the lion, held effortlessly in her embrace, does look as if he could be on his last gasp! Apollo was so impressed by the nymph's strength that he made her his bride.

A narrow stairway led from the fountain to a grotto reserved for the ceremonial ablutions of the priests of Apollo. Here, on twin rock pillars supporting the roof, Roman inscriptions of the priests' names have been inscribed. More flamboyant graffiti in Arabic has been daubed on the walls. A sign of the times but also of the past: it was an art form not unknown to the Romans and recorded by Strabo on a trip up the Nile in 24 BC. Strabo observed that Romans (trippers) had used the smoke of torches to write their names on the ceiling of the lower chamber of the Great Pyramid.

From the grotto we climbed the gentle outer slope of the hill towards the village of Shahat and Valley Street from where Gerry first glimpsed the sculptured relief. It was a long haul over rough ground but with an interesting diversion. We literally stumbled upon a row of Greek baths. Complete with niches for oil lamps and water jars the baths were said to have been used by the maidens of Cyrene, when they came to dedicate themselves to Artemis. The twin sister of Apollo and virgin goddess of light, Artemis was more interested in protecting the vulnerable and oppressed than in romance and marriage. Happiest when hunting or bathing in the company of her band of nymphs, her appeal is as great to independent women of the modern world as it was to the women of ancient Greece.

Finally, we were standing before the remaining sections of the bas-relief. Once part of the artwork from an imposing propylon dedicated to Septimius Severus, the huge carved marble sections had been conveniently propped at eye level: action-packed scenes of helmeted Roman soldiers on horseback, armed with swords and shields, in close combat with naked tribesmen wielding massive clubs were right before us. The more unfortunate victims were being trampled underfoot by both men and horses! Elaborate sculptures showing the Romans defeating barbarian tribes and aided by the gods were a traditional form of imperial propaganda. However, the Romans were not always the victors! Herodotus tells us that fierce local tribes did have some success against the might of Rome.

During the first century of Roman rule of Cyrenaica, the Nasamones' attacks on the walls of the city and piratical activity in the Syrtic region to the west caused the Romans many headaches. In fact, the territory of the Nasamones lay within the Roman frontier, making them subject to taxation. Haynes tells the story of a Roman-led expedition against the Nasamones, who had risen in protest against extortionate tax demands and put to death some of the tax collectors. Not only were the Romans defeated but the Nasamones succeeded in taking over their camp. The tragic irony of their success was that it was to lead to their downfall. Seduced by the large quantities of available food and wine in the camp, they overindulged to such an extent that when the Romans returned seeking revenge they were incapable of defending themselves and all but a handful who escaped perished by the sword.

Getting into the right position to take photographs wasn't easy. Sections of the relief propped up and facing a ditch were backed by thorny trees and surrounded by equally thorny shrubs. Our activities had caught the attention of a group of youths from the adjacent village. Distracted from idling and listening to Arabic pop music in the shade of a ficus tree, they stared in fascination at the sight of two foreigners attempting to extricate themselves from the tangle of thorny branches in the litter-strewn ditch.

Battle scarred but mission complete, we made our way to the café near the North Gate to find a rather forlorn and damp Simon waiting. He was lamenting that he'd spent most of his time and energy battling with strong currents and tides before giving up and returning to meet us. His despondency was such that he was bitterly regretting the failed acquisition of Roman coins on offer during our visit to Apollonia. The only solace we could offer was to buy him a drink. There were no prizes for guessing what was on offer!

Entrance to the Palace of Dux: Apollonia

Marble columns, marked with the symbol of a cross, outline the nave of the Eastern Church: Apollonia

Reassembled columns of the Temple of Apollo: Cyrene

Roman soldiers shown defeating local tribes on sculptured relief of battle scenes

An obelisk, guarded by solemn lions, marks the Fountain of Apollo

Resting in the Sacred Way: a place where journeys begin and end

Return to Tripoli

Countdown

One of the idiosyncratic methods of people control in Libya is to make it impossible to book the return half of your ticket when you make the original reservation. You can reserve a ticket for the outward journey but the return can only be booked at the place of your destination on the day of your return. The airline offices had been closed since the start of the Eid, increasing the chances of being left behind. We had two fears: if we failed to get on the flight we would be absent from work on the following day. This would not be looked upon favourably. Secondly, our late return would give some satisfaction to pessimistic friends whose warnings about the dangers and unreliability of travel in Libya we had ignored all year.

We faced the usual scrum conditions at the airline office. Since we were not literally travelling security was notably absent. Without the now customary 'priority treatment' we were left to our own devices; we knew that the only way to survive was to follow the same practices as our fellow passengers. That meant taking up a position at the back and pressing forward whenever the opportunity arose.

Waiting has certain advantages, one of which is it provides an opportunity to observe people and make notes in my head about what I see and hear and think. Just now I was examining the turbans worn by the men. Called *emaha*, *esaba* or *kasa* they are worn in a similar casual fashion as the towel I wrap round my head after a shower – as if they were about to collapse and fall off. One thing was certain – Libyan Arabs lacked the more elaborate style and rakish appeal of the Tuareg, their desert neighbours.

My attention wandered to Simon. His head bobbed and weaved above the turbans. He hated waiting and doing nothing.

He was restless, fiddling with dog-eared tickets and examining torn bits of paper entangled with crumpled dinars extricated from the crumb and fluff depths of his pockets. He preferred to plod through filthy streets than to stand still or rest. Suddenly, he announced that if I'd get his ticket he'd go to the Omar Khiam Hotel to see if they had my sarong that I'd been bewailing the loss of since our overnight stay. An ageing Galahad, he left on his mission. I had my doubts about his success in making himself understood. How does one describe a sarong to an Arab who doesn't speak English? Nevertheless, I was grateful for his offer.

"Hi, where are you guys from?" enquired a friendly voice from behind.

Gerry and I introduced ourselves to a dark-haired, broad-shouldered British man with a just detectable north-country accent, who had emerged from the body of waiting Arabs.

"David," he responded and explained that he worked at a language institute at Marsa el Brega, a top oil company in the Syrte Desert. His rugged good looks: a square jaw and deep-set blue eyes and a head of thick, brown wavy hair were matched by an easy, friendly manner. We exchanged notes about our travels and he offered his card, saying that he was staying at the modern Uzu Hotel.

"Overlooks the Inner Harbour. Quiet and good value," he said. "If you've no other plans why don't you join me later, for a drink – soft, unfortunately," he added with a wry smile.

An hour later with tickets in our hands for the 10 p.m. and last flight to Tripoli, we had resorted to sitting on the pavement outside the airline office, wondering if we'd ever see Simon again when, looking as if he'd just conquered Everest, he appeared. He was carrying the scrunched-up sarong – a crumpled trophy in his huge hand. Momentarily, I was engulfed in memories and nostalgia for tropical islands and a yacht called the *Star of Siam* then I stuffed the sarong along with my nostalgia into my backpack.

Reality was sitting on a sand-strewn pavement. Reality was

females wrapped in sheets showing one eye. Reality was the unmitigating midday sun in Benghazi.

In fact, the sun was directly overhead and we were hungry. Simon was determined to go native by trying local food and doing some back-street exploring. I was determined to spend the last hot hours quietly in luxury at the Uzu Hotel and take up David's suggestion to meet for a drink. Gerry agreed to the same plan. We'd had our fill of the 'flavour of the place!' So we parted company with Simon, arranging to meet him at the airport at 9 p.m. for the flight to Tripoli.

Elegant fountains and bowers of fresh flowers adorned the entrance hall and adjoining lounges of the Uzu Hotel. It was a scene from a forgotten world. My room too was luxurious. It had all the things you take for granted in the real world that we had been deprived of for so long: a bed with two clean cotton sheets, a quiet air conditioner that worked, a hot-water shower. In addition, there was a telephone with international dialling facilities and a balcony with a view over the still waters of the deserted Inner Harbour. Swallows wheeling and dipping over mirrored sky were the only visible signs of life – not one yacht – not one boat. It was unreal and it was unnatural but it was blissfully quiet. I looked at my watch. A long awaited telephone call followed by a shower, room service and rest between cool, clean sheets before dinner and our rendezvous with David.

It was one of those meetings that are not so much coincidence as meant. It transpired that David was the manager of a team teaching English to adult Libyans employed in various sectors of the oil industry in the Syrte Desert and was on his way back to England to recruit new staff for the next academic year. It was a male preserve but he insisted they were not averse to recruiting females. Appointments depended on qualifications and experience not gender, he assured me. The work was on a sixty-day-rotation basis followed by three weeks' leave but the tax-free salary was good and paid regularly into UK bank accounts. Sixty days was a long haul but David explained you could opt for occasional days off – these would be deducted from the leave. It sounded more efficient and financially worthwhile than the Tripoli package and there were other advantages. In distant Brega I could lose my CIA status and would have the opportunity to explore the oases of the eastern Sahara. I left with David's card in my pocket, promised to think about it and to ring him when I returned to the UK for my summer leave.

By the time we arrived at the airport for our return flight Simon had taken up residence in a green plastic bucket chair. One minute he was engrossed in his book and the next he was on his feet with the 'out of character' alacrity he drew upon for specific occasions. In fact, the entire room had responded to some hidden sign that Simon had been tuned in to. In one body the room rose to its feet and lurched towards the check-in desk. Simon was third in line from the front.

We struggled forwards, stretching to hand him our tickets and almost immediately found ourselves propelled by the body of travellers towards the departure lounge. The bad news was that the flight was three hours late. Predictably, there were no facilities at the airport, just two rows of plastic bucket seats facing each other across an empty room. We resigned ourselves to a long, uncomfortable wait. The one female passenger, sitting directly opposite across the aisle, spent the entire time staring at me with her uncovered eye through the hole in her *farashiya*, reminding me of Miss Moppet peeping through a hole in a duster in Beatrice Potter's *Tale of Samuel Whiskers*.

***

The high days of my last weeks in Tripoli, like the high days of previous months when we weren't travelling, were Fridays. Not because I'd been converted to Islam, although some of my colleagues had tried hard enough, but because Fridays were dive days, and dive days were escape days. Escape from the compound and litter-strewn, police-controlled streets – escape from the rumours, horror stories and gossip. I wasn't exactly converted to shore diving in the Mediterranean – my tropical baptism had spoiled me – but I was becoming accustomed to its vicissitudes. I also enjoyed the company of the divers. There was a good mix of eccentric people; you have to be eccentric to agree to work in Libya and eccentric people are inevitably interesting people. You also have to be eccentric to dive in Libya. By my standards there's not a great deal to see and conditions are frequently more conducive to punishment than pleasure.

Nevertheless, a diving expedition was a good antidote to problems beyond our control, and for the divers, at least, a time-proven remedy for clearing the mind. My previous diving experiences were limited to dives from boats by abandoned oil rigs in the tropical South China Sea off the coast of Brunei and some spectacular dives from a yacht off the coast of the southern Philippine island of Palawan. For me the Tripoli West 809 Branch of BSAC was a school of diving with a difference.

We headed west out of our Tripoli suburb along the freeway towards Tunisia to a prearranged meeting point. Travelling in a convoy is part of a safety campaign: should you run into difficulties or become entangled with Libyans practising racetrack skills or high speed U-turns on the freeway there are no working telephone points and no rescue services. A complete lack of road signs is another good reason for group travel. Not only is it difficult to know where you are, but also it's unlikely that you'll find the track leading to the venue for the day's dive. This has to be spotted off the freeway which passes through a nondescript fifty-kilometre stretch of shabby modern shop-houses resembling rows of lock-up garages. Between these the road is strung with scattered settlements, roadside markets, olive and date plantations. White mosques, each capped by a green cupola and spiralling minaret, punctuate the route like beads on a rosary. Layers of fine desert sand that coat buildings and vegetation contribute to the impression of Libya as a forgotten slice of the world.

In fact, there were road signs but the information has been blotted out. When Gaddafi came to power part of his anti-imperialist campaign was to get rid of all information given in English. Rumour also had it that at some time in the previous decade, fearing that Libya was about to be invaded, an army of men was let loose with ladders and pots of green paint to blot out all the road signs along the freeway between Egypt and

Tunisia, in the belief that the enemy would be confused! It was surmised that the paint was probably left over from painting Green Square green!

The only invaders, expatriate workers in the oil and oil-related industries, have compensated for the lack of information by inventing their own place names and signposts. The designated meeting place for dives west of Tripoli is in a lay-by, just off the freeway, clearly marked by a gigantic stone phallus. This unmistakable symbol, also marking the entrance to an oil company's compound, was appropriately named Big Dick Corner by the dive club.

Once everyone had assembled beneath Big Dick we headed for the 'Chicken Shop' for take-away picnic lunches of roasted chickens, straight off the spit, small fresh loaves and plastic bags of ready-chopped salad. The proprietor, a friendly and helpful Libyan, has adopted the Friday divers, displays a BSAC logo on the window above his counter and at 8.30 on a Friday morning has enough chickens turning on his spits to satisfy up to thirty, including divers, family members and friends.

Our destination was a beach, christened Dawn Dive by our predecessors, and renamed Dead Man's Beach by current members who retrieved the body of a man from the sea at that spot sometime last year. It seems that an increasing number of Libyans are taking to the sea without any knowledge of swimming, providing divers with opportunities to practise rescue skills on real victims. As the descendants of nomadic desert people the sea has been of remarkably little interest to the average Libyan. This is evident from the extraordinary absence of local fishing boats and from the use of accessible beaches as dumping grounds for rubble and rubbish. Perhaps the Libyan eye is more tuned to the aesthetic beauty of undulating desert landscape – their 'Sand Sea' as the Arabic word Sahara suggests – than the shoreline that they desecrate so liberally.

The approach to Dead Man's Beach through olive plantations that open out to sand hills resembled a miniature desert landscape. We followed tracks gouged by lorries on their way to sandstone quarries. Dust flying, the convoy of laden saloon cars bounced their way between hedgerows of prickly pear across burning hummocks of sand, like boats bouncing across rough sea. The absence of four-wheel drives is accounted for in the same way as the absence of boats: you need a licence, which is virtually impossible to get. This was just one more confirmation of the premise that it may be difficult to get into Libya but it is even more difficult to get out: four-wheel drives and boats are a means to escape across desert or sea. Finally, we crested a ridge and followed a track along a line of dunes. Beyond them the sea tumbled onto a coarse sandstone beach held between two rocky peninsulas.

By the time cars had been unloaded and encampments set up under beach umbrellas, the dive leader was organising the first shift. On this occasion the water temperature of seventeen degrees required 3-mm wet suits but the air temperature, of over fifty degrees, exacerbated by the hot desert wind, meant being trapped in your own private sauna. What is more, snake-easing sweating limbs into black rubber is an art. The sight of us doing so was attracting larger and larger crowds of Libyan onlookers. It must have been the nearest thing to a sex show available in Libya. It didn't end there either. That was only the curtain raiser. Part two included struggling into an inflatable jacket with a massive phallic cylinder attached to the back; strapping a lethal sheathed knife to your thigh; then sprouting rubber tubes and a plethora of instruments to measure breathing rates, among other things; and finally, standing in buddy pairs on the edge of the ocean checking each other's equipment before submerging.

The diving group included a large representation of people from the embassies. For such a small population Libya has a plethora of embassies. As far as I could make out embassy staff did very little apart from enjoy privileges: they could make international calls and drive fast air-conditioned cars through border posts as if they didn't exist; attend cocktails parties where there were ample supplies of real drink; they could plead they were busy when one of us was caught in a tricky political situation. In other words, they enjoyed diplomatic immunity to the full.

Finally, there was Don, our dive leader – a Canadian diving enthusiast – under whose warmth, enthusiasm and expertise the club has grown and continued to grow from half a dozen people to over eighty in a handful of years. I thought back to my first dive with Don when, unsuitably clad in my pink tropical skin-suit, I was not prepared for either the cold or the onslaught of waves. Entry, from the far side of one of the rocky headlands, entailed crossing a platform of rock. I was used to kitting up in a dive-boat and tumbling backwards into sea that was always warm, if not always friendly. Neither was I prepared for the fifty-metre trek across slippery uneven rocks with a cylinder strapped to my back. Feeling like Christian carrying the sins of the world on my shoulders, I staggered and then crawled over slippery rock towards my Slough of Despond to be confronted by the challenge of Don's backward lean and tilt entry into churning water and crashing waves.

"Wait for a pause," Don instructed.

I watched nervously as he stuffed his demand valve into his mouth, leaned and tilted at a twenty-five-degree angle and dropped out of sight. I had learnt a range of conventional entries including: a backward roll, a forward roll, stepping in forwards or stepping in backwards but this was my first encounter with the lean and tilt entry. Suddenly, Don surfaced and was bobbing between lunging waves, looking as happy as an expectant seal. I waited until the next charge had receded and then, hunched and drenched, I pulled on my mask, wedged my dummy between my teeth and, sucking furiously, glanced briefly and nervously at the water, leaned, tilted and dropped. As soon as I'd surfaced and spotted Don I finned away from the rocks and towards him as fast as incoming waves would allow.

Once we were at a safe distance he gave the thumbs-down sign and we descended into the murky underworld of muted autumnal tones. Tumbled rocks covered in rusty, tossing creepers resembled wooded hills tugged by wind. Puffballs, soft as thistledown, drifted from side to side. Huge porous cavities in a wall of rock gaped like skulls. Some opened into murky caverns. In this mottled world lit by shafts of dust-flecked light, fish, striped horizontally, vertically or blotched in a sort of camouflage, reflected the colours of the surroundings. Only the painted comber with a luminous mauve spot on its belly was not in uniform. Even massive groupers conformed, stared and swam away. Meanwhile, buffeted by overhead currents and subjected to constant depth changes as we crossed rocky hummocks and dropped into sandy hollows, I was feverishly correcting my buoyancy and clearing my ears. Cold crept through me. Cold took possession of me. I was suffering from subterranean culture shock.

Now, on the morning of my last dive, acting as shore marshal, I was disappointed to discover that I had missed an encounter with friendly dolphins that swam circles round all the delighted submerged buddy pairs. However, I had the pleasure and fun of sharing the afternoon dive with Bob, one of the club's veteran divers. He had introduced barbequed chicken to the local fish by hand-feeding them on the weekly dive and had attracted a large following of primeval-looking groupers that lurk in rock caves waiting for their weekend treat. On this Friday the groupers were either too lazy or had decided to vary their diet and we were followed by a shoal of saddle bream. Surprised by the voracity of their attacks on the proffered pieces, I nearly lost my thumb to one greedy fellow who swallowed half a chicken leg whole, in the manner of a python.

On our way back Bob gestured to me to stay close to a boulder of rock. He pointed to the floor. As if on cue for my final curtain, in the rippled sand of the ocean's bottom I saw two eyes, still as marbles. We stayed behind the boulder, watching until with a flurry of sand a gigantic stingray with widespread wings rose and hovered before taking flight and melting into the deepening blue as graceful and ghostly as a shadow.

***

Administration's combination of incompetence, ignorance and psychological warfare reached its height at the end of the academic year when teaching contracts had been completed and it was time for the annual leave. Retribution was taken on those who had not toed the line, or had stirred up trouble or caused offence in any way by the application of delaying tactics. Passports were never returned until the day of departure and some were deliberately held back. Like a number of my colleagues my teaching contract was complete. Before I could leave Libya all that remained was the fulfilment of the terms specified in the small print of my contract: the return of my passport and exit visa as well as air tickets to my point of origin.

The most effective weapon, primarily used as an incentive to make sure people who were renewing contracts did return, was delayed and non-payment of salaries. In some cases a vicious circle evolved so that the victim was never in a position to leave unless, like Kate, she was prepared to accept her losses in order to get out. Blatant lies concerning the transfer of hard-currency salaries to UK bank accounts were supported by the production of fake telexes as proof that the instructions for the transfer had been given.

It was difficult not to be caught up in the general hysteria, especially since I had reasons to be anxious about my own safe exit. My suspected CIA involvement apart, I wasn't renewing my contract and that would be seen as a slight. Then to my surprise and to the chagrin of finger-wagging colleagues I received everything I needed for escape including club class air tickets to London. I was one of few issued with the right documents on time. There had to be an ulterior motive. A colleague enlightened me.

"You're a CIA suspect. They want to get rid of you. Don't hang about. Get out now!"

However, before I could make an exodus I had a problem to solve. How to get out with my computer and printer? I considered abandoning them. All my writing was on disks. It would be easier to take the disks and abandon the computer. Then an embassy friend came to my rescue and made arrangements to have the computer and printer taken to a hotel in Djerba in a red-plated embassy car. There remained one major problem. I had been issued with tickets from Malta to London and not from Tunis as requested. I had some juggling to do. It was Sunday and my forbidden items were being taken to a hotel on Djerba Island, on Tuesday. My brain slipped into fifth gear. It would be more convenient if I travelled to Djerba in the embassy car at the same time.

I got on the phone to the embassy and in a heavily coded, monosyllabic conversation discovered that, yet again, the gods were on my side. I could leave with my bags and baggage at 8 a.m. on Tuesday morning. Once in Djerba I would have to arrange a flight to Malta, either via Monastir or Tunis, to pick up a flight to London. It was a long way round but it avoided the ferry, I could get my gear out and I was unlikely to have problems at customs. Now all I had to do was pack and make some hasty farewells.

At 8 a.m. on the morning of my departure I sailed past the shabby security office and through the iron gates for the last time in the luxury of an air-conditioned embassy limousine. Fear of jeopardising my exit prevented me making a less than polite farewell gesture to the Weasel. I contented myself with muttered 'pleasantries' and a royal wave. It wasn't over yet, I reminded myself; nevertheless, I felt good. A fleeting wave of nostalgia, as we passed the track lined with prickly pear that led to our favourite dive site, resurfaced when I caught a last glimpse of the elegant outline of Sabratha's Roman theatre. As we approached the border with Tunisia and its numerous checkpoints I began to feel less complacent. I was not an embassy official as my passport readily declared and, therefore, although travelling in an embassy car I was not immune from investigation.

All too soon I discovered that my apprehension was not unfounded: an overzealous Tunisian guard was interrogating the driver about the *Inglesse*. There is no love lost between Tunisians and Libyans and red embassy plates from Libya don't command respect in Tunisia. The interrogation went on for so long that my fear was growing out of proportion. Were they in league? What was the driver saying? Maybe he wasn't on my side. Maybe he was bargaining to exchange me and my computer for more than he'd get for delivering me safely to Djerba. Apart from '*Inglesse*',

I understood nothing. Suddenly the guard swopped Arabic for French and, directing his attention to me, asked,

"*Avez-vous des articles électroniques?*"

"*Non,*" I replied, feeling the skin on my scalp prick and my heart rate increase.

He looked at me hard. I turned to face him and smiled a sickly Mona Lisa smile. He motioned the driver to go. My whole body went limp. I knew there was one more checkpoint. Again, a lengthy interrogation took place, engendering a further rush of paranoia. They'd given me all my papers, waited for me to attempt to leave and then would pounce! Or were they going to let me taste freedom and then close in? Then, it was over, and was I restraining myself from whooping with joy? With four and a half hours behind us we were approaching Bahiret el Bibane and Tunisia's wide inland salt lakes – like huge mirrors holding images of flat blue sky they border the main road.

We trundled over the Roman-built causeway, cruised along the coastline past the huge flat expanse of sea creeping over the bay, past the old fort on a headland that marked the start of Zone Touriste and I began to relax. Stage one of my escape was nearly over but I reminded myself it was the height of the tourist season. Now fears about full hotels were surfacing. Fortunately, Zone Touriste has as many hotels as palm trees and before long I was bidding the driver farewell, had checked in and collapsed in relief onto the luxurious bed in my room at the hotel, 'Les Sirens'.

The windows overlooked two pools. In one the water was aquamarine, crystal clear and empty and in the other murky brown and full. Elderly overweight Germans dressed in pre-war style, one-piece black bathing suits were wallowing like hippopotamuses in its therapeutic waters – females distinguishable from the males by rubber bathing caps. Transfixed by the scene for some minutes, I began to have misgivings. If this was the real world, was I ready for it? Just now, I reminded myself, I had to remain focused on the last stage of my exit: first room service and refreshments and then a taxi to the airline office in Houmt Souk to arrange flights to Malta.

I had never been fully converted to the *Insh'a allah* syndrome and once again alarmist warnings of friends were responsible for the overdose of adrenalin pumping round my arteries. It was the tourist season. I would never get a flight out of Djerba. There were limited flights to Malta. I had to link up with a connecting flight at Tunis or Monastir. I could be marooned in Djerba for weeks. On the other hand, my safe arrival had increased my confidence and I felt that once again Allah was with me. By early afternoon I was back in my hotel room with connecting tickets from Djerba to Tunis to Malta and London for the day after tomorrow. I had a full day to relax in murky therapeutic waters and grow accustomed to indulging in the comforts of the almost real world until my departure 'at the appointed hour'.

The Gulf of Syrte

Degrees of Madness

The day earmarked for my return to Libya, 1st September 1994, was also the day celebrating twenty-five years since Gaddafi took power. However, this time I would not be making for Tripoli – the focus of the anniversary celebrations – instead I was destined for a top-security desert oil site, the most profitable and highly developed centre of the Libyan oil industry at Marsa el Brega, situated off the Gulf of Syrte some ten hours east of the Libyan capital by road.

The coastal settlement of Syrte, the most prominent town of this remote desert region between the two coastal provinces of Tripolitania and Cyrenaica, received its name from the Greeks. The fear inspired in sailors by this harbourless coast with its sudden storms and treacherous shoals is reflected in the name of Syrtes, or drag nets. In ancient history it is also the legendary meeting place of the Carthaginian Philanoi brothers who sacrificed their lives in order that the boundary between the ancient Greek and Punic worlds remained at Syrte.

In modern times Syrte is famed as the home town of Gaddafi. Born less then twenty kilometres from the city, he first attended school there at the age of ten. Today, it is the meeting place of the Popular Congresses of the Jamahiriya and there have been plans to make it the new capital of Libya. However, it was the discovery of oil in the region in the 1960s that brought Syrte into the economic limelight and inadvertently provided me with an opportunity to return to a country I had become fascinated with exploring.

I arrived at Djerba Airport, congratulating myself on the smoothness of the journey so far and with expectations that with the extra care and attention promised by my new employers I had nothing to fear. Once outside the airport my confidence faded. Not only was there no waiting limousine or even a minibus sporting the company's logo of an oil rig sprouting from a puddle of oil, but there were no taxis either. Every ten minutes or so when a taxi did appear it was flagged down before it reached the forecourt. Handicapped by the amount of luggage required by a new recruit, I could not compete with the alacrity of fellow travellers whose sudden appearance and nimble sprint to a favourable position heralded the arrival and departure of another cab.

Finally, just as I was succumbing to despair, a vehicle carrying two female passengers pulled alongside me. Needing no further invitation, I climbed in. The driver set off towards Homt Souk, an ancient market and favourite shopping place for visitors and the destination of my fellow passengers. Beyond the souk the journey to the Hotel Sina on the undeveloped side of the island took us past cupola-domed farms with olive groves and ancient wells sunk deep between parallel stone walls against a backdrop of sleek expanses of water dotted with fishing boats. Totally unspoilt, it was the stuff of picture postcards and dreams.

The marble-fronted hotel, fragrant from the sweet-scented blooms of a huge frangipani framing the entrance porch, was a welcome retreat between the main stages of the journey from London to Tripoli. The balcony from my room looked down on the still waters of a swimming pool as deserted as it was inviting. Minutes later I arrived at the poolside to find a complete change of scene. It had been taken over by a group of middle-aged men with the physiques and boisterous tones of a Celtic rugger team celebrating victory after a match! On further consideration I deduced that they too must be employed in oil-related industry and in all probability they were my fellow passengers for the next day's journey by road to Tripoli and by air to Brega. Convinced that, before long, they would succumb to the temptations of the bar I decided to remain incognito and slipped away. I could have the pool to myself later. Tomorrow promised to be a long day and would be soon enough for introductions.

At 7.30 a.m. I boarded the company bus with, as I had

suspected, a selection of future inmates destined for Marsa el Brega. Before long, my head throbbing with risqué stories and jokes, I was doing my best to avoid causing offence by refusing repeated offers of rum and coke, whisky or accommodation once we arrived and bracing myself for a further six hours of alcohol-induced hilarity until we reached Tripoli!

A diversion at the Libyan border post brought about a change of mood. Believing he was in possession of all Syrte employees' passports, the driver queued in direct sun for forty-five minutes. Attempting to survive sauna conditions on the bus, the rest of us had been reduced to a state of torpor. Suddenly, the driver returned and was in heated confrontation with one of the men.

"Didn't hand in his passport!" one of his companions informed me. "Too drunk. Silly sod! This'll take another hour. Don't know about you, love, but I'm losing the will to live!"

Thirty minutes later we were on the move again. Audible sighs of relief reverberated at the safe passage of beer- and wine-making ingredients hidden in the luggage. My primary fear was the safe transport of my computer. Although this time I had a company letter of permission to bring the laptop into Libya for work purposes, I knew that security had their own rules. That it had remained undetected so far was an added relief. As we neared Tripoli I became the target for horror stories about my destination. 'Top-rate security prison' and similar complimentary descriptions of my new place of abode kept my companions amused. Accustomed to such initiation treatment, I was unmoved until I heard the rumour about the grounded Fokker F28 – the company plane used for the last leg of the trip between Tripoli and Marsa el Brega.

"You'll be lucky to get a seat on the substitute. A Shorts cos it's shorter," my informant joked. "It's much smaller and you can bet on your life that seats will go to priority Libyans. Could mean the 'hell run' with us lot. Ten bleedin' hours across bleedin' desert by bleedin' bus!"

I held my breath and hoped for the best. I'd heard that the flight took one hour from Tripoli to Brega. Ten more hours on a bus across desert with my present companions didn't bear thinking about. Now, I was losing the will to live!

Less than an hour after we reached the airport my fears were dispelled. I was handed a boarding pass for the F28 and escorted to the plane by the Libyan pilot. "Let me," he said, offering to take one of my pieces of hand luggage. Both carried high risk items. I decided to hang on to the briefcase holding my laptop and handed him the second bag in which a freeze-dried winemaking kit had been carefully distributed between a camera and toiletries!

There were no air crew and no services but, unlike the Libyan-controlled domestic flights, the oil-company plane was regularly serviced and the pilots regularly tested. Seating was first come first choice. Soon after take-off we were cruising over the now familiar and beautiful Great Sand Sea. In evening light the rolling shadowed dunes were streaked in myriad shades of burnished gold, blues and greens.

By the time we started to lose height bright stars were emerging from a bruised sky and a blurred landscape dotted with orange lights rose to meet us. Minutes after landing and a journey of thirty-six hours, that under normal circumstances with direct air transport via Tripoli would have taken no more than six, I was speeding from the airport and surrounding desert in a company car towards Brega.

A small sand-coloured house in an all-female street generally known as 'Secretary Row' was my new home. Forbidden territory to the alternative sex, the street was nicknamed by them 'Street of a Thousand Virgins'. Whether this title was wishful thinking or chagrin at the lack of opportunities for access I had yet to discover! My initial reaction was delight at the privilege of having a place to myself fronted by a small courtyard, bordered by beds of geraniums and Saharan daisies glowing in the last of evening light.

On closer inspection the building and furnishings had seen better days. The ill-fitting front door opened on to a living room-cum-kitchen. The far end was furnished with a sink, a small refrigerator and a black enamel electric cooker and had a door leading to a small backyard. The near end, representing the living area, held an ancient two-seater sofa, an upright winged armchair, a coffee table and a wooden standard lamp with a crumpled shade. The furniture was arranged to focus on the pièce de résistance: a huge black 1950s-looking TV. A small dining room connected to the kitchen by a hatch I immediately assigned for use as a study and for winemaking. A second door from the lounge opened on to a corridor leading to a room filled with a good-sized double bed and fitted wall-to-wall wardrobes plus an en suite housing an ancient bath and toilet and smelling of mould. It was basic but it was liveable in. One thing was worrying me. In theory I had the house to myself, but from the minute I entered I was convinced that I was not alone!

A sense of the sudden cessation of the scurrying of countless insects and creatures had greeted me. I imagined them silently tunnelling and squeezing into cracks and crevices, hiding behind wainscoting, creeping under furniture and taking up lifeless poses. The ultimate survivors that even neurotically clinical Singapore hasn't succeeded in eliminating included columns of gigantic ants, syringe-armed mosquitoes, armour-plated cockroaches, bedbugs, beetles, and countless microscopic versions I was unable to identify. Armed with weapons of attack, they were certain to have taken up residence and would regard me as a plentiful supply of nourishment. I thought and hoped I'd glimpsed a gecko as it darted behind a faded picture of an oasis hanging on the lounge wall. If I were right it was relief, for I knew a gecko would be on my side. At the same time its presence confirmed a ready supply of living meals.

For the time being I had more pressing things to deal with. When the driver handed me a key to the house he instructed me to be ready for a 7 a.m. pick-up the following morning. I hadn't eaten since we left the hotel in Djerba and there was no sign of a Gargaresh-style welcome committee with offerings to keep me going. A quick inspection of the cupboards revealed supplies of tea bags, instant coffee and a packet of biscuits while the fridge held a carton of long-life milk and six eggs. In positive mode I set about preparing my first evening meal of scrambled eggs – not on toast, as I envisaged, for there was neither bread nor a toaster. Resolving to set up my winemaking kit as soon as possible, I settled down with a plate of scrambled eggs and a cup of coffee to read what Herodotus had to say about exploring the desert beyond Syrte.

In ancient times the coastal region bordering the Gulf of Syrte was a serious barrier to movement along the North African coast while the great desert wastes to the south were held in equal awe. Syrte was home to the Nasamones. Ruthless lords of their domain, they travelled with upright birds' wings on their heads and had a reputation for driving lesser encroaching tribes into the desert to perish. Equal in numbers and ferocity to the Garamantes they controlled the Syrte region as successfully as the Garamantes did the Fezzan.

Each year the Nasamones left their cattle on the coast and travelled some 400 kilometres to harvest their crop of date palms at Augila Oasis. An age-old stop on the caravan route from Egypt and Cyrenaica to the Fezzan, it was one of the places I hoped to visit during my stay. Taken by the Arabs in the seventh century, Augila disappeared under the sands during the Ottoman occupation of Libya. Rediscovered and resettled after the Ottoman retreat, its appeal for travellers today lies in two early Islamic multi-domed mosques. Accounts of their egg-box-shaped roofs reminded me of my favourite similarly domed ancient Naga mosque in Tripoli.

I knew that if the opportunity arose to travel south to the ancient oases and beyond to regions where 'rhinoceros congregate' and 'a great river with crocodiles in it' flows it would be a temptation I would be unable to resist.

***

At first light I was picked up in a company minibus and taken past security into the cordoned-off high security region of Area 1. The oil compound at Marsa el Brega is divided into two zones: Area 1 – ostensibly the industrial zone – and Area 2 – the main residential zone. Area 1, housing the vast complex of the oil industry, was also the location of the training and language centre. The journey to the centre was through a landscape of crude oil and liquid gas containers and their supporting network of elaborate metal structures and machinery, not unlike rocket launching pads.

Driving through this alien landscape in the half-light of early morning, I was having grave doubts about my decision to live and work here and began to wonder exactly what I had let myself in for. But this time, I consoled myself, I had my passport with a business visa and return ticket, enabling me to get out of Libya should the need arise. I was yet to discover that a major stumbling block remained. The tight security procedures of the compound included the necessity of a desert pass to get out of the site.

First impressions of the centre and introductions to my colleagues helped to restore my confidence. The first and only woman to be employed in this all-male preserve, my arrival was eagerly awaited. I wasn't sure what my colleagues expected but if they were disappointed they didn't show it. I wasn't disappointed either. I was warmly welcomed by David, the recruiting manager I'd first met in Benghazi, and the current team of three 'bachelors', Don, Graham and Josh. In fact, all except one of the men were married with families, but the company saved money by employing expatriate staff on single or bachelor terms only.

A quick tour of the purpose-built, air-conditioned centre allayed remaining fears. Spacious and with resources which included the luxury of shelves of books, overhead projectors, a workroom as well as a lounge area furnished with easy chairs and an on-the-go coffee percolator, by Libyan standards the facilities were good. In spite of diminishing administrative standards the staff had made valiant efforts to continue running the centre as efficiently as the Americans had in Esso days. Even the initials of the name, Syrte Oil – SO – are a derivation of the name of the former company.

In comparison with the modern world the place was technologically backwards, but in comparison with the rest of Libya the whole complex appeared well maintained, functional and amazingly clear of rubbish. Confidence restored, it was down to business but not too exacting. "Just sit here and relax," David directed as we returned from the tour. "Ahmed will bring you coffee," he added, gesturing to a young Arab standing nearby. "My next class starts in thirty minutes. Come along and join the fun. Today, I'll do all the work. Tomorrow it will be your turn."

During the next few days I met a range of people employed in different sections of the oil and oil-related industries and, in spite of the first impressions of order and progress at the training centre, I heard such disturbing stories about the working environment at Brega and the effects it had on some residents that I became convinced of the truth of the Mad Hatter's pronouncement that 'Everybody is mad'. Top of the league in the madness stakes was the Leader and his dream turned nightmare. It was in Brega that I learnt about some of the more horrifying policies of the revolution and the chilling behaviour of the revolutionary guards who ensured that they were put into practice.

"It's the hot-bed environment," a colleague enlightened me. "Libyan employees are taught that they are superior. They seem to believe it. You may have heard the slogan, 'partners not wage earners'. Taken quite literally, Libyans here believe they are joint partners in the land, the oil and the oil company. And that's not all. They believe that they are the master race and all foreigners their slaves. That means us. We're here to serve them."

"My students don't act like they believe that."

"It's not in their interest. They need to work and to succeed in order to get grants to escape. This way they get recognised qualifications as well as having the facility to open up Swiss bank accounts providing the opportunity to siphon company money overseas once they return; they're paid peanuts; it's their way of accumulating savings; for some it's the only way of recovering loses made when his Nibs changed the currency overnight, leaving even the former wealthy poor! The reality is that most of the Libyans employed in Brega do not have the opportunity to get out, do very little work and go out of their way to make life as difficult as possible for us – the expatriates who do all the work and attempt to run the place! They may have reasons to be confused but they have a massive attitude problem!"

It didn't take long for me to realise that life in this isolated top-security desert site was more intense than life in Tripoli. As a place to live and work Brega was highly unnatural, and like a carefully engineered stage the setting provided the perfect environment for perpetrating 'madness' in its various forms.

One of the reasons for high stress levels, especially for those on 'bachelor' contracts, was not only the working conditions but the reality of a sixty-day work cycle with no breaks. In the first week of my new post I learned that I was the replacement for a colleague who had terminated his contract after completing one work cycle only. Sensory deprivation and an inability to cope with displays of open antagonism were the reasons given for his short length of stay. Two weeks after my arrival another colleague was refusing to leave his accommodation. A few days later, heavily sedated, he was taken to Tripoli for medication and then escorted back to the UK.

Both men, breaking their contracts, were employed on a single-status basis and accommodated in back-to-back trailers – one room units linked by a shared bathroom. The trailers, housed in rows on an open gravel site with just sufficient room for walking between them, were a depressing and demoralising sight. When not at work the bachelors were confined to the trailers and completely ostracised from the more normal living conditions of families and single women in Area 2. Now, the engineers' need of liquid fortification on the journey to Brega made sense!

"What's your recipe for survival?" I asked Josh, who'd been working at the site for some seven years.

"Cricket, when it's not too hot. Bridge when it is. Home-made beer helps. I've installed a small cooker. When I go on leave I bring back dried and tinned food – just to vary the diet and make me feel independent. My trailer-mate has a TV but without satellite viewing it's limited to local programmes, centred on his Nibs promoting himself at great length as 'the only eagle'. It's a laugh really. Himself ranting on about crushing imperialistic dogs and satanic Americans as well as pontificating on the glories of the Great Libyan Jamahiriya. If you didn't laugh you'd cry!"

From my own black and white screen I was familiar with the start of local television programmes featuring an eagle, symbolising Gaddafi, descending on the globe. Prominence was given to countries occupied by Arabs by flooding them with green light; non-Arab countries were grey while those not in favour were removed from the world map. At that time the United States of America had ceased to exist! Not surprisingly, video recorders were in great demand and there was a lively trade in smuggled cassettes. Just one of the privileges for residents in Area 2 was the availability of Sky TV but, even so, viewing was limited as one by one the channels had been cut off until the residents were left with nothing more than the news. For variations in presentation Sky News could be alternated with CNN. At least those of us fortunate enough to have this facility could keep up to date with global happenings. My female single status gave me distinct social advantages over my colleagues. I was fortunate indeed to have a small if run-down house in the purely residential section of the complex where expatriate family and social life offered a degree of normality. The most outstanding facility was undoubtedly a lovely beach of white sand. On the downside my long working hours and work rota meant that I had limited time to use the beach in daylight hours.

Non-working wives and married men who enjoyed weekend breaks could make use of the beach and attached facilities, including a boat-shed complete with Sun Fish dinghies, sailboards and a compressor for diving cylinders – leftovers from Esso days. As were a golf course, tennis courts and family club with a pool and restaurant. Today, it functioned without alcohol and, of course, bachelors were prohibited!

A major drawback for Western women wanting to sunbathe or swim was the fear that stripping down to a swimming costume could result in being reported to the religious police. It was a risk. Libyan women went onto the beach and even into the sea, completely covered in black from head to foot. I still remember the shock I received when the black tent I'd spotted surrounded by sea suddenly got to its feet and walked up the beach, black folds clinging to its legs!

Shopping and facilities for eating out were non-existent or abysmal. Both single and married men had the dubious privilege of free meals at appropriately named Mess Halls. Females and children relied on limited supplies of essential foodstuffs in the supermarket. National women were allowed to visit the supermarket on Friday mornings escorted by their husbands and suitably covered in black from head to toe, and on two other designated 'housewives only' occasions.

Erratic opening hours and rules about when female camp residents could shop turned this into a nightmare for the lone female working in Area 1! Other females employed at Brega were secretaries and school teachers at the oil company primary school. The primary school teachers worked relatively short hours and had weekends off, giving them more freedom to shop and socialise. By the time I got back from Area 1, on the evenings when I was permitted to shop, bread (white sticks only) and the best of the locally grown fruit and vegetables had gone.

All too often I found myself picking through near-empty containers of rotten tomatoes, brown bananas and wrinkled apples. Floor-to-ceiling freezer compartments, which I was told bulged with luxuries in Esso days, were invariably empty. Supplies of fresh milk ran out almost as soon as they were delivered. From time to time supplies of butter appeared and disappeared, long-life milk and processed cheese was usually available. The metal shelves in the main body of the supermarket stocked some tinned foods, varieties of pasta, jars of jam, dried milk, cans of coke and oversweetened fruit drinks loaded with additives. I don't eat red meat and didn't see a chicken or fresh fish in the place from the day I arrived. I dreamed about wholegrain bread, yoghurt, fresh orange juice, real cheese of any variety, cereals and Marmite.

On my first shopping expedition I was unprepared for the obligatory door check. As I tried to leave I was stopped by a security guard standing at the door, repeating in a loud and threatening tone: "Bill! Bill!" while tugging on the bags holding my shopping. I was, and must have looked, totally confused. Fortunately, two local women came to my rescue. While one returned to the till the other searched through my shopping. Seconds later the first woman was walking towards me holding aloft a receipt she had picked up from the checkout. This she handed to the guard. Meanwhile, the other was handing him my bags and repeating behind her veiled mouth: "Must keep! Arrest! Stealing is arrest!"

Only then did it become clear. To make sure you hadn't stolen anything a guard was on duty to check your itemised bill against the contents of your plastic bags. Failure to produce shopping receipts was tantamount to admitting theft! My heart was still hammering as I walked to my house, asking myself what else this madhouse had in store for me. The incident also indicated that theft from the supermarket was not uncommon.

"We should have warned you," was the response to my story from one of my colleagues. "You are the one who should be checking the bill. It's common practice to overcharge expatriates. Theft from the oil company is also common practice. Not just food, electrical stuff, even company four-wheel drives. What you have to remember is, if you're Libyan it's not theft. The company belongs to them. It's called Brega logic!"

The alternative shopping experience was a visit to 'Crossroads' – a row of shanty shops set up by Sudanese immigrants and some enterprising locals – a kilometre or so from the camp. Located where the roads from Tripoli to Benghazi cross with a road from the desert oil sites into the camp, Crossroads had developed into the most popular shopping area in Brega. There was one problem. In order to get past security and out of the camp to the makeshift shops you needed a car or a lift and a desert pass. To get or renew a desert pass depended on having the right contacts. In Libya the right contacts made life a lot more pleasant and the benefits from having a pass were twofold: the wonderful sense of freedom experienced from being on the other side of the barbed wire; the shopping experience and, if you knew the right people, it was also possible to exchange black-market American dollars.

The bachelors saw to it that I had a pass and a lift to accompany them on shopping expeditions to Crossroads.

A service station, a tyre repair shop and a row of shabby and rundown mud-brick buildings with corrugated iron rooftops formed the heart of the settlement. Ankle deep in garbage and sand we made our way along a row of shanty shops past two tethered goats and the fly-blown head of a sheep hanging in a shop doorway. It was customary throughout Libya for butchers to advertise meat available in the shop by displaying the head of the animal(s) outside. The sight of the blood-stained head revived memories of the near arrest of a fellow expatriate who attempted to take a photograph of the heads of a camel, a goat and a long-horned cow hanging outside a shop in Gargaresh. Within minutes she had been surrounded by angry locals accusing her of making fun of Libya and threatening arrest. Pursued by the excited crowd, she was lucky to escape on her bicycle to the nearby compound.

I poked my head round the doorway. Under a single naked light bulb a man with blood-stained hands, wearing an apron stained deep red and with a cigarette hanging from his bottom lip, was arranging hunks of meat on a tray. With the sickly smell of blood and circling flies it wasn't a place to hang about.

Just a few doors away I was guided into a narrow windowless shack. As my eyes adjusted to the dust-freckled light three woven reed baskets each filled with freshly baked loaves took shape. The room was filled with the mouth-watering smell of new bread. We exchanged dinars for bags of still warm, sweet-smelling bread and, clutching our purchases, made our way in single file through the narrow walkways of an adjoining shop literally overflowing with goods. From overpacked shelves spilled everything from cosmetics to outdated clothes: domestic and electrical goods; carpets and dairy products; cereals, tinned food, vegetables and fruit of a quality and range that was far superior to supplies available inside the camp.

On my first visit I came across and bought a whole Edam cheese, albeit rock hard with the red skin peeling off, but there was no sign of mould. I couldn't resist such luxury. In fact, it was so old that to my deprived taste buds it had the tang of mature Farmhouse Cheddar and was at its best grated and used to add piquancy to a variety of otherwise bland dishes. That was until Don, one of the bachelors, enlightened me.

"Stolen from Famine Relief."

"You're kidding!"

"God's own truth. Probably destined for Somalia or Sudan."

I'd invited Don to test my first brew of white wine and was showing off by serving the luxury of cheese and biscuits to go with it.

"Common practice," he assured me, taking another nibble.

"Wouldn't have bought it if I'd known. I'll never feel the same about Crossroads."

"You're not to blame. Government officials and soldiers hijack supplies, transporting them for sale to countries like Libya. In fact, an eyewitness tells the story of planes landing. As soon as the goods were unloaded lorries appeared from the bushes and took the supplies to waiting Russian aircraft."

****

Reading extracts from Herodotus was an antidote to the deprived and depressing side of life in Brega, especially his tales about the colourful lives of ancient people of the region. In contrast to the lives of current nationals under their repressive regime, the practices of both male and female members of indigenous tribes were highly liberated as these humorous episode reveal:

Each of them [the Nasamones] has a number of wives, which they use in common, like the Massagetae – when a man wants to lie with a woman, he puts up a tent pole to indicate his intention. [Not to be outdone in exhibitionism, the women of the Gindanes tribe] wear leather bands round their ankles, which are supposed to indicate the number of their lovers; each woman puts on one band for every man she has gone to bed with, so that whoever has the greatest number enjoys the greatest reputation because she has been loved by the greatest number of men.

Such stories were a far cry from the way of life in Brega. However, in spite of the strict gender separation rules, expatriate Bachelors and Virgins did manage to get together on occasions. Less ostentatious about their intentions and accomplishments than the Nasamones and Gindanes, they resorted to cloak-and-dagger arrivals and departures in the half-light of dusk and dawn. Rumours of sightings of nondescript figures fleeing on bicycles through the dimly lit Street of a Thousand Virgins were not uncommon!

Home entertainments, especially barbeques, were the main source of socialising and meeting people for the expatriate community, but once again they were not an option for the bachelors. At times of expatriate festivals a general exodus took place, especially at Christmas and New Year. This year, with four of my colleagues, I was destined to spend both festivals in Brega. Weeks before the events we began speculating on the chances of getting a day off. Then on Christmas Eve a dictum from 'On High' decreed that one day's holiday could be given to Christians at the discretion of the manager of each department.

Just two days before Christmas, David called us into his office. "Don't get too excited, guys. We've been graciously awarded half a day – we're free from noon on Christmas Day!" A cacophony of groans was interrupted. "Hang on. There's more joy to come. The Muslim manager and Libyan staff have taken off three days, including Christmas."

"Is this a sick joke?" Josh asked.

"I'm afraid not. We the Christians have to be up and ready for the 7 a.m. pickup for work on Christmas morning while our fellow Muslims lie in their hot beds!"

Expecting a day's holiday, we had planned a picnic lunch at the remains of the great Roman fortress of Boreum on the coast just an hour or so from the compound by taxi. Built to defend coastal approaches to the province of North Africa during the reign of Justinian it promised to be a memorable venue for our celebration. Depressed by the shortened time for festivities but undeterred in resolution, we decided to continue with our plans and ordered a taxi from Crossroads to pick us up at noon.

A peerless blue sky flecked by scudding tilted clouds made it seem more like Easter than Christmas. Squeezed into an ancient taxi held together by string, we rattled past sullen security guards, calling, *"Mar hab!"* through the open windows, more in anxiety than greeting. Nothing was certain and a change of heart from security could mean a hasty end to our expedition. After a brief inspection of our passes the double set of gates was unlocked and opened and we were free of the barbed-wire barricade.

Before us desert wastes as blond as harvested summer fields stretched into the distance. Finally, the taxi growled to the top of a hill and tipped over the horizon. There before us lay the honeycombed peninsula where the remains of the Roman fort tunnelled into the rock face and clung to the coast. The sun dangled obligingly over sparkling sea like an oversized Christmas-tree bauble.

Dumped on the headland, we arranged a pickup time with our driver, gathered our baggage and yahooing like excited kids let out from school, slithered and raced towards the beach. Initial explorations of the cliff face had us crawling through tunnels and peering down vertical shafts that led into further tunnels and a series of interlocking caves. Apart from the underground passageways and remaining sections of stone walls nothing else had survived the ravages of the sea. While David and Graham kitted up in wet suits and snorkels and set off into the choppy waters to catch fish for our Christmas barbeque, I went in search of driftwood for the fire with Josh and Don. There was no shortage. We took over a cave with a convenient hole in the roof for smoke and made preparations for cooking and serving lunch.

By the time the shivering and empty-handed divers had returned we had the fire burning, the alternative menu of frankfurter sausages sizzling in the pan and glasses of naturally chilled white wine at hand. Clinking glasses and Happy Christmases echoed between the cliff walls. While we savoured the delicious taste of sausages blackened by woodsmoke, wedged between fresh bread rolls with a choice of mustard or *horrica*, the local hot chilli sauce, we debated about how long it was going to take to cook the oversized turkey squeezed into in my archaic oven back on the compound.

When we ordered the turkey there was uncertainty over its size. It wasn't until I went to collect it and it was handed to me in a dustbin sack that I discovered it weighed 50 lbs! I struggled to carry it home, its great legs bursting through torn black plastic, feeling as if I were carting a dead human body through the streets.

Now, with the sound of waves reverberating through the caves like a column of marching feet, the smell of wood smoke and home-made wine to accompany pork sausages, we decided to leave the turkey in the hands of Allah and concentrate on enjoying the forbidden joys of Islam and a pre-Christmas lunch as different as it was distant from family celebrations taking place across the sea.

***

We were too far removed from the political stage in Libya to be affected by the intrigue, attempted coups and police activities that had so coloured life in Tripoli. In Syrte excitement on the political front was limited to gunfights at Crossroads. This usually took the form of shoot-outs with sawn-off shotguns when disputes arose between local tribes. A major cause of arguments and subsequent gunfights was disagreement over those elected to represent the area in the People's Congress. Excitement at the training centre was more Orwellian in nature. A system of spying and reporting on the comings and goings of our department and labels such as 'Holiday Inn' for such frivolities as laughter heard in the corridors or issuing from our offices were common place and more often than not the cause of more laughter.

Then a major disruption was added to our limited lives. The life-saving F28 had been grounded. This was no rumour. Engineers were waiting for imported spare parts. The ban on international flights made this a long process and employees due to return or go on leave had to face the dreaded ten-hour hell run across desert. The importance of the F28 to the expatriate residents was demonstrated by their reactions when the sky overhead suddenly roared into life as the pilot took the resurrected plane through its paces. The entire camp came to a standstill as everyone dropped what they were doing and rushed to windows, or outside, and stood transfixed, gazing skywards at the sound and sight of the aircraft and its plume of vapour soaring and roaring above the camp. That evening a grand barbeque was arranged, the pilot was given a hero's welcome and dubbed 'the only eagle' in the desert sky!

Apart from the vicissitudes of the F28, excitement in the daily lives of the inmates of Brega was restricted to horror stories about the past and present lives of residents and gossip.

"You must have heard of the dreaded white letter?" Josh teased.

"White letter?" I repeated mindlessly.

''Yes, a letter delivered in a white envelope – notification that your contract has been terminated. No reasons. No explanation. Usually happens as the result of a sweeping Libyanisation policy in a particular department. Depends on the whim of some official who has taken exception or dislike to an individual – frequently with disastrous results for the company.''

"Could be a relief!''

"Depends. Tax-free dosh is a great lure.''

Another topic of conversation was the non-payment of contractors in key jobs who were owed millions. If a contractor appeared to be on the verge of walking out a token amount would be paid. This was an incentive to stay with the added incentive of promises of further payment. If a contractor pulled out his hope of recovering financial losses was minimised and replacements were easy enough to find. Rumours were floating about a Dutch company responsible for dredging the harbour, providing access for oil tankers. Apparently, the company hadn't been paid for two years and was on strike. The latest report was that only one small remaining channel was deep enough for the safe passage of vessels.

Then I heard about a non-payment of more immediate concern to us. Graham had returned from leave and the hotel in Djerba had insisted that he pay for his own overnight stay. Part of the contract was that hotel bills for staff travelling to and from Brega were company funded.

"The hotel hasn't been paid for months. Gave me a receipt and told me to get a refund. I'm still waiting!"

"It's an old story," Josh added. "They'll set up a deal with another hotel until the same thing happens. Eventually they could run out of hotels!"

Then two events took place with both immediate and far-reaching consequences. The first was a report that the current head manager of Marsa el Brega and his assistant had been killed in a car crash and were to be replaced by a new management team from Tripoli. This news was received with deep suspicion and scepticism. It was not unusual for out-of-favour characters, especially those in high positions, to disappear overnight with no questions asked.

Shortly after I was sent for by the Libyan manager of the language training centre; a non-event in terms of personality and management, on this occasion he was the bearer of bad news. Records of my espionage activities from Central Intelligence at Tripoli had been forwarded to the new senior management at Brega. As a result of this I was told that I was under surveillance and my work was being closely monitored. Furthermore, I was warned that on no account was I to write anything about Libya. I felt my heart drop.

My unrealised plans for travel were now out of the question. If travel from Tripoli had been regarded with suspicion then, given the recent warning, travel from Brega would be a warrant for arrest. In spite of increasing hurdles I made the decision to continue working at the centre until I had completed the academic year. In order to do so successfully I resolved to follow the example of my single-minded colleagues: keep my head down, collect my salary and take my leave out of Libya. There are times, however, when even the best intentions do not cover all contingencies.

The second event acted as a catalyst. The majority of mature students released by their companies to attend courses at the training centre, ranging from technicians, engineers, management and even doctors, were genuine, highly motivated and hard-working. The reward for successful students who gained a pass in the final examination was that the company would pay for them to attend further courses at colleges of higher education in the UK.

One of my students did not fit into this category. He was in the group not on merit, but through the decree of management. His dress-code: a base-ball cap worn back to front, a denim bomber jacket and jeans; his below-average standard of work and behaviour – frequent outbursts and open complaints of boredom – were more in keeping with the disruptive behaviour of a low-ability teenager. One of his regular complaints centred on the subject matter in the course books. Designed for the acquisition of particular language skills needed by students to take and pass the series of fortnightly tests leading to the final examination, the texts were not inspiring but purpose written and focused on the practicalities of daily life in England. They were the only teaching material the staff had access to and the majority of students had no problem with this.

When the time arrived for the group's fortnightly interim test, the student in question was unprepared and resorted to leaning over a fellow student's work and openly copying his answers. The tests and the results were taken very seriously and a pass was necessary for progress to the next stage. I was supervising the class and gave the offending student two verbal warnings. In a demonstration of bravado he then moved in the opposite direction to overlook the work of the student on his left side and proceeded to copy the answers onto his paper. At this, I told him his paper was cancelled and instructed him to hand it to me.

Rising to his feet, he went into a manic rage of shouting, arm waving and clenched-fist gesticulations. In spite of not understanding his Arabic threats – the tone of his voice and his voluble anger were unnerving. Uncertain how to respond the class were keeping their heads down. Calling to one of the students, I directed him to go to for help. The rest of the class remained in their seats, silently watching the enraged student as he edged his way towards me. Meanwhile, my heart was hammering the seconds and minutes away until the sound of marching feet heralded the arrival of two of my colleagues. Without attempting dialogue with me or reasoning with the irate offender, they took hold of one arm each and escorted him from the room, still ranting and raving.

Shortly afterwards I learned on the grapevine that the student in question was a member of a powerful tribe related to Gaddafi and had a chilling history. In jail for murder in Greece he had been rescued and brought back to Libya by Gaddafi's gunrunners. As exaggerated as this may seem it was not considered unusual in Libya. This, after all, was Gaddafi's home territory and tribal affiliations and rivalries were strong as testified by the gunfights outside the camp. It was also a well-known fact that opponents to Gaddafi or his regime who were under threat and had escaped overseas were pursued and assassinated by the Leader's gunrunners. The return of the rescued Libyan had previously led to much speculation about the reasons behind the murder. This news served to strengthen my decision to ban the student from my class.

In the post-mortem following this episode I made my feelings clear. The newly installed Powers were not happy but I was not in a kissing mood. The final outcome was a message from head office. My days in Libya were numbered. By this stage I was neither surprised nor disappointed. Without the facility to travel, life in Brega was turning into a prison sentence that not even golden handcuffs could compensate.

"I'm surprised your days aren't numbered!" was David's response to my announcement of a hasty departure. "You'd be behind bars if you were a bloke. I'm not kidding," he added. "Horror stories circulating about overseas staff in confrontation with Libyan students include a member of staff being publicly flogged in front of the students and fellow teaching colleagues. The horrified staff reacted by en masse on-the-spot resignation. More recently, a British lecturer at the university in Tripoli was jailed for upsetting a student from his class."

Uncomfortable reminders of the interrogation in Tripoli and

the lecturer I had been linked with as a spy surfaced. It was time to make a final exit.

***

If I thought that Libya had no further surprises to offer me I was wrong. The first stage of my exit was the luxury of a flight in the resurrected F28 from Brega to Tripoli. Stage two was the usual six-hour journey in the company bus from Tripoli to Tunisia. I boarded with five oil-company engineers and a Libyan wearing a discontented expression and a dull grey European suit. He, I surmised, was my minder. His duty: to ensure I left the country. Emboldened, no doubt, by the company of the engineers, I felt a certain smug satisfaction about having my own private revolutionary guard to see me off, even if he didn't look the part!

Then an hour or so into the journey we were caught up in a police road check and the subsequent traffic jam. Most of the traffic was waved on but we were directed off the main road and down a track to a local settlement. Parking alongside a fleet of taxis and minibuses outside a sandstone building marked with the recognisable hospital emblem of a red crescent moon, the driver disappeared inside. We sat wondering and debating what sort of emergency was taking place and what it had to do with us.

Minutes later the driver appeared waving a yellow card and beckoning us to get out of the vehicle while miming an injection in the arm. Alarmed, I followed my companions. The minder too got off the bus, lit a cigarette and remained on the spot, smoking. It appeared that he was exempt. No such luck for the rest of us. We could get no information except that we were going for an injection without which we couldn't leave the country. Inside the doorway of the clinic we joined the end of a lengthy queue straggling down the corridor, all waiting for the compulsory jab.

"Bubonic plague!" joked one of my companions. "Outbreak in India."

I could feel my paranoia about unclean needles and dangerous doses of unwanted serum rising.

"You won't get out without it, love, and I'm not stopping in any longer than I have to," another of my companions warned. "At this rate I'll miss my flight," he added, tapping his watch and claiming the attention of our driver.

The driver responded by negotiating the dubious advantage of getting us to the head of the queue. Meanwhile, we discovered that talk of an outbreak of cholera in Italy had influenced a decision by the Powers who decreed that any person leaving or entering the country was to be given the serum. Although I had received all necessary jabs before coming to Libya and had the documentation to prove it I knew that it would be futile to attempt to apply logic to their practices. I also knew that to refuse could jeopardise my exit. Libya was having its revenge!

The sight of a nurse tearing plastic wrappers off each of a diminishing pile of needles was the only source of comfort. Meanwhile, discarded needles were growing into a mountain on the floor. Obediently rolling up my sleeve, I steeled myself for what I hoped would be the last act of madness to be perpetrated on me in Libya.

Afterword

The year 2003, when Libya opened its doors to the outside world, created a turning point for tourism. Purpose-built tourist hotels continue to sprout along the coastal strip while campsites proliferate in the Fezzan. Although the dawn of the era of mass tourism has arrived in Libya, it is still in its infancy and highly controlled. Visitors must travel in groups with approved tour companies, accompanied by government-trained Libyan guides/minders, stay in purpose-built or approved tourist hotels and campsites and see only what the authorities want them to see. This way, at least, tourists should be safe.

My story takes readers to the world behind the facade. The essential Libya hidden from today's tourists did not change overnight. While Gaddafi continues to hold centre stage and has made a number of commendable political changes, behind the scenes members of the revolutionary committee and security forces continue to hold sway. A great deal of the Libya I experienced – including summary arrests and imprisonments on spurious charges of both nationals and members of the expatriate community – may be out of sight but still exist. Recent findings of the Amnesty International Rights Group make this clear.

Selective Bibliography

(International copyright laws do not apply to books published in Libya; those books republished by Fergiani in Tripoli do not indicate the original date, publisher or place of publication.)

Al Gaddafi, Muammar, *The Green Book* (1976).

Ashiurakis, Ahmed Mohamed, *Your Guide to Libya Past and Present* (Tripoli) (publisher and date not given).

Azema, James, *Libyan Handbook* (1st edn, Bath: Footprint Handbooks, 2000).

Barth, Heinrich, *Travels & Discoveries in North and Central Africa* (London: Ward, Lock & Co., 1890).

Cooper, Paul E., *Libya, The Dream or Nightmare* (Mesa, Arizona: The Quiet Leaf Group, 2004).

Cowper, H. S., *The Hill of Graces* (London: Methuen & Co., 1897).

Goodchild, Professor Richard, *Cyrene and Apollonia*, *An Historic Guide* (2nd edn) (place, publisher and date not given).

Hamilton, James, *Wanderings in North Africa* (London: John Murray, 1856).

Haynes, D. E. L., *The Antiquities of Tripolitania* (Tripoli: Department of Antiquities, 1981).

Herodotus, *The Histories*, trans. Aubrey de Selincourt (1954), rev. John Marincola (London: Penguin Classics, 1996).

Kapuscinski, Ryszard, *The Shadow of the Sun*, trans. Klara Glowczewska (London: Penguin Books, 2001).

Salak, Kira, *The Cruellest Journey* (London: Bantam Books, 2005).

Simpson, John, *A Mad World, My Masters* (London: Pan Books, 2001).

Stark, Freya, *The Valley of the Assassins* (London: Arrow Books, 1991).

Strabo, *The Geography of Strabo*, trans. Horace Leonard Jones (London: William Heinemann, 1932).

Tully, Miss, *Narrative of Ten Years' Residence at Tripoli in Africa* (London: A. Barker, 1957).